Books by Charles M. Schulz

Peanuts

More Peanuts

Good Grief, Charlie Brown!

Good Ol' Charlie Brown

Snoopy

You're Out of Your Mind, Charlie Brown

But We Love You, Charlie Brown

Peanuts Revisited

Go Fly a Kite, Charlie Brown

You Can't Win, Charlie Brown

Peanuts Every Sunday

Snoopy, Come Home

Sunday's Fun Day, Charlie Brown

It's a Dog's Life, Charlie Brown

And a Woodstock in a Birch Tree

Here's to you, Charlie Brown

YOU'RE THE GREATEST, CHARLIE BROWN

Charles M. Schulz

Selected Cartoons from
AS YOU LIKE IT, CHARLIE BROWN Vol.II

TITAN COMICS

YOU'RE THE GREATEST, CHARLIE BROWN

ISBN: 9781787742703

ORIGINALLY PUBLISHED CORONET BOOKS, 1971.
FACSIMILE EDITION PUBLISHED BY TITAN COMICS 2024. PUBLISHED BY TITAN COMICS,
A DIVISION OF TITAN PUBLISHING GROUP, LTD. 144 SOUTHWARK STREET, LONDON SE1
0UP. TITAN COMICS IS A REGISTERED TRADEMARK OF TITAN PUBLISHING GROUP, LTD.

FIRST EDITION NOVEMBER 2024
PRINTED IN INDIA
10 9 8 7 6 5 4 3 2 1

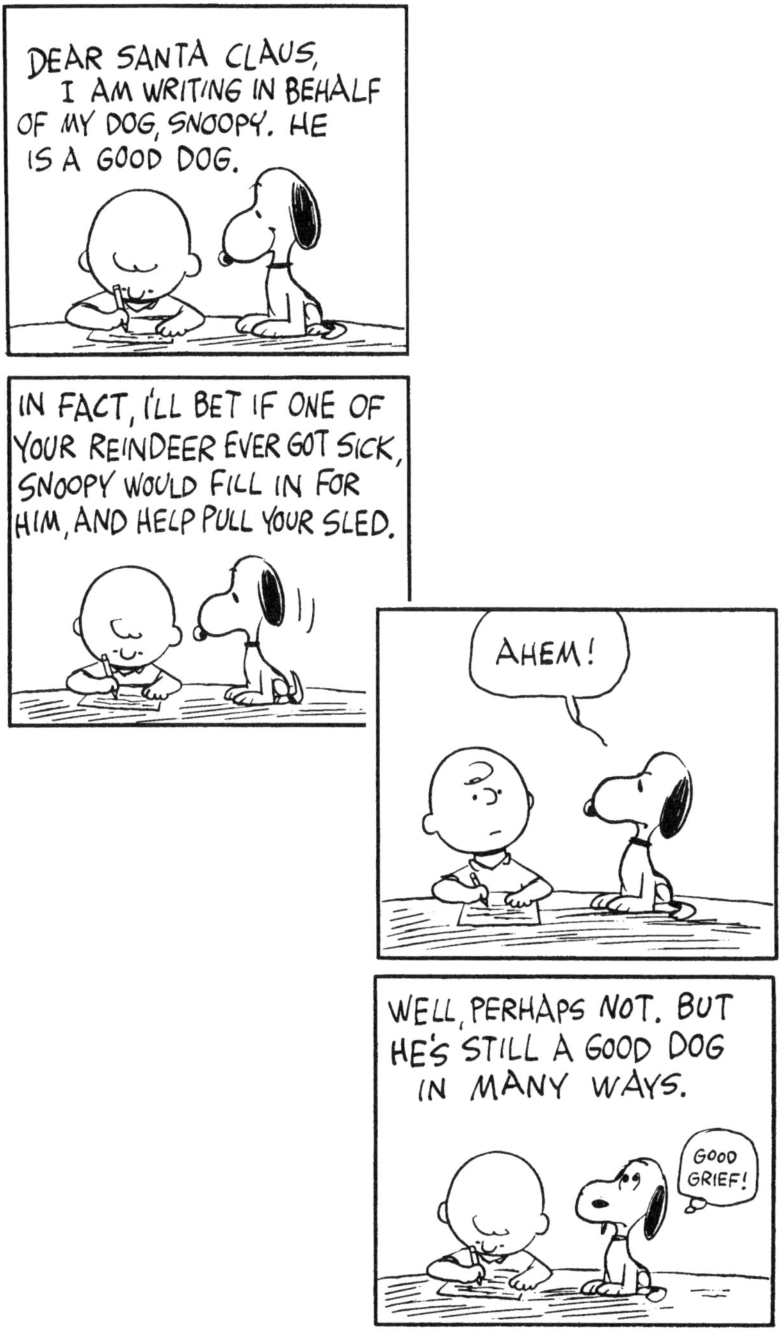
DEAR SANTA CLAUS,
I AM WRITING IN BEHALF OF MY DOG, SNOOPY. HE IS A GOOD DOG.
IN FACT, I'LL BET IF ONE OF YOUR REINDEER EVER GOT SICK, SNOOPY WOULD FILL IN FOR HIM, AND HELP PULL YOUR SLED.
AHEM!
WELL, PERHAPS NOT. BUT HE'S STILL A GOOD DOG IN MANY WAYS.
GOOD GRIEF!

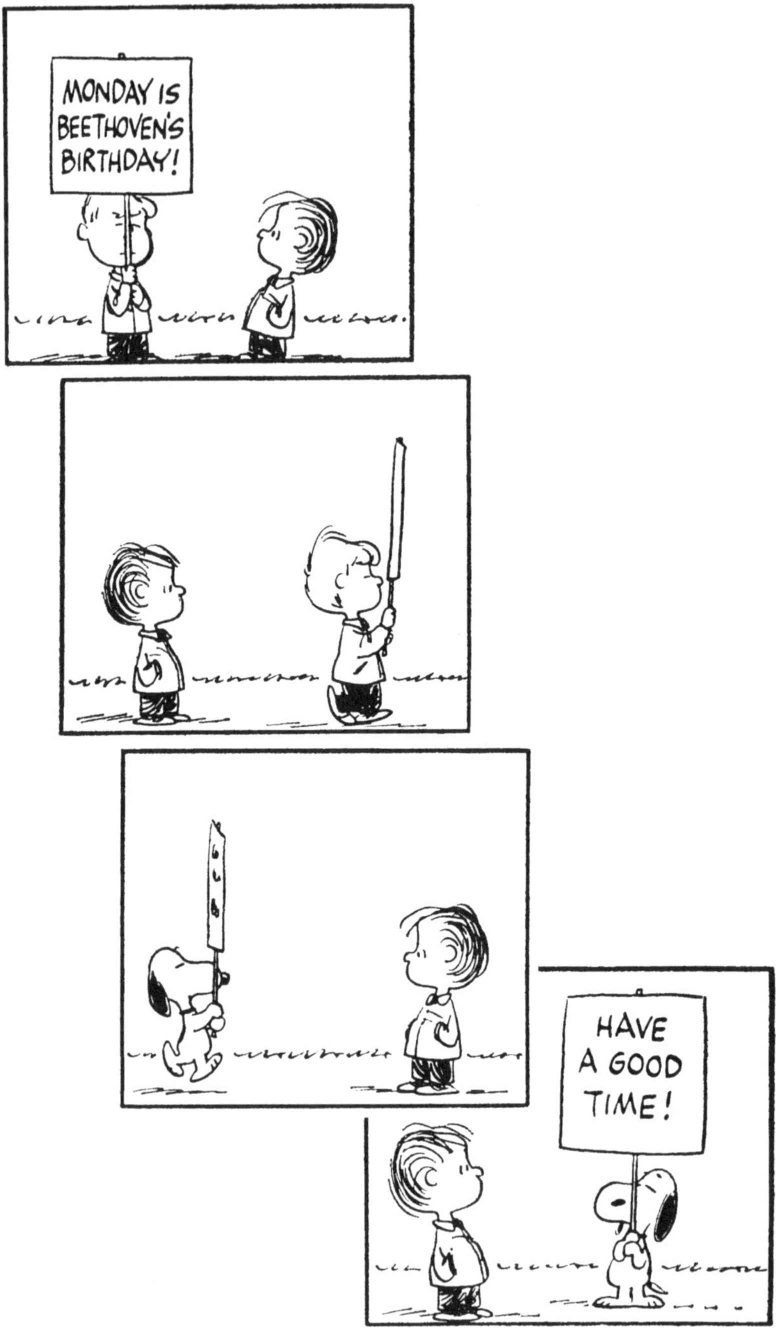
MONDAY IS BEETHOVEN'S BIRTHDAY!
HAVE A GOOD TIME!

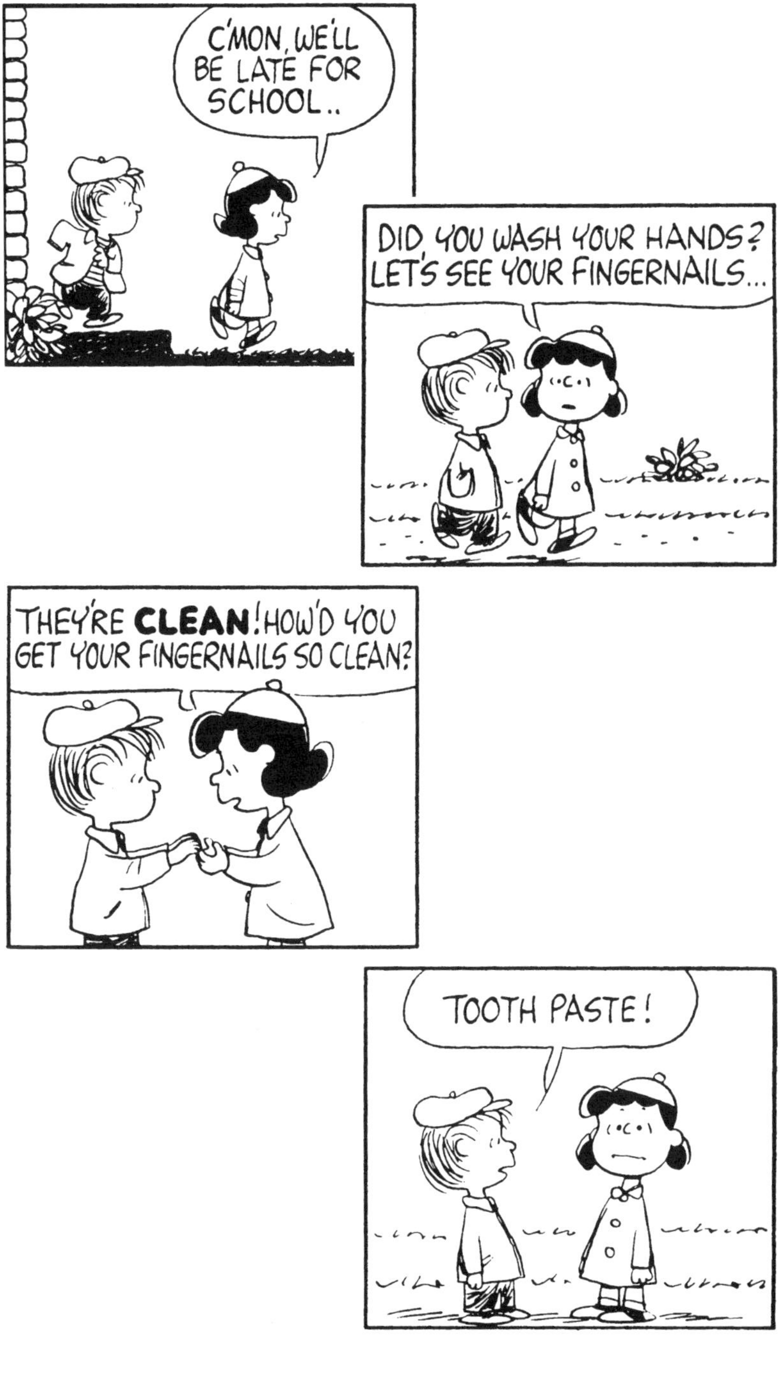
C'MON, WE'LL BE LATE FOR SCHOOL..
DID YOU WASH YOUR HANDS? LET'S SEE YOUR FINGERNAILS...
THEY'RE **CLEAN**! HOW'D YOU GET YOUR FINGERNAILS SO CLEAN?
TOOTH PASTE!

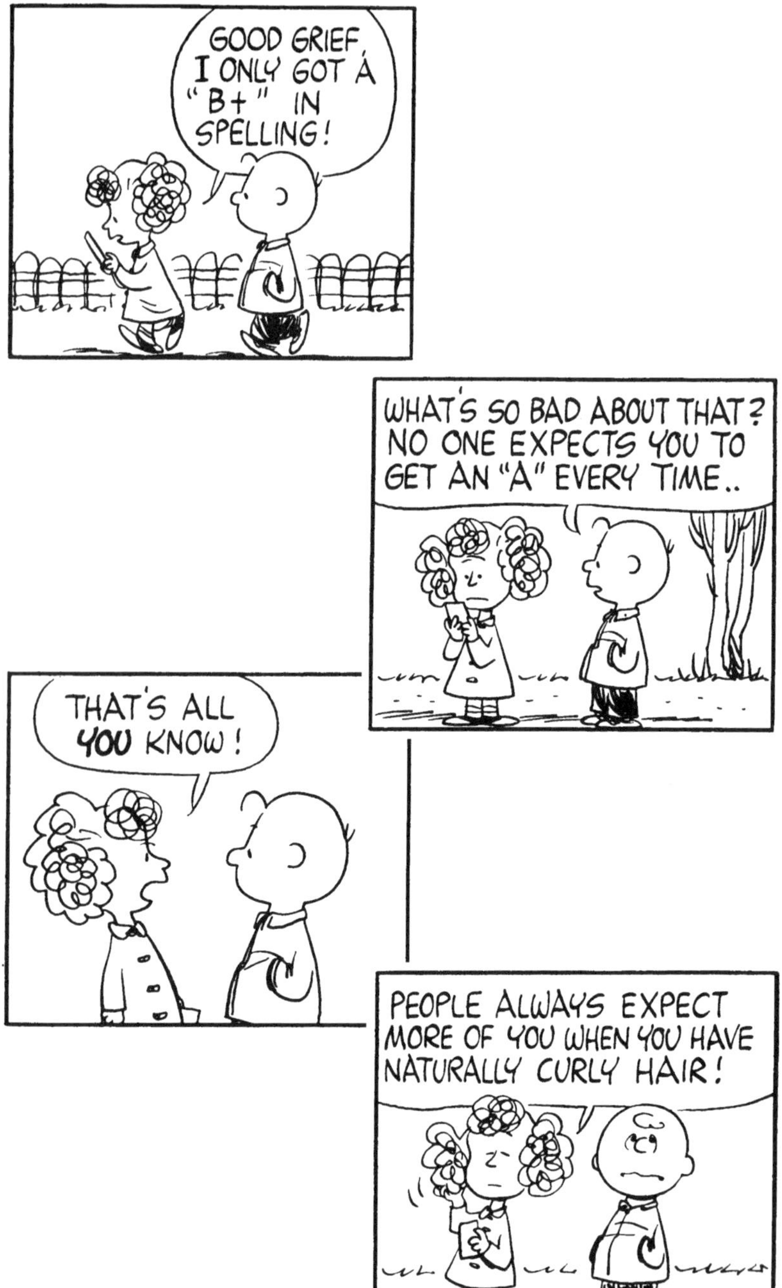
GOOD GRIEF, I ONLY GOT A "B+" IN SPELLING!
WHAT'S SO BAD ABOUT THAT? NO ONE EXPECTS YOU TO GET AN "A" EVERY TIME..
THAT'S ALL YOU KNOW!
PEOPLE ALWAYS EXPECT MORE OF YOU WHEN YOU HAVE NATURALLY CURLY HAIR!

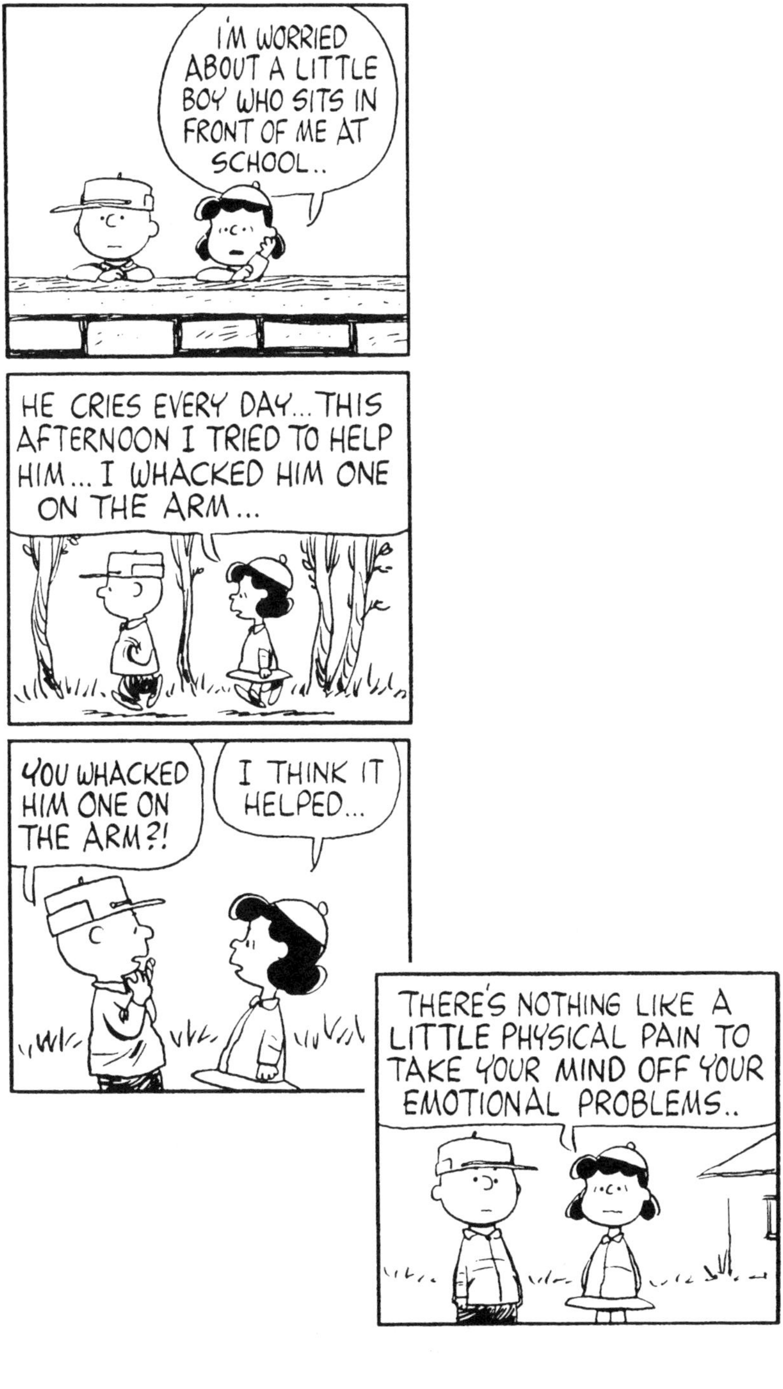
I'M WORRIED ABOUT A LITTLE BOY WHO SITS IN FRONT OF ME AT SCHOOL..
HE CRIES EVERY DAY... THIS AFTERNOON I TRIED TO HELP HIM... I WHACKED HIM ONE ON THE ARM...
YOU WHACKED HIM ONE ON THE ARM?!
I THINK IT HELPED...
THERE'S NOTHING LIKE A LITTLE PHYSICAL PAIN TO TAKE YOUR MIND OFF YOUR EMOTIONAL PROBLEMS..

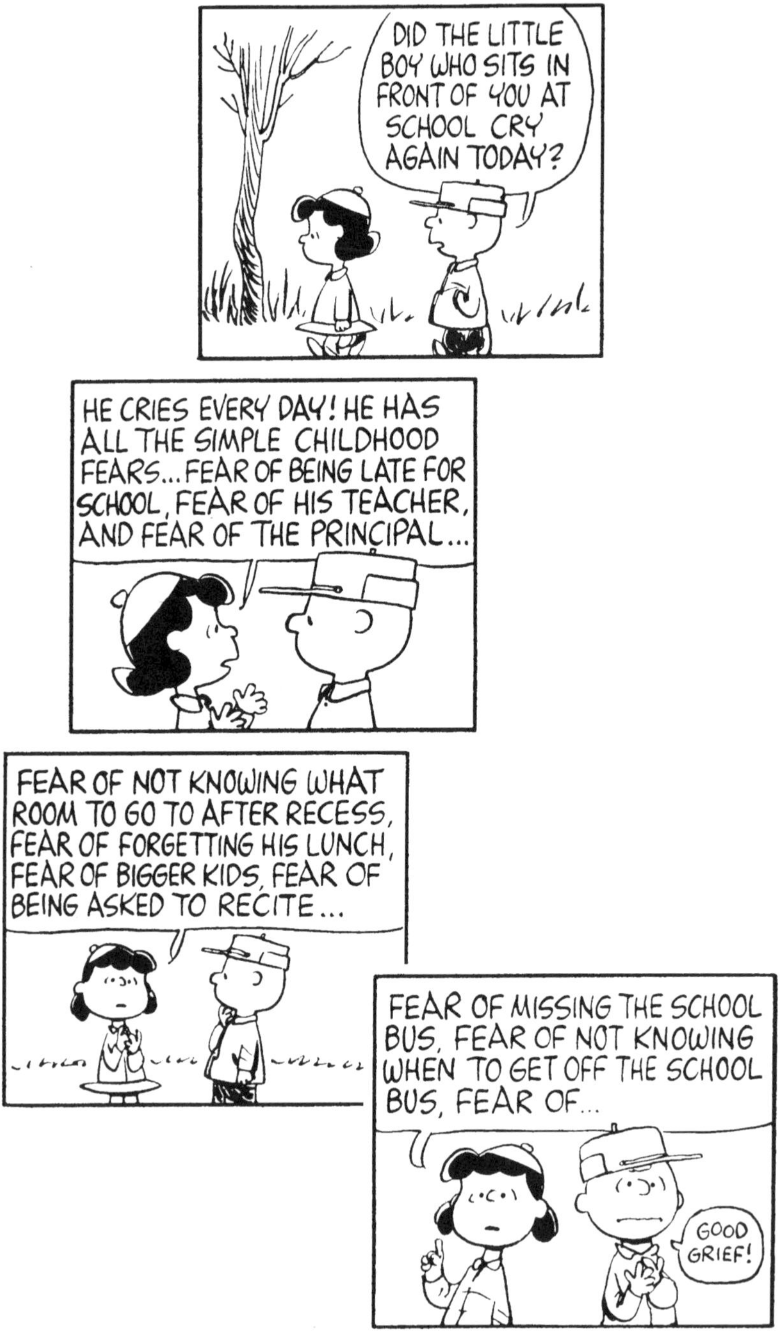
DID THE LITTLE BOY WHO SITS IN FRONT OF YOU AT SCHOOL CRY AGAIN TODAY?
HE CRIES EVERY DAY! HE HAS ALL THE SIMPLE CHILDHOOD FEARS...FEAR OF BEING LATE FOR SCHOOL, FEAR OF HIS TEACHER, AND FEAR OF THE PRINCIPAL...
FEAR OF NOT KNOWING WHAT ROOM TO GO TO AFTER RECESS, FEAR OF FORGETTING HIS LUNCH, FEAR OF BIGGER KIDS, FEAR OF BEING ASKED TO RECITE...
FEAR OF MISSING THE SCHOOL BUS, FEAR OF NOT KNOWING WHEN TO GET OFF THE SCHOOL BUS, FEAR OF...
GOOD GRIEF!

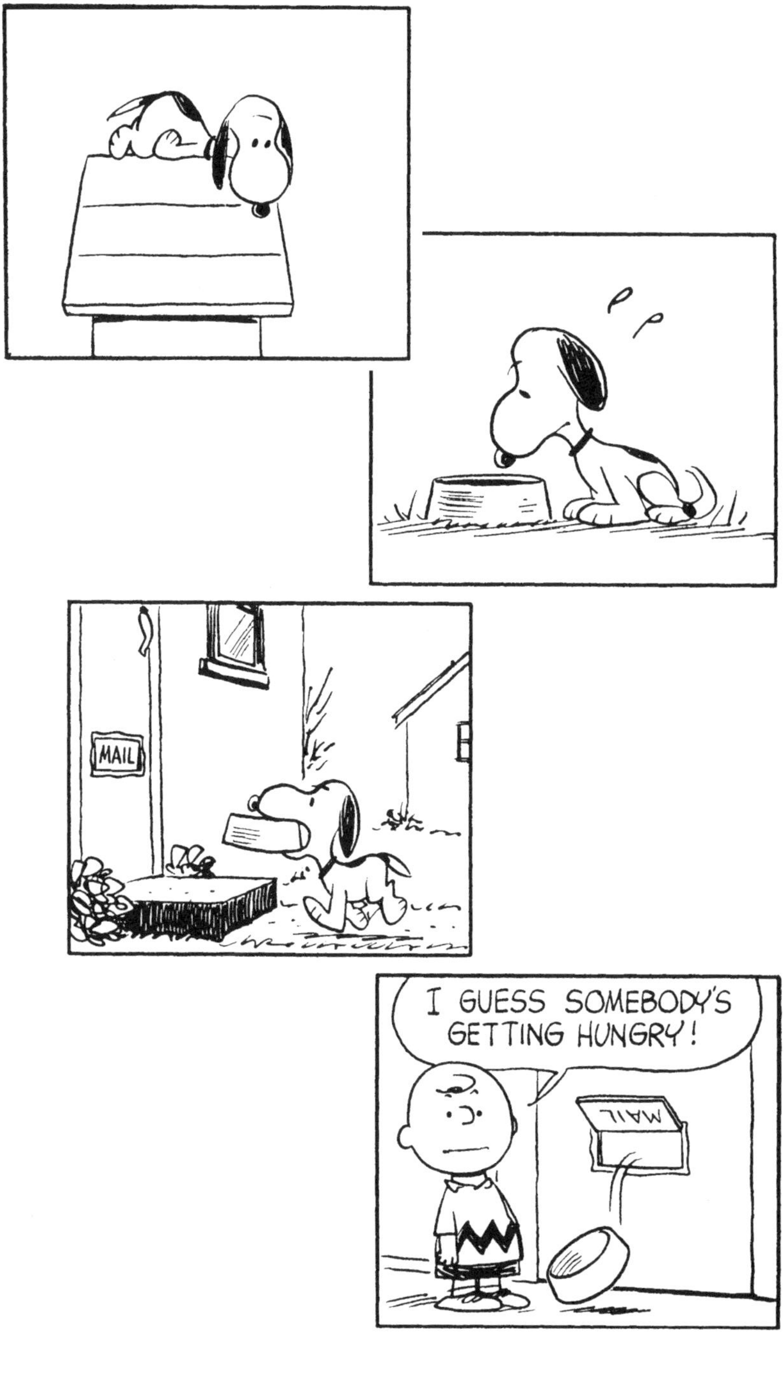
MAIL
I GUESS SOMEBODY'S GETTING HUNGRY!
MAIL

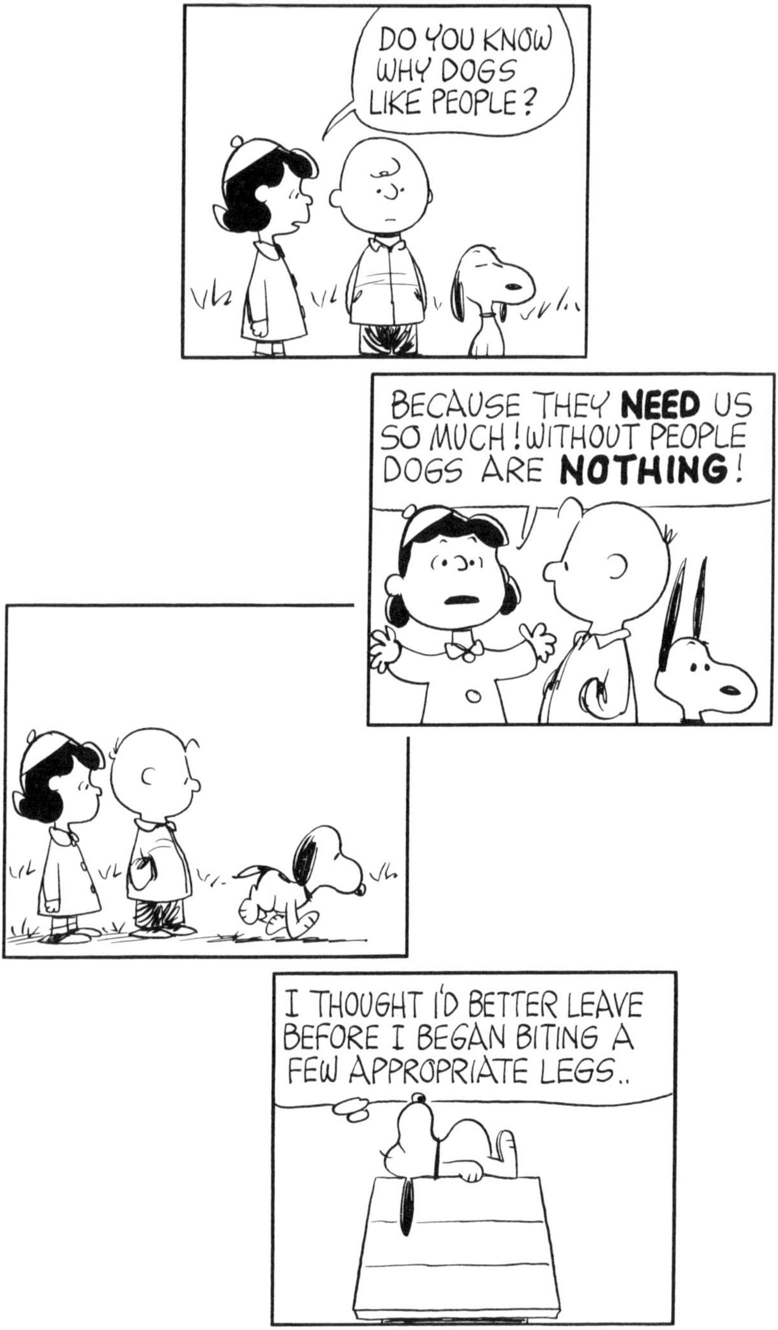
DO YOU KNOW WHY DOGS LIKE PEOPLE?
BECAUSE THEY **NEED** US SO MUCH! WITHOUT PEOPLE DOGS ARE **NOTHING**!
I THOUGHT I'D BETTER LEAVE BEFORE I BEGAN BITING A FEW APPROPRIATE LEGS..

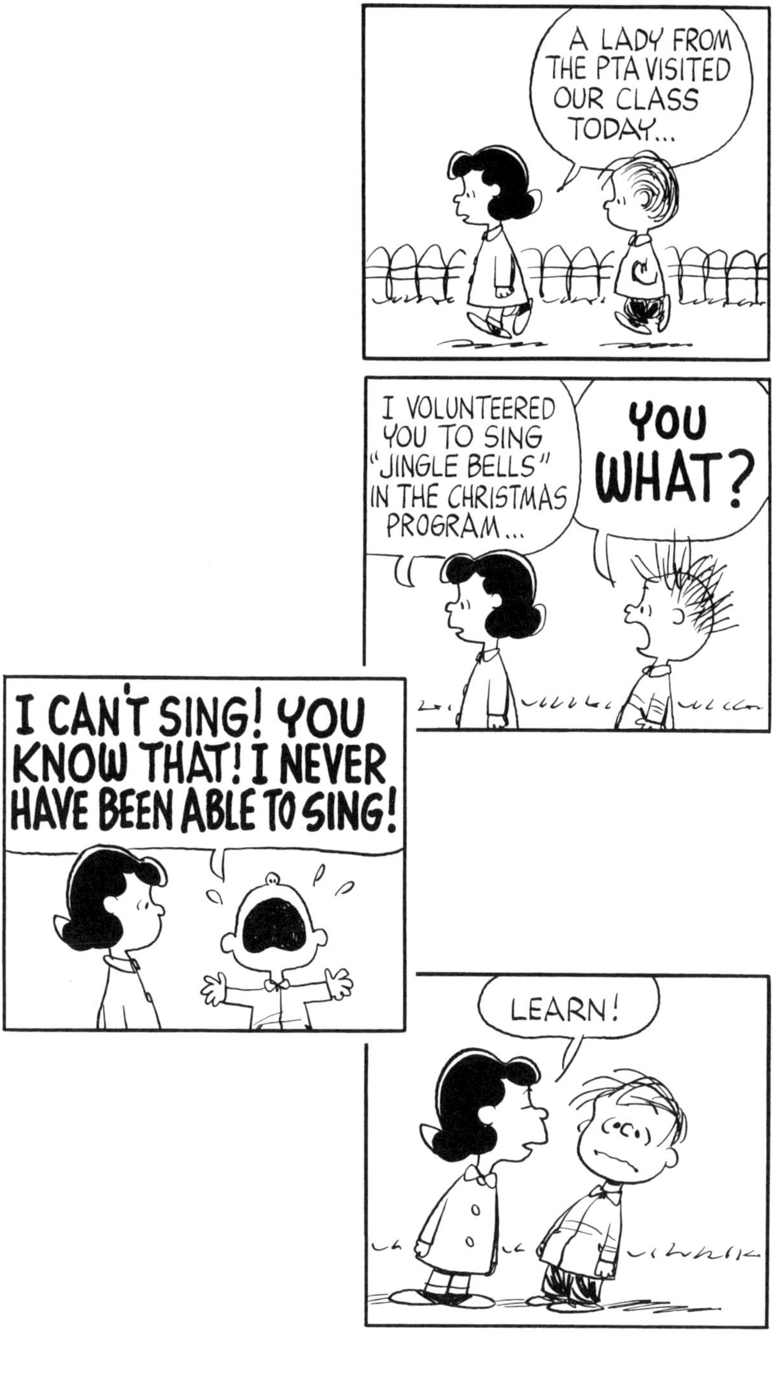
A LADY FROM THE PTA VISITED OUR CLASS TODAY...
I VOLUNTEERED YOU TO SING "JINGLE BELLS" IN THE CHRISTMAS PROGRAM...
YOU WHAT?
I CAN'T SING! YOU KNOW THAT! I NEVER HAVE BEEN ABLE TO SING!
LEARN!

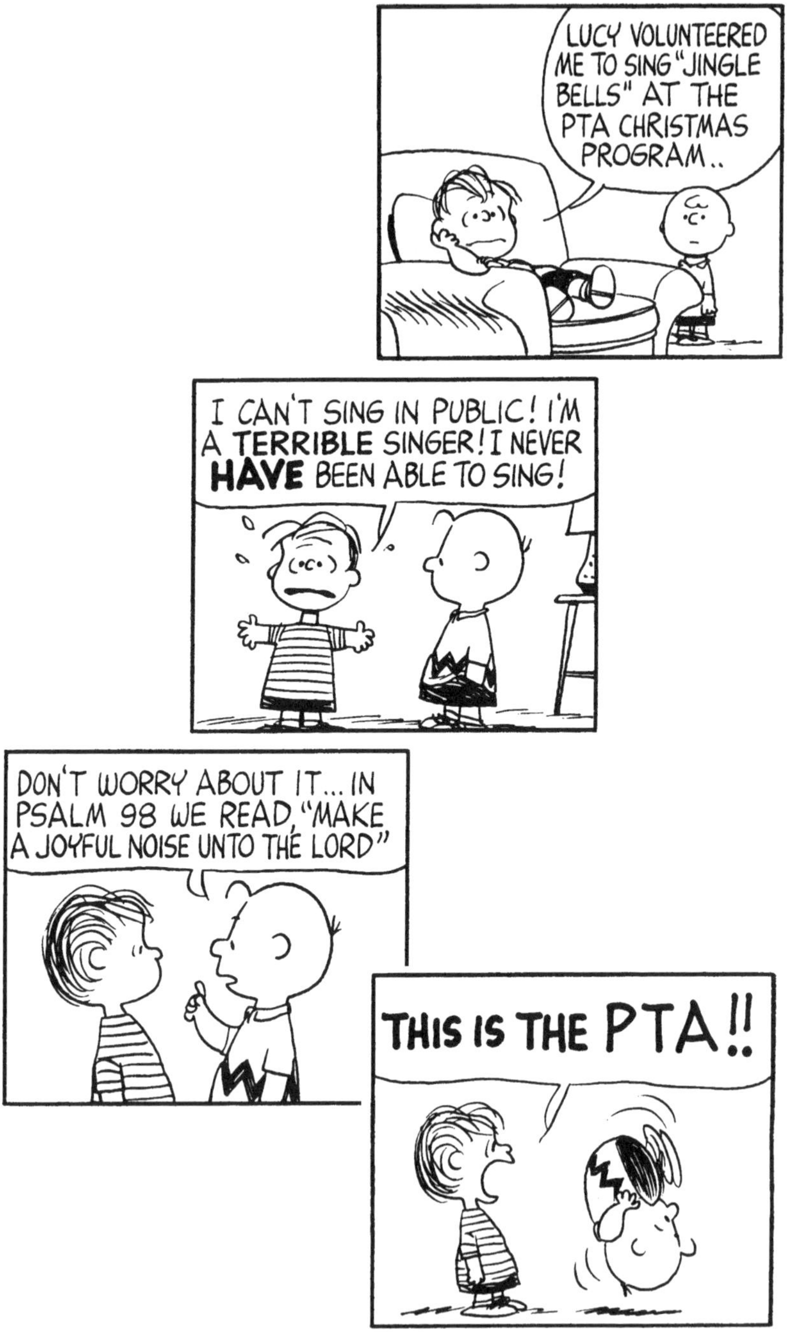
LUCY VOLUNTEERED ME TO SING "JINGLE BELLS" AT THE PTA CHRISTMAS PROGRAM..
I CAN'T SING IN PUBLIC! I'M A TERRIBLE SINGER! I NEVER HAVE BEEN ABLE TO SING!
DON'T WORRY ABOUT IT... IN PSALM 98 WE READ, "MAKE A JOYFUL NOISE UNTO THE LORD"
THIS IS THE PTA!!

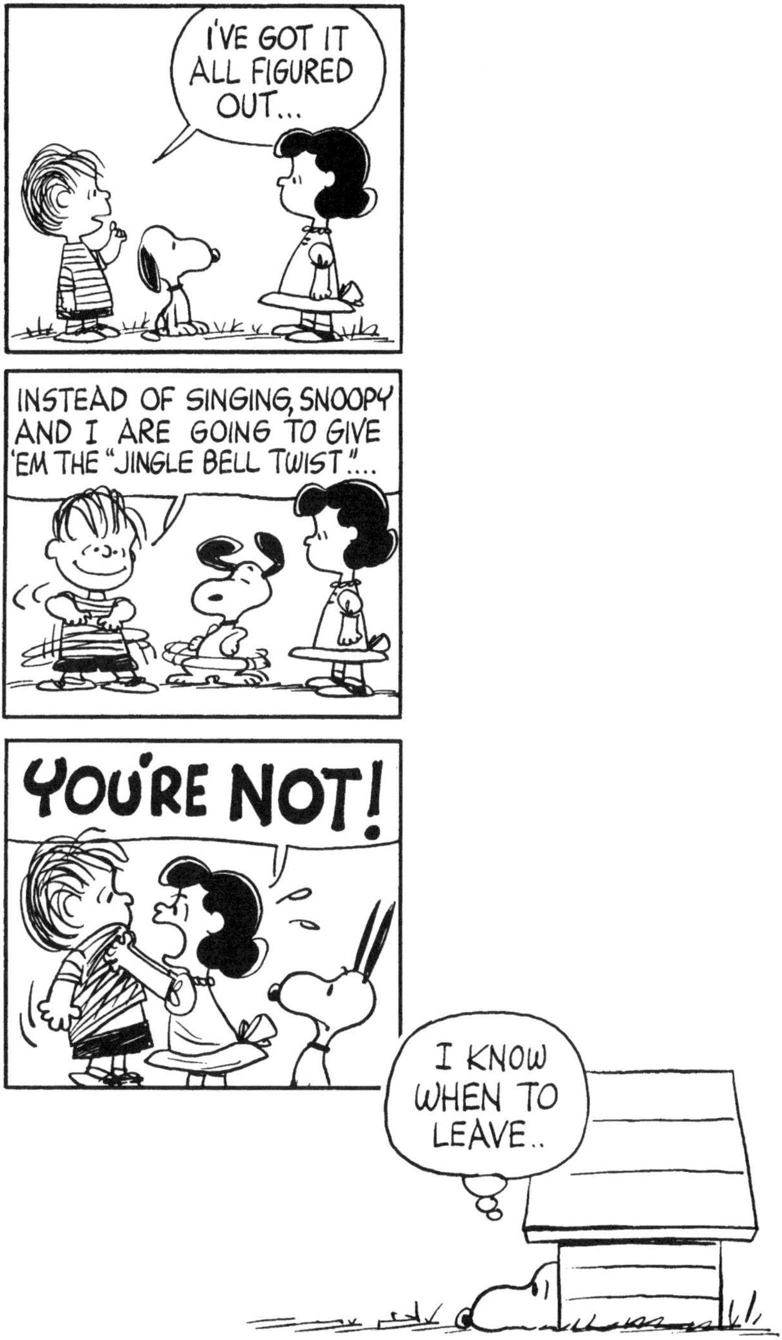
I'VE GOT IT ALL FIGURED OUT...
INSTEAD OF SINGING, SNOOPY AND I ARE GOING TO GIVE 'EM THE "JINGLE BELL TWIST."...
YOU'RE NOT!
I KNOW WHEN TO LEAVE..

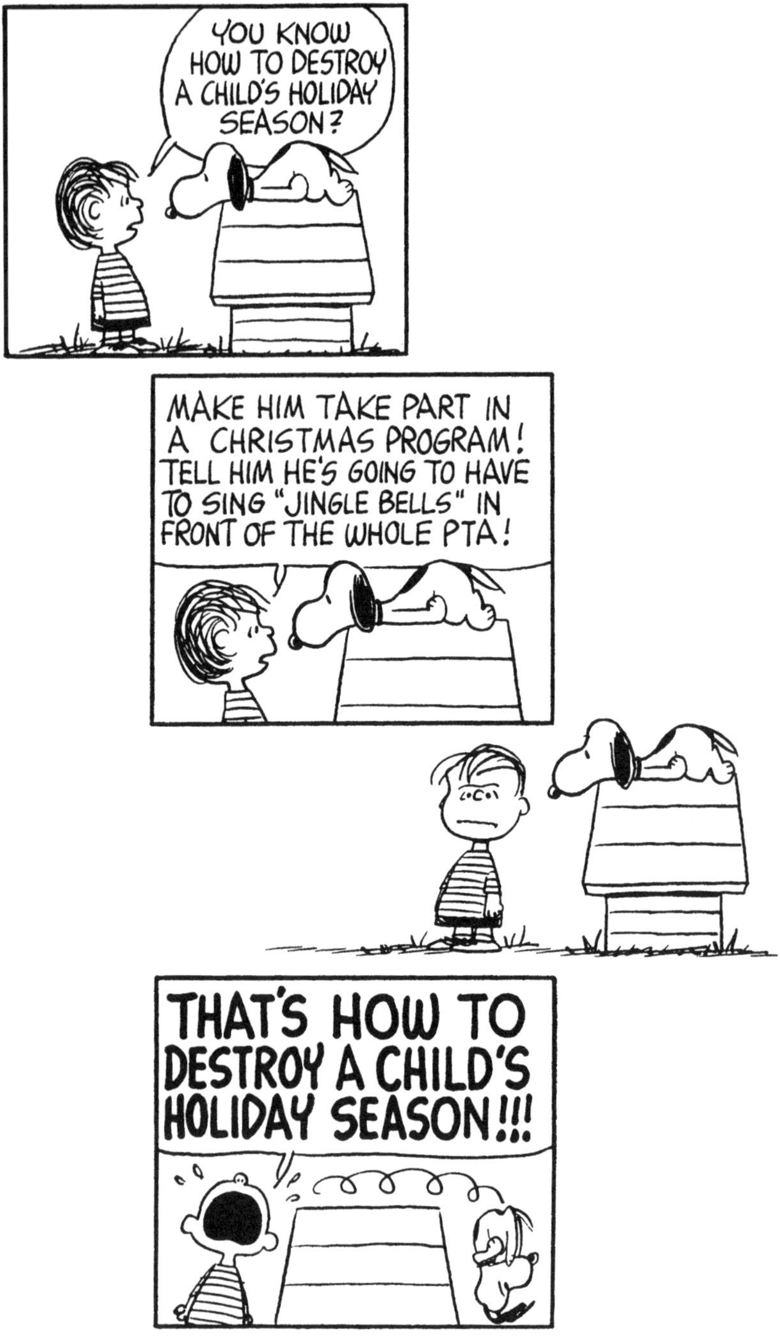
YOU KNOW HOW TO DESTROY A CHILD'S HOLIDAY SEASON?
MAKE HIM TAKE PART IN A CHRISTMAS PROGRAM! TELL HIM HE'S GOING TO HAVE TO SING "JINGLE BELLS" IN FRONT OF THE WHOLE PTA!
THAT'S HOW TO DESTROY A CHILD'S HOLIDAY SEASON!!!

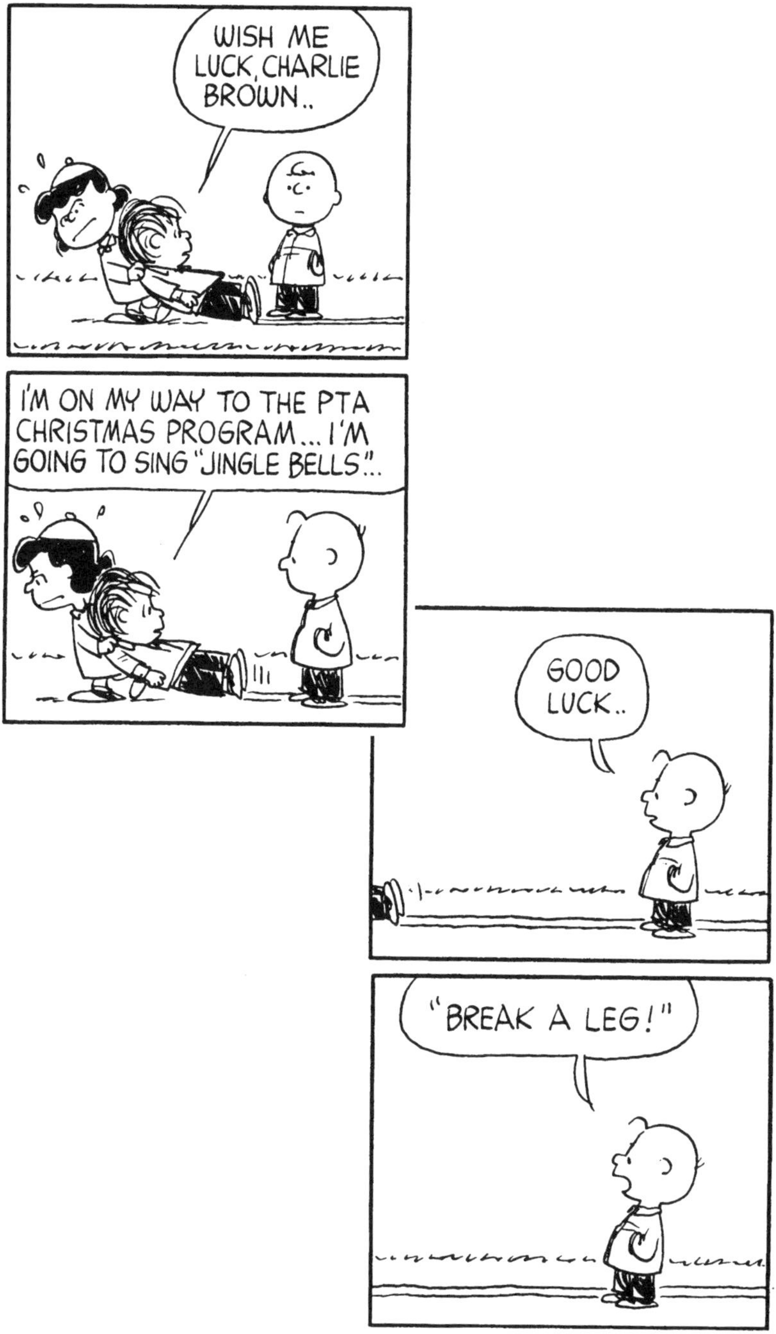

WISH ME LUCK, CHARLIE BROWN..
I'M ON MY WAY TO THE PTA CHRISTMAS PROGRAM... I'M GOING TO SING "JINGLE BELLS"..
GOOD LUCK..
"BREAK A LEG!"

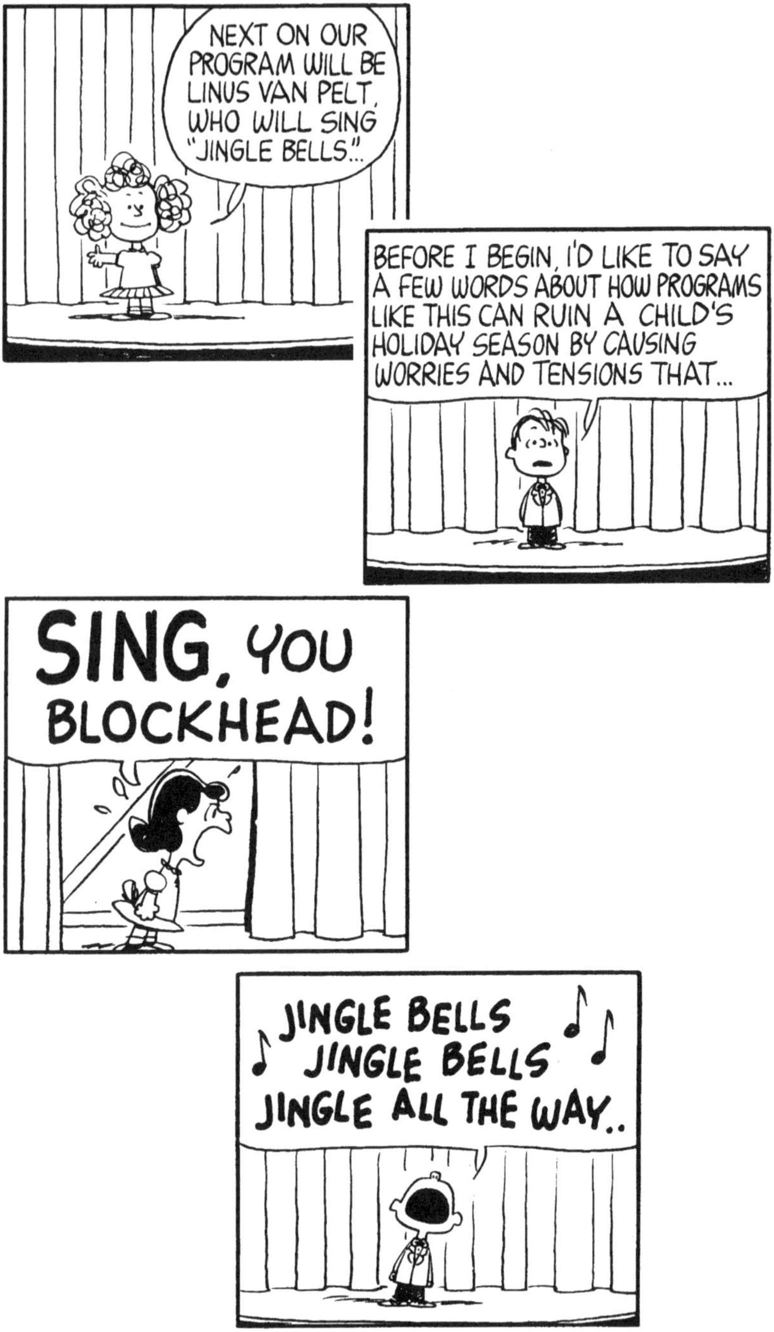
NEXT ON OUR PROGRAM WILL BE LINUS VAN PELT, WHO WILL SING "JINGLE BELLS."..
BEFORE I BEGIN, I'D LIKE TO SAY A FEW WORDS ABOUT HOW PROGRAMS LIKE THIS CAN RUIN A CHILD'S HOLIDAY SEASON BY CAUSING WORRIES AND TENSIONS THAT...
SING, YOU BLOCKHEAD!
JINGLE BELLS
JINGLE BELLS
JINGLE ALL THE WAY..

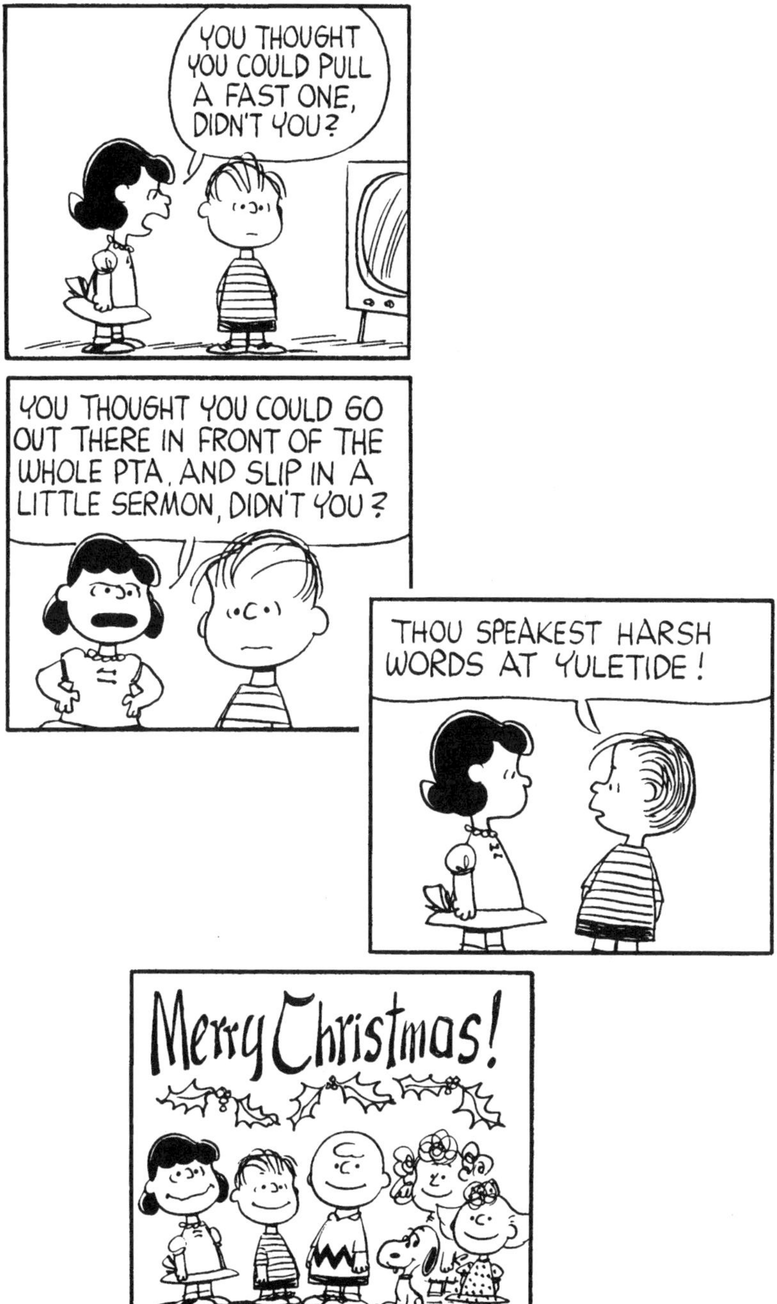
YOU THOUGHT YOU COULD PULL A FAST ONE, DIDN'T YOU?
YOU THOUGHT YOU COULD GO OUT THERE IN FRONT OF THE WHOLE PTA, AND SLIP IN A LITTLE SERMON, DIDN'T YOU?
THOU SPEAKEST HARSH WORDS AT YULETIDE!
Merry Christmas!

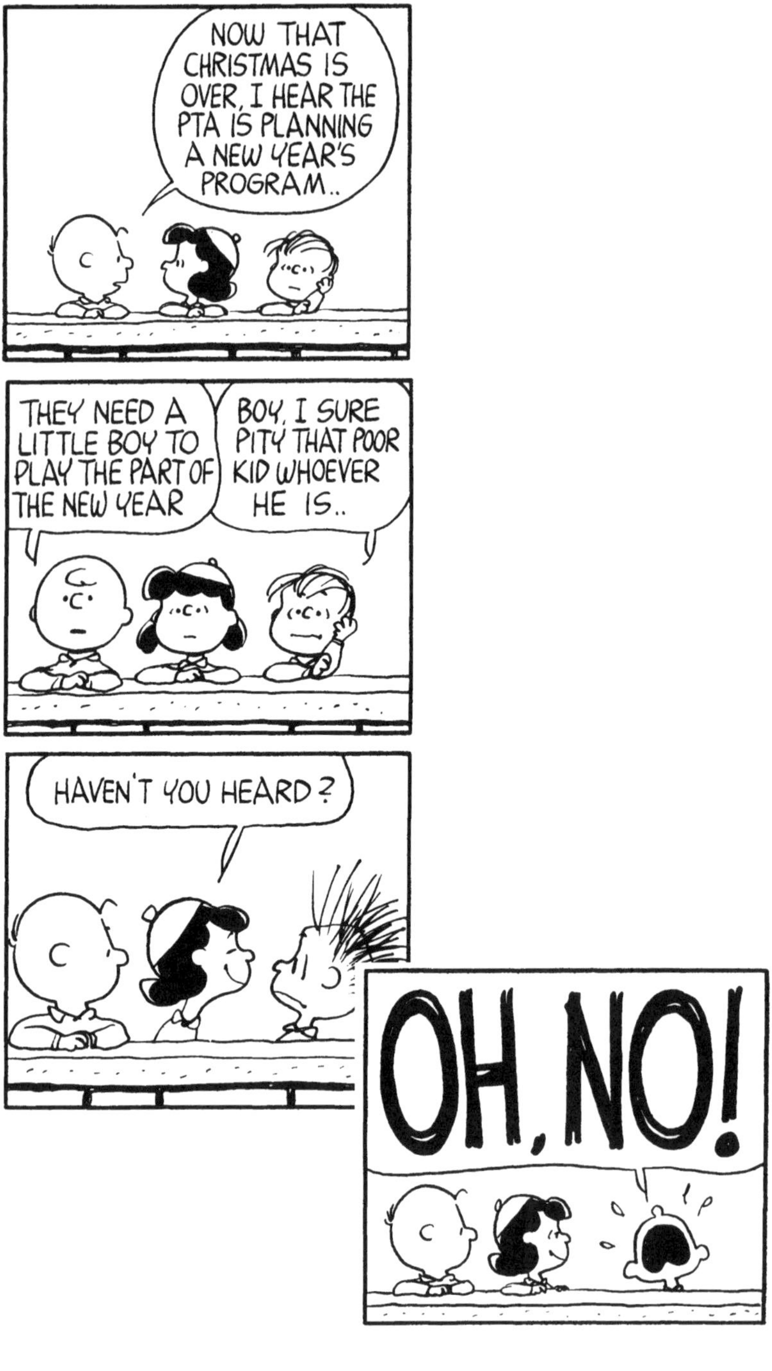
NOW THAT CHRISTMAS IS OVER, I HEAR THE PTA IS PLANNING A NEW YEAR'S PROGRAM..
THEY NEED A LITTLE BOY TO PLAY THE PART OF THE NEW YEAR
BOY, I SURE PITY THAT POOR KID WHOEVER HE IS..
HAVEN'T YOU HEARD?
OH, NO!

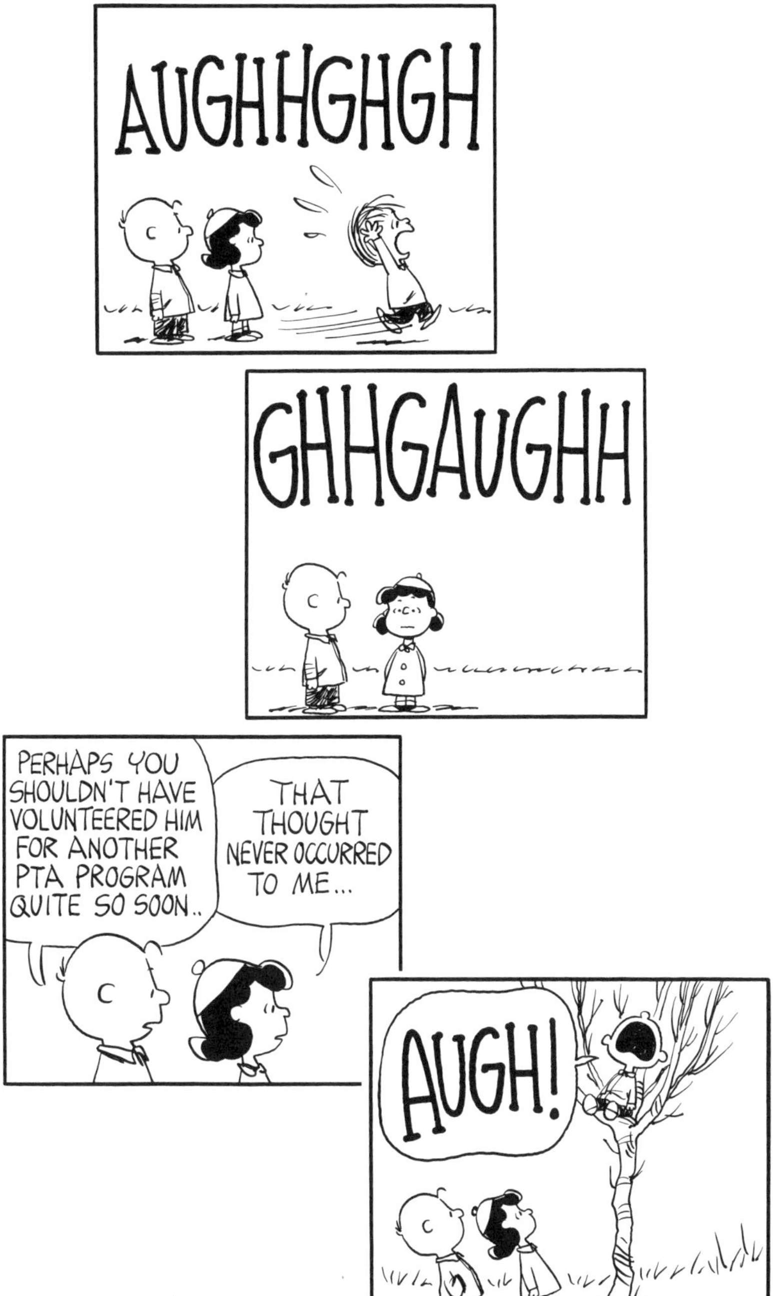
AUGHHGHGH
GHHGAUGHH
PERHAPS YOU SHOULDN'T HAVE VOLUNTEERED HIM FOR ANOTHER PTA PROGRAM QUITE SO SOON..
THAT THOUGHT NEVER OCCURRED TO ME...
AUGH!

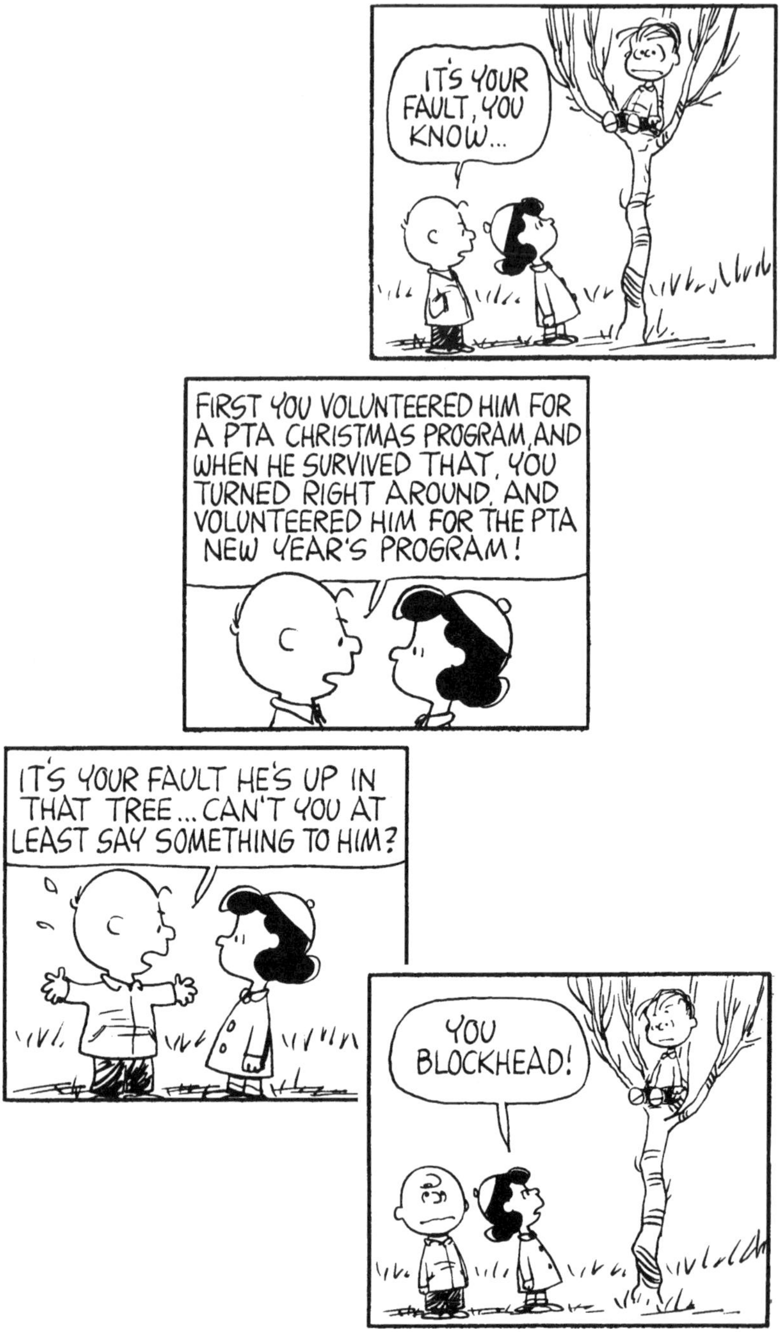
IT'S YOUR FAULT, YOU KNOW...
FIRST YOU VOLUNTEERED HIM FOR A PTA CHRISTMAS PROGRAM, AND WHEN HE SURVIVED THAT, YOU TURNED RIGHT AROUND, AND VOLUNTEERED HIM FOR THE PTA NEW YEAR'S PROGRAM!
IT'S YOUR FAULT HE'S UP IN THAT TREE... CAN'T YOU AT LEAST SAY SOMETHING TO HIM?
YOU BLOCKHEAD!

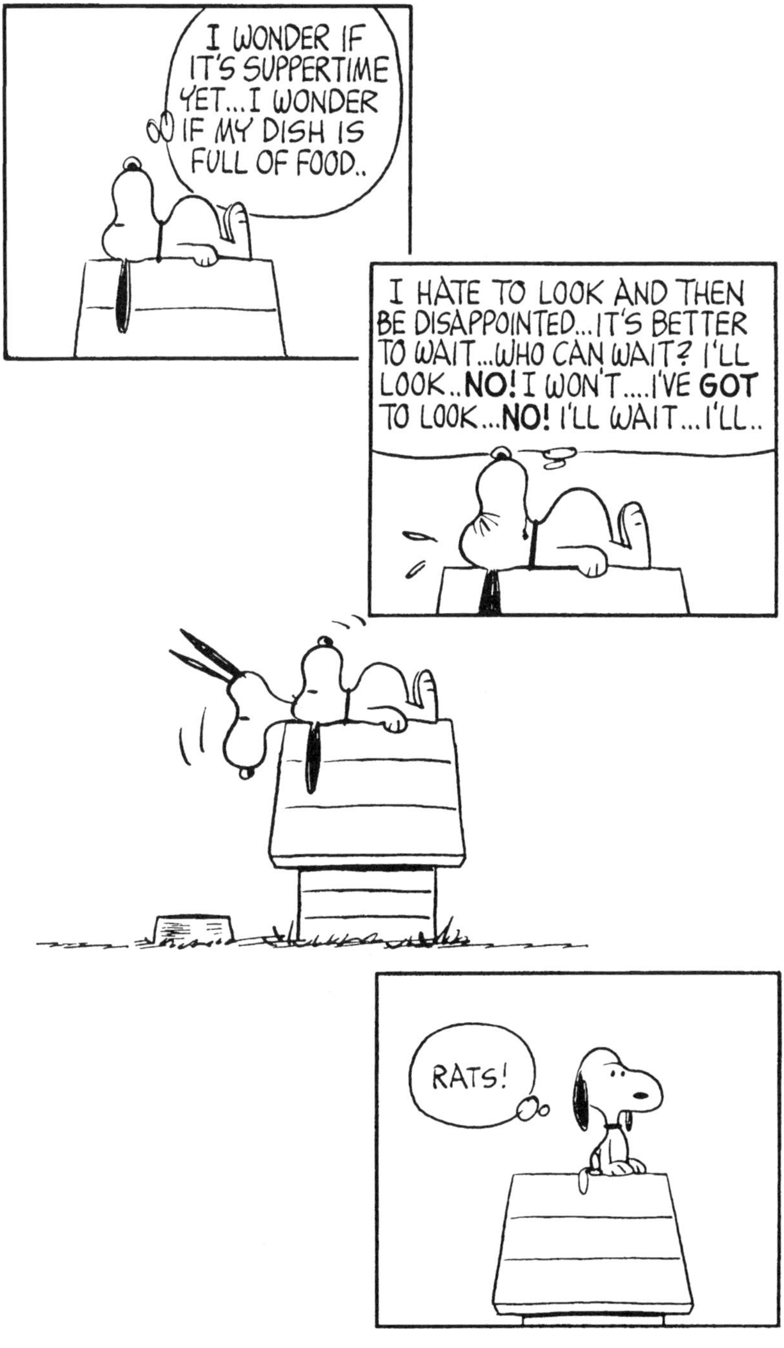
I WONDER IF IT'S SUPPERTIME YET...I WONDER IF MY DISH IS FULL OF FOOD..
I HATE TO LOOK AND THEN BE DISAPPOINTED...IT'S BETTER TO WAIT...WHO CAN WAIT? I'LL LOOK..NO! I WON'T....I'VE GOT TO LOOK...NO! I'LL WAIT...I'LL..
RATS!

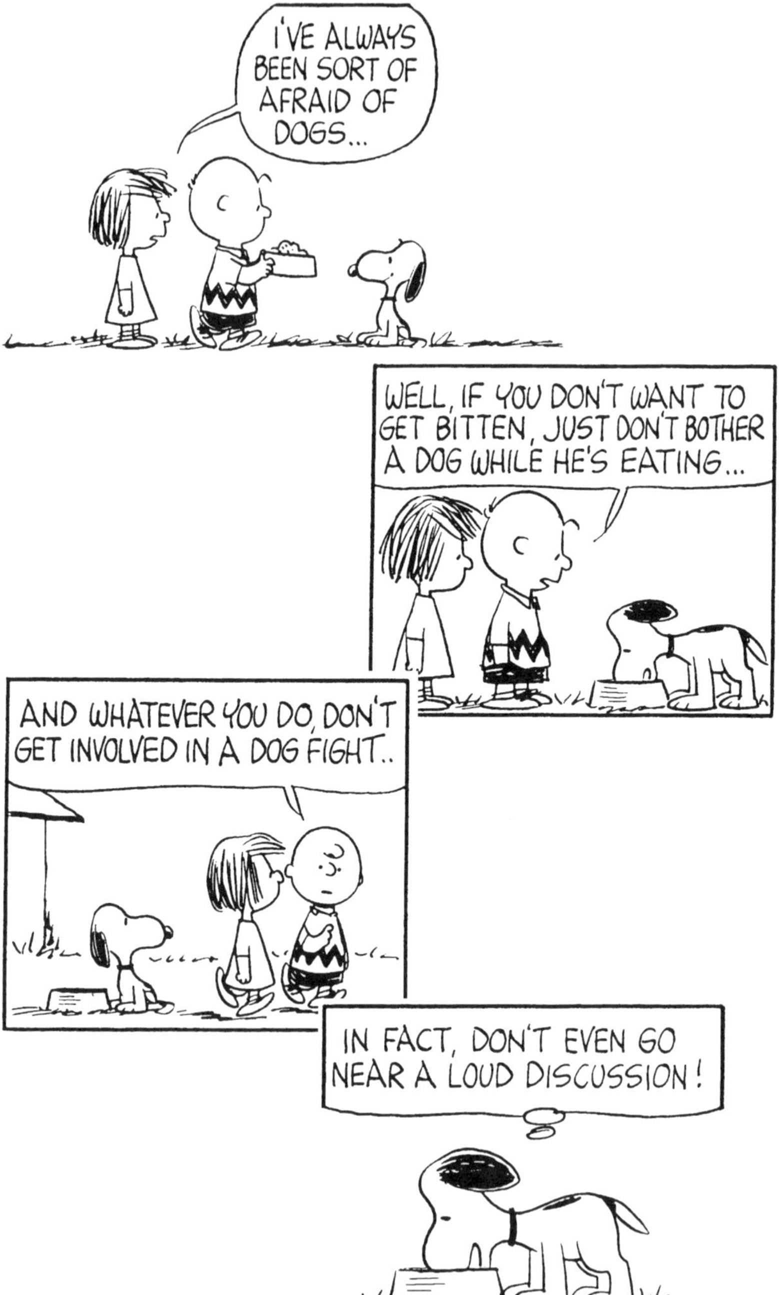
I'VE ALWAYS BEEN SORT OF AFRAID OF DOGS...
WELL, IF YOU DON'T WANT TO GET BITTEN, JUST DON'T BOTHER A DOG WHILE HE'S EATING...
AND WHATEVER YOU DO, DON'T GET INVOLVED IN A DOG FIGHT..
IN FACT, DON'T EVEN GO NEAR A LOUD DISCUSSION!

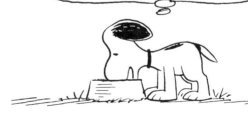

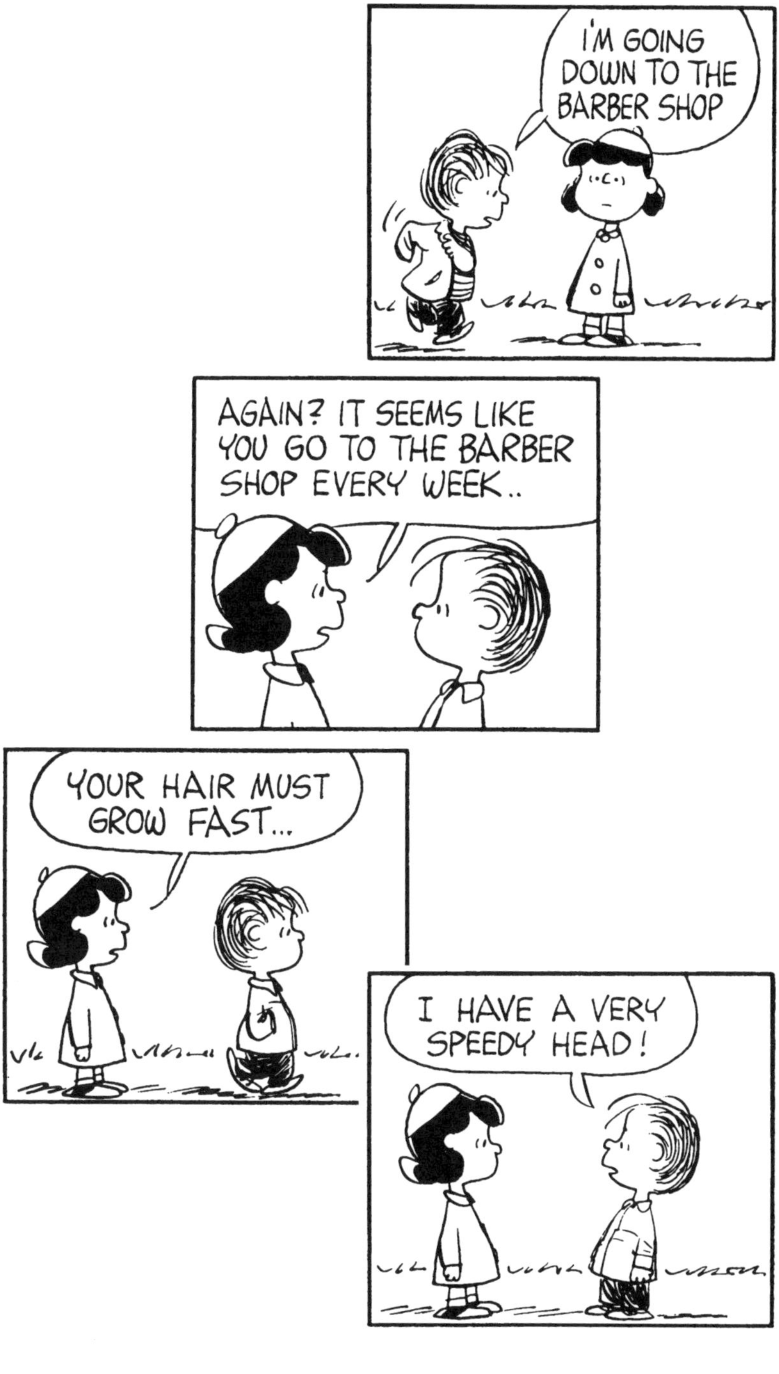
I'M GOING DOWN TO THE BARBER SHOP
AGAIN? IT SEEMS LIKE YOU GO TO THE BARBER SHOP EVERY WEEK..
YOUR HAIR MUST GROW FAST...
I HAVE A VERY SPEEDY HEAD!

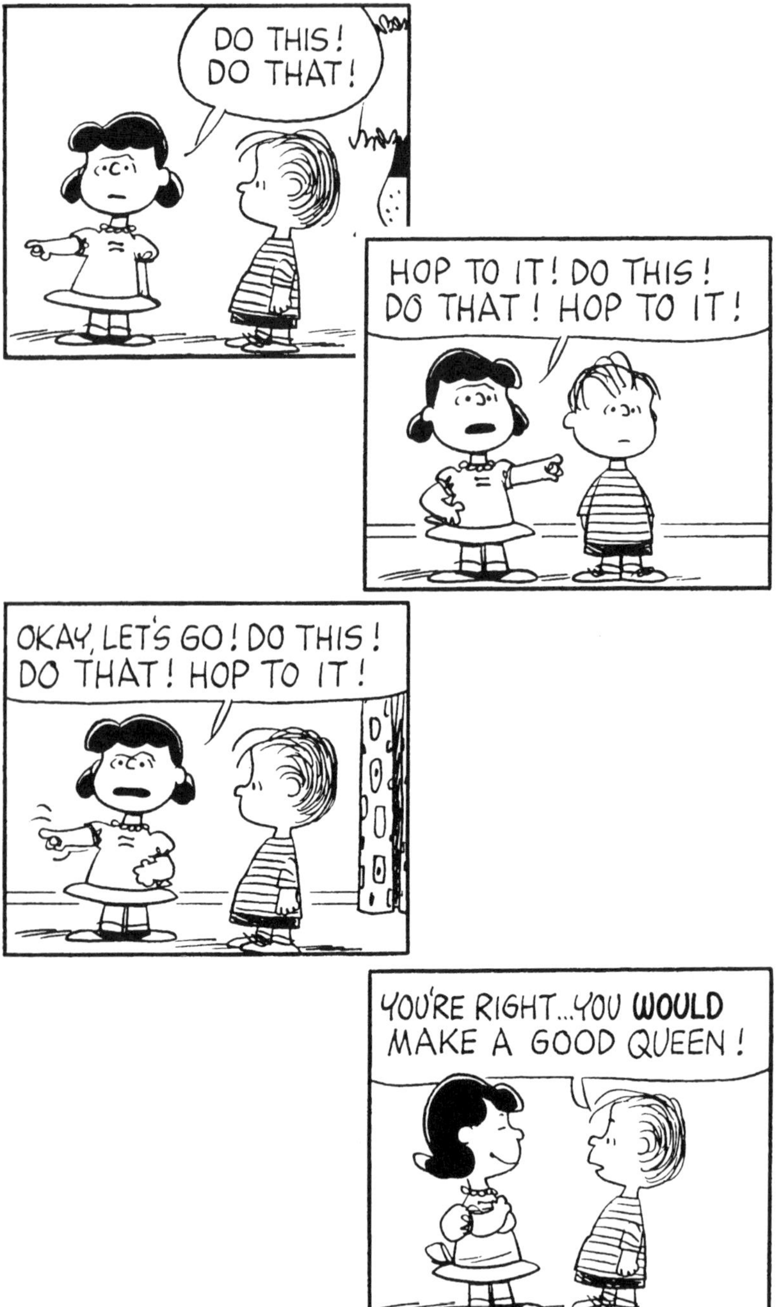
DO THIS! DO THAT!
HOP TO IT! DO THIS! DO THAT! HOP TO IT!
OKAY, LET'S GO! DO THIS! DO THAT! HOP TO IT!
YOU'RE RIGHT...YOU **WOULD** MAKE A GOOD QUEEN!

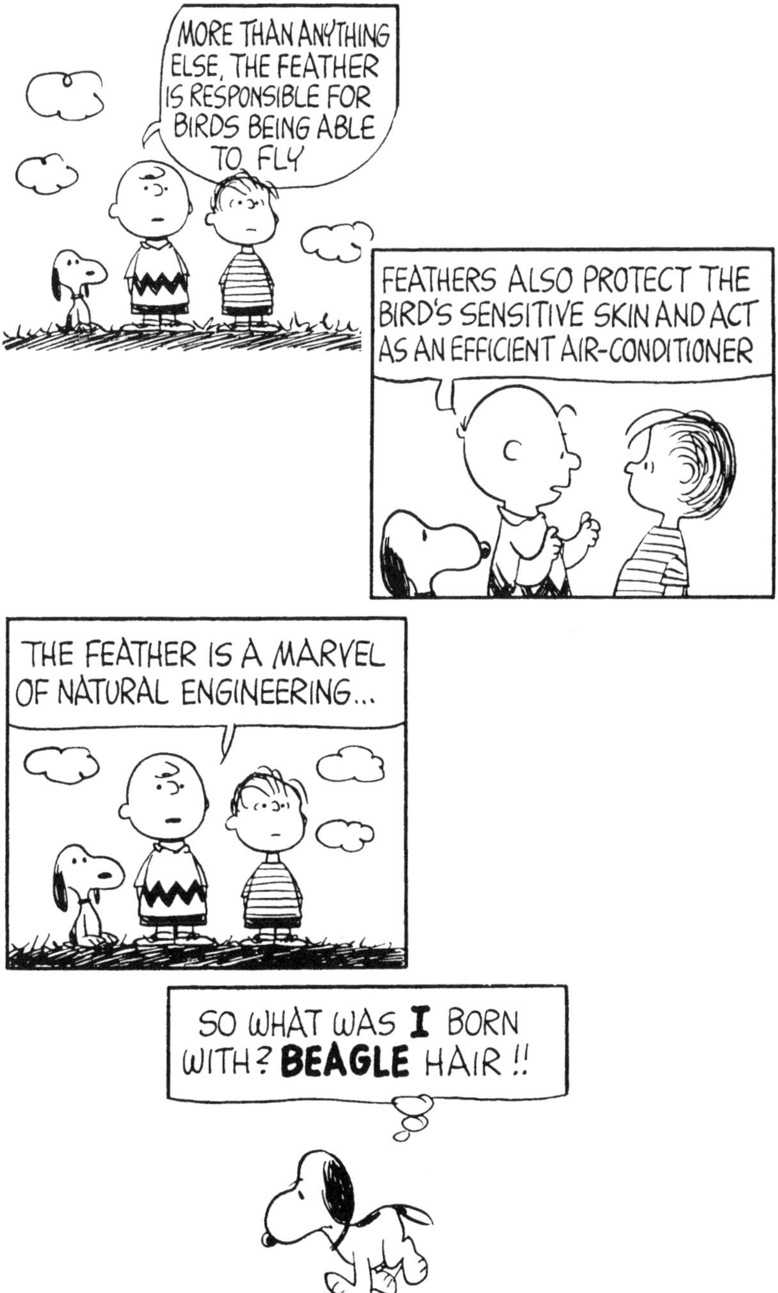
MORE THAN ANYTHING ELSE, THE FEATHER IS RESPONSIBLE FOR BIRDS BEING ABLE TO FLY
FEATHERS ALSO PROTECT THE BIRD'S SENSITIVE SKIN AND ACT AS AN EFFICIENT AIR-CONDITIONER
THE FEATHER IS A MARVEL OF NATURAL ENGINEERING...
SO WHAT WAS **I** BORN WITH? **BEAGLE** HAIR !!

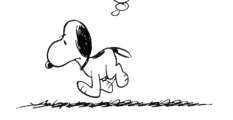

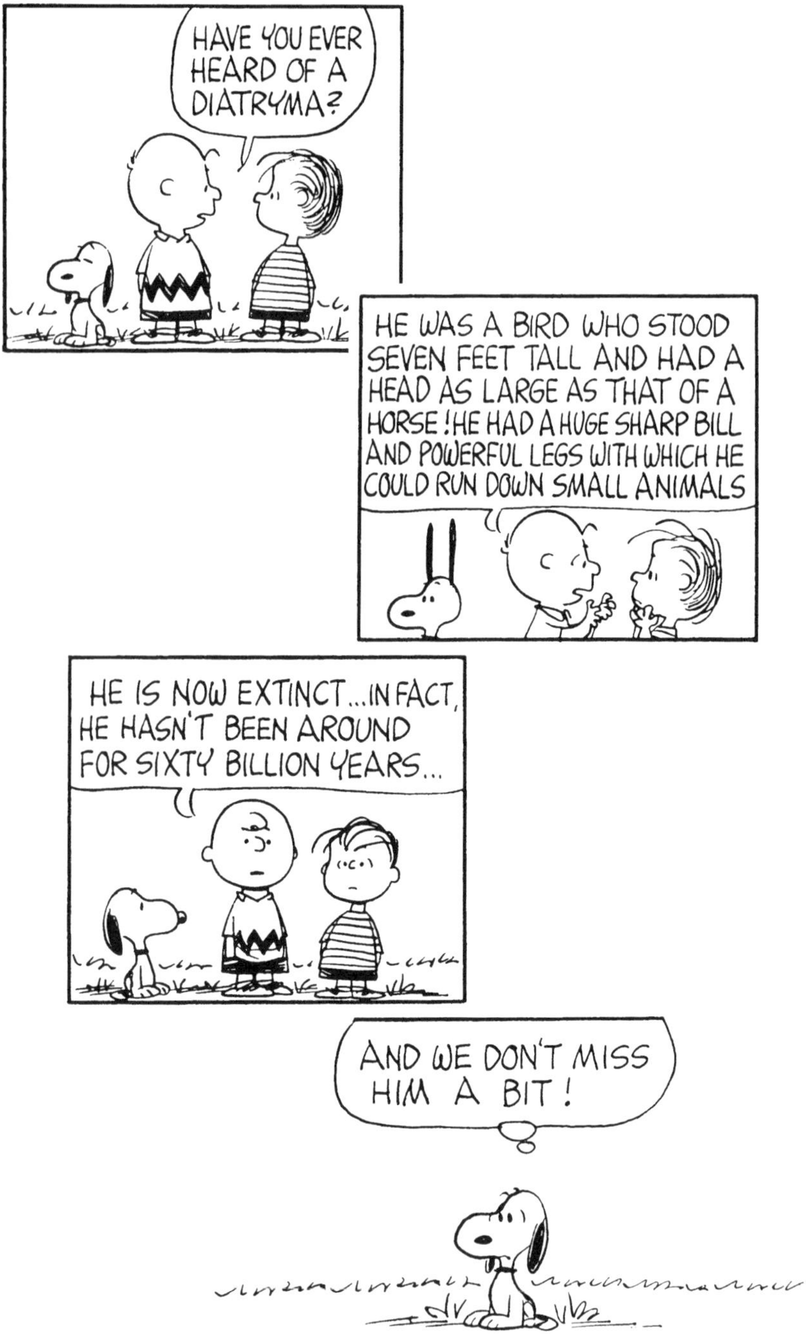
HAVE YOU EVER HEARD OF A DIATRYMA?
HE WAS A BIRD WHO STOOD SEVEN FEET TALL AND HAD A HEAD AS LARGE AS THAT OF A HORSE! HE HAD A HUGE SHARP BILL AND POWERFUL LEGS WITH WHICH HE COULD RUN DOWN SMALL ANIMALS
HE IS NOW EXTINCT...IN FACT, HE HASN'T BEEN AROUND FOR SIXTY BILLION YEARS...
AND WE DON'T MISS HIM A BIT!

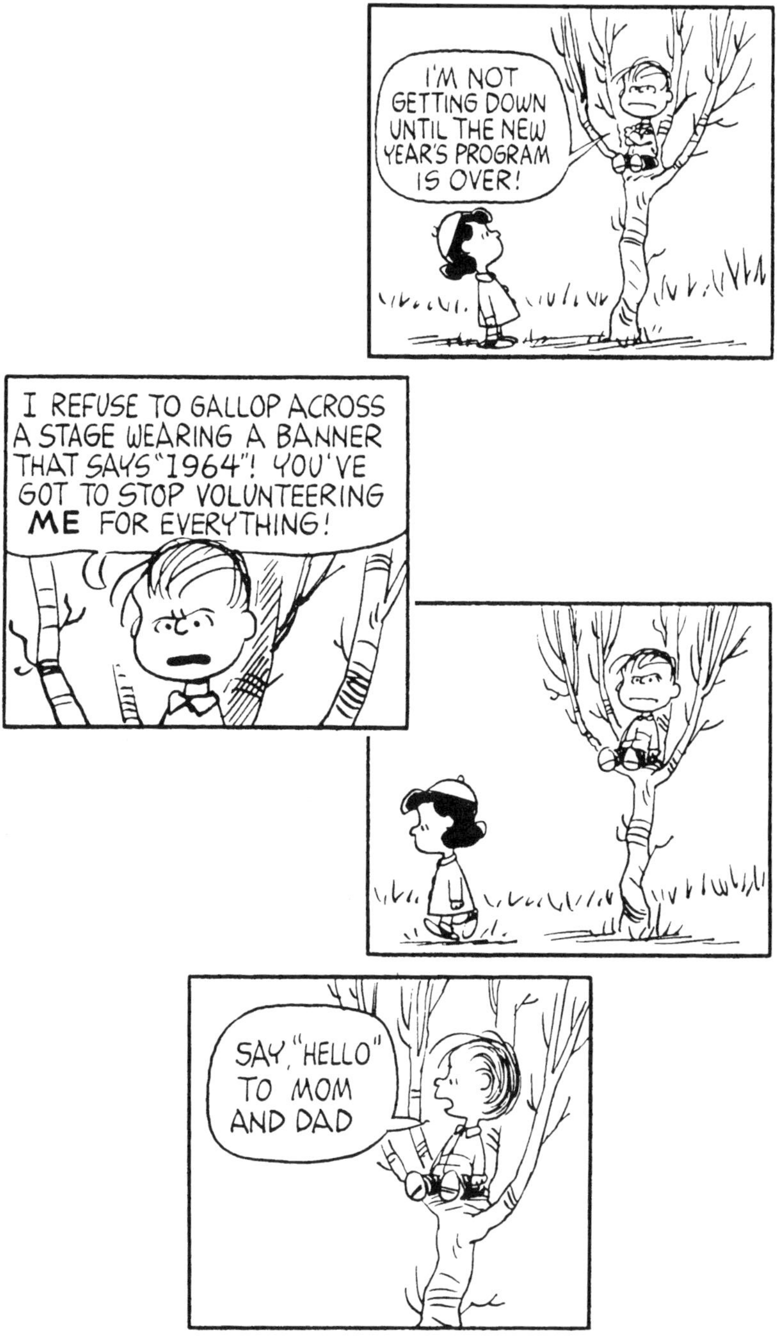
I'M NOT GETTING DOWN UNTIL THE NEW YEAR'S PROGRAM IS OVER!
I REFUSE TO GALLOP ACROSS A STAGE WEARING A BANNER THAT SAYS "1964"! YOU'VE GOT TO STOP VOLUNTEERING **ME** FOR EVERYTHING!
SAY, "HELLO" TO MOM AND DAD

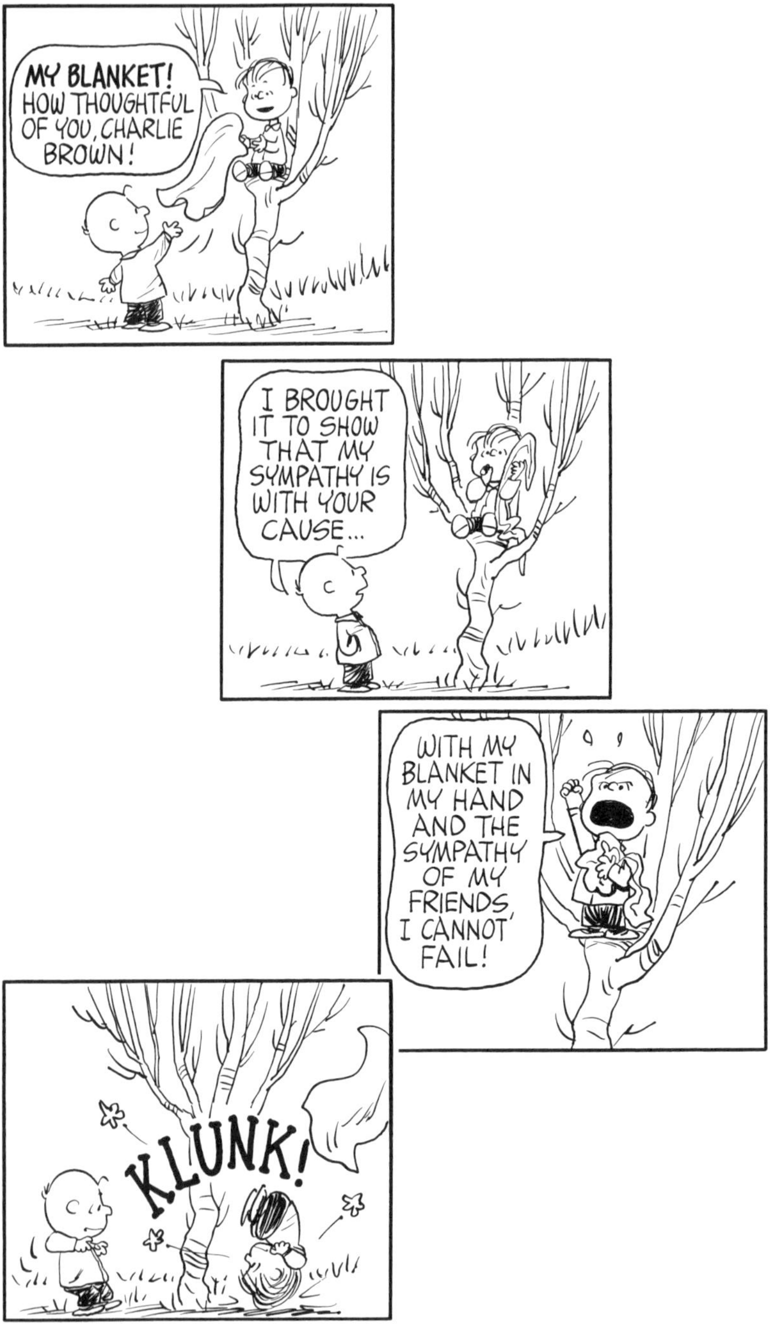
MY BLANKET! HOW THOUGHTFUL OF YOU, CHARLIE BROWN!
I BROUGHT IT TO SHOW THAT MY SYMPATHY IS WITH YOUR CAUSE...
WITH MY BLANKET IN MY HAND AND THE SYMPATHY OF MY FRIENDS, I CANNOT FAIL!
KLUNK!

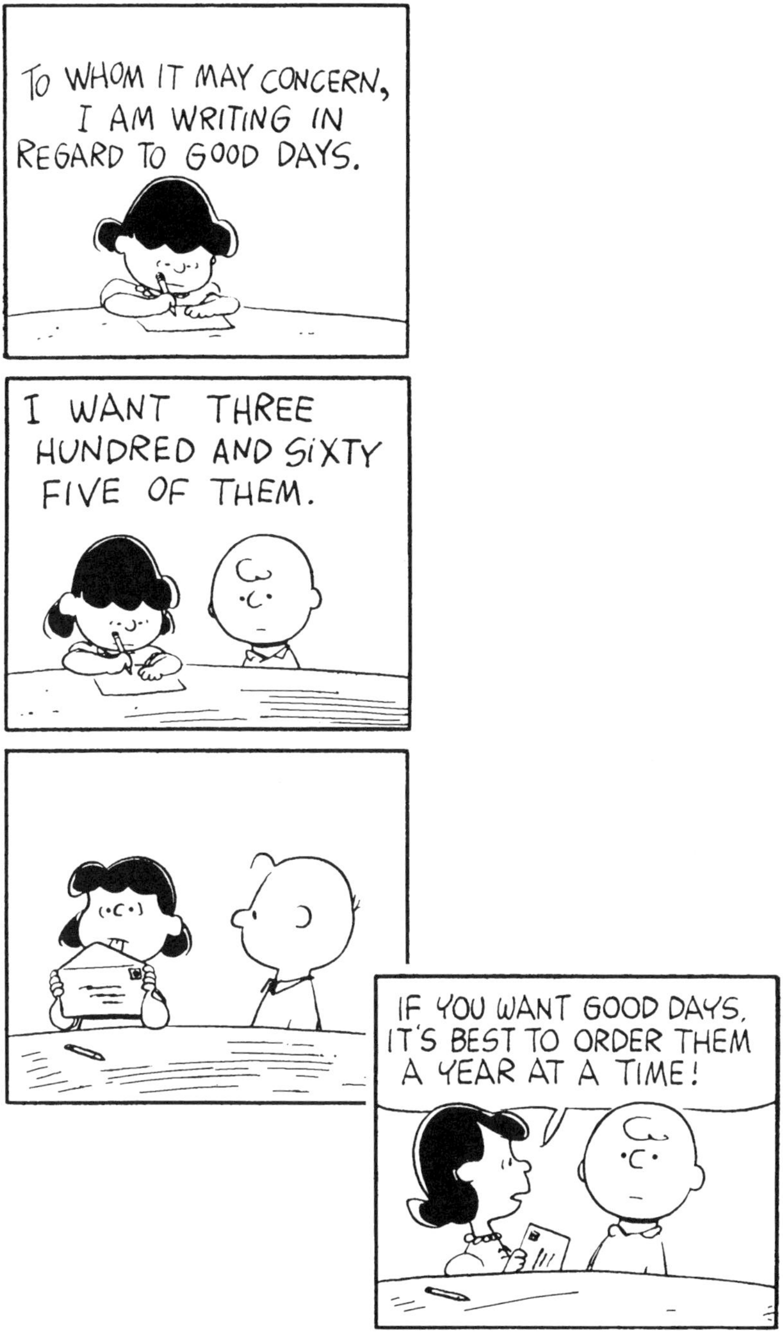
TO WHOM IT MAY CONCERN, I AM WRITING IN REGARD TO GOOD DAYS.
I WANT THREE HUNDRED AND SIXTY FIVE OF THEM.
IF YOU WANT GOOD DAYS, IT'S BEST TO ORDER THEM A YEAR AT A TIME!

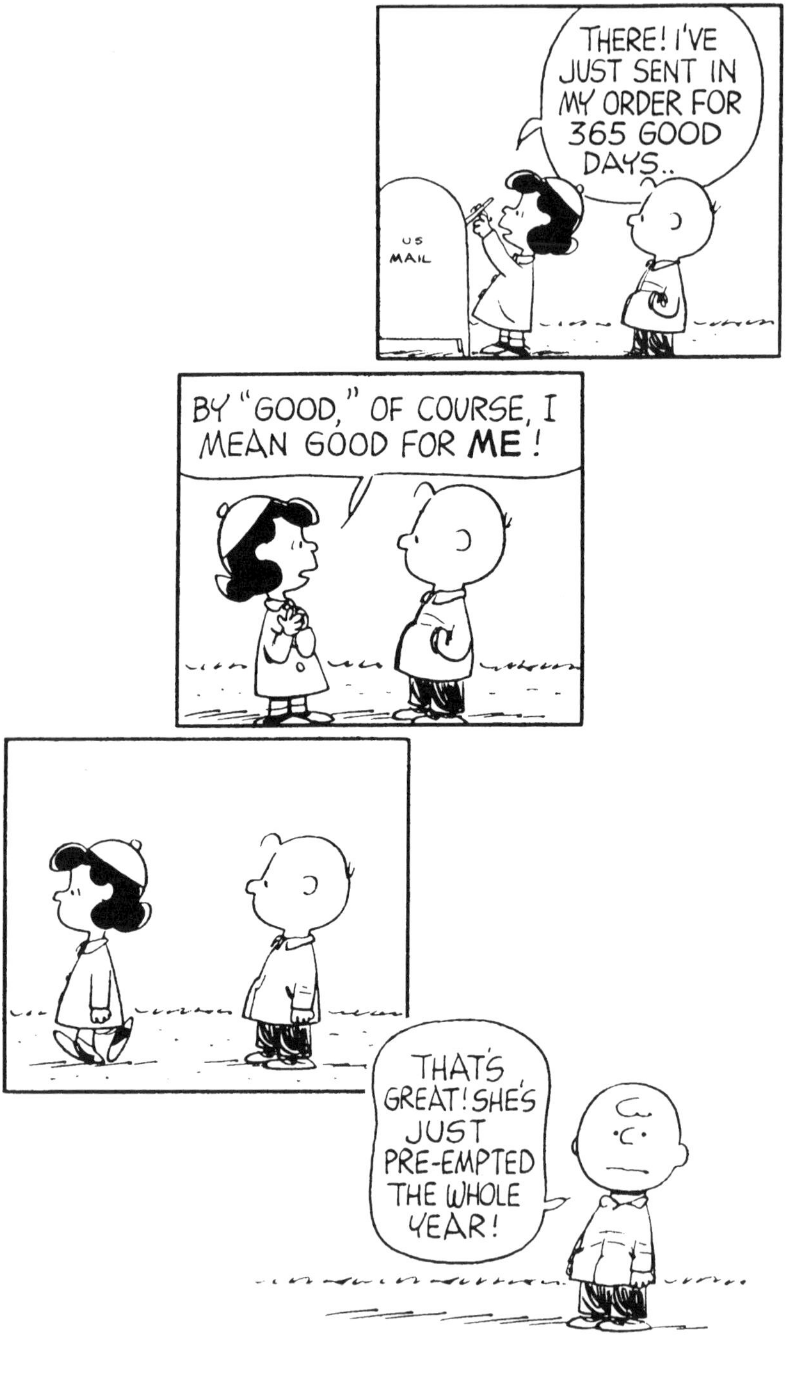
THERE! I'VE JUST SENT IN MY ORDER FOR 365 GOOD DAYS..
US MAIL
BY "GOOD," OF COURSE, I MEAN GOOD FOR **ME**!
THAT'S GREAT! SHE'S JUST PRE-EMPTED THE WHOLE YEAR!

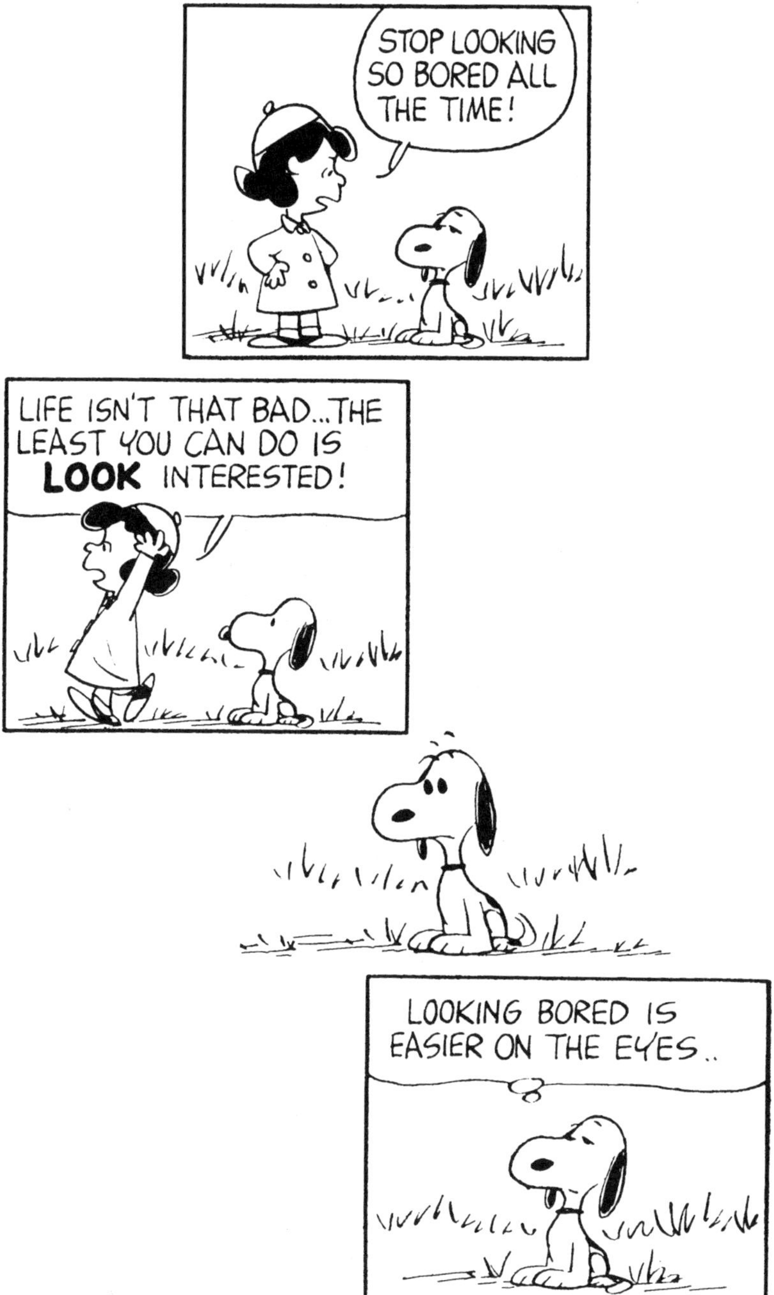
STOP LOOKING SO BORED ALL THE TIME!
LIFE ISN'T THAT BAD...THE LEAST YOU CAN DO IS **LOOK** INTERESTED!
LOOKING BORED IS EASIER ON THE EYES..

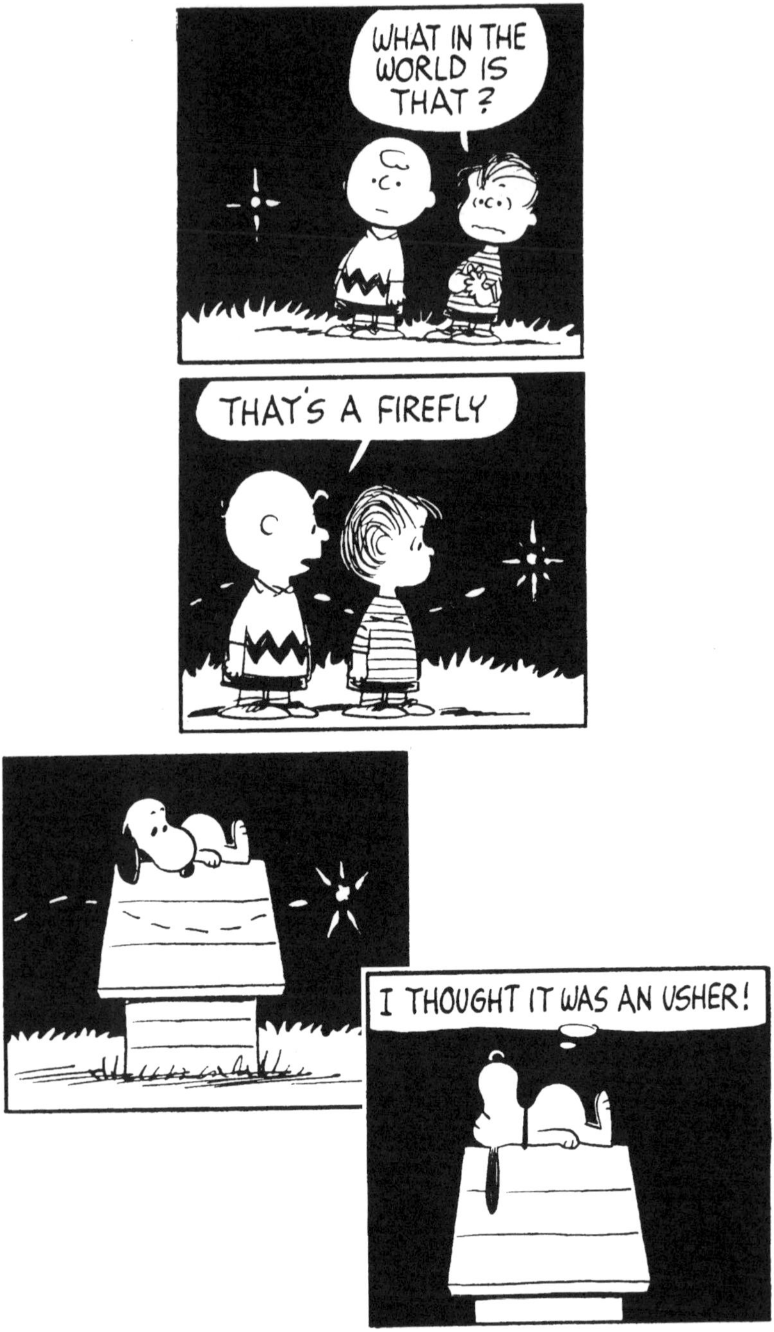
WHAT IN THE WORLD IS THAT?
THAT'S A FIREFLY
I THOUGHT IT WAS AN USHER!

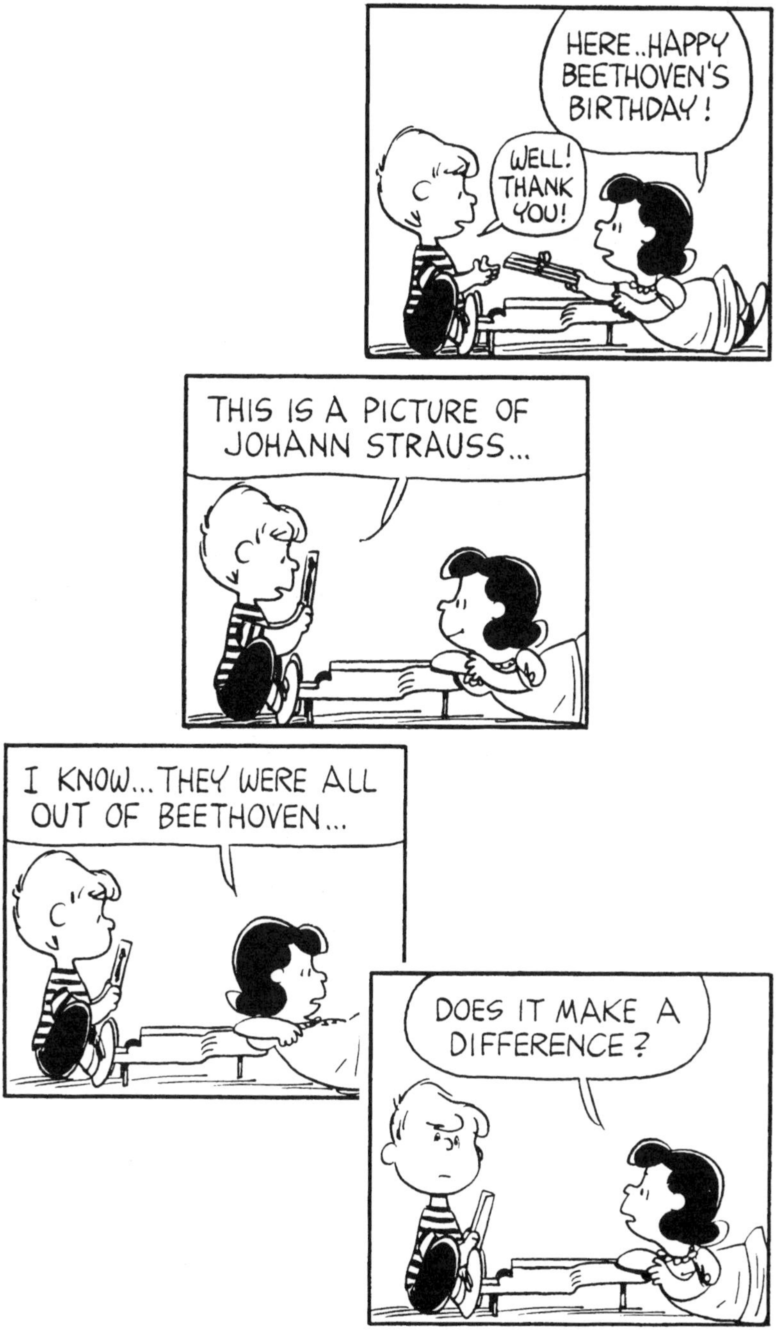
HERE..HAPPY BEETHOVEN'S BIRTHDAY!
WELL! THANK YOU!
THIS IS A PICTURE OF JOHANN STRAUSS...
I KNOW...THEY WERE ALL OUT OF BEETHOVEN...
DOES IT MAKE A DIFFERENCE?

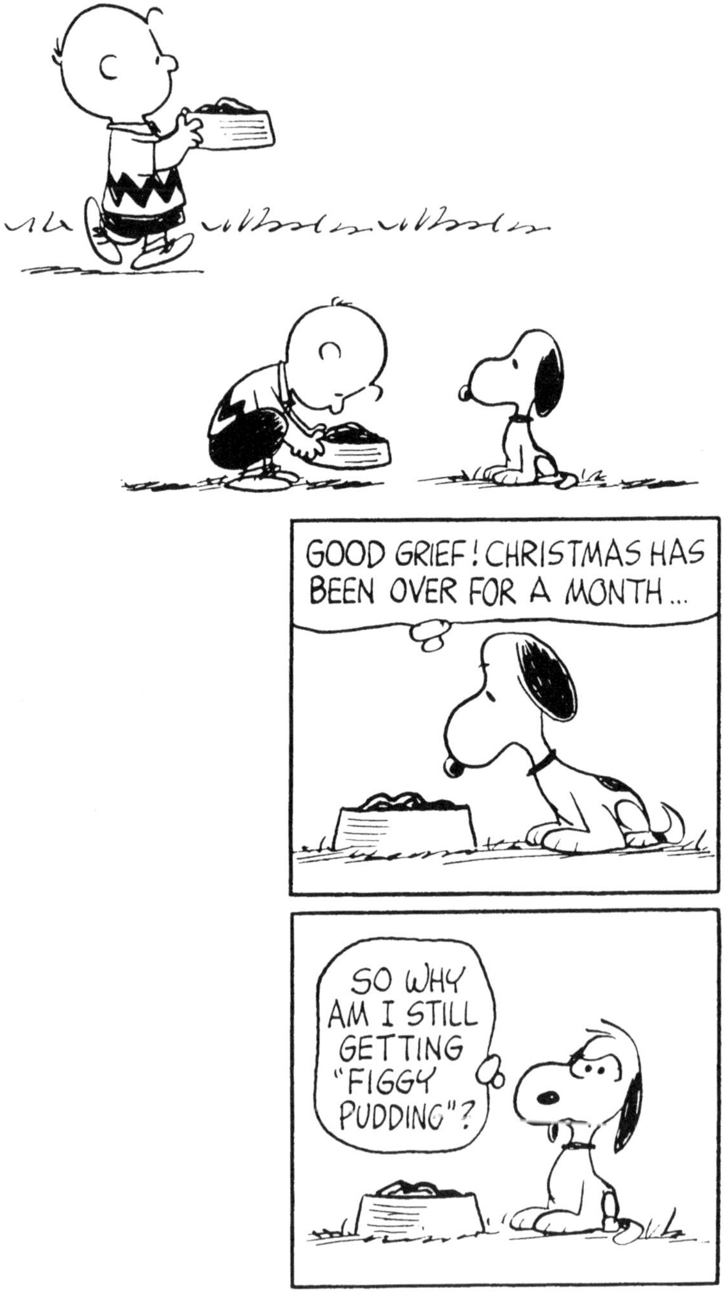

GOOD GRIEF! CHRISTMAS HAS BEEN OVER FOR A MONTH...
SO WHY AM I STILL GETTING "FIGGY PUDDING"?

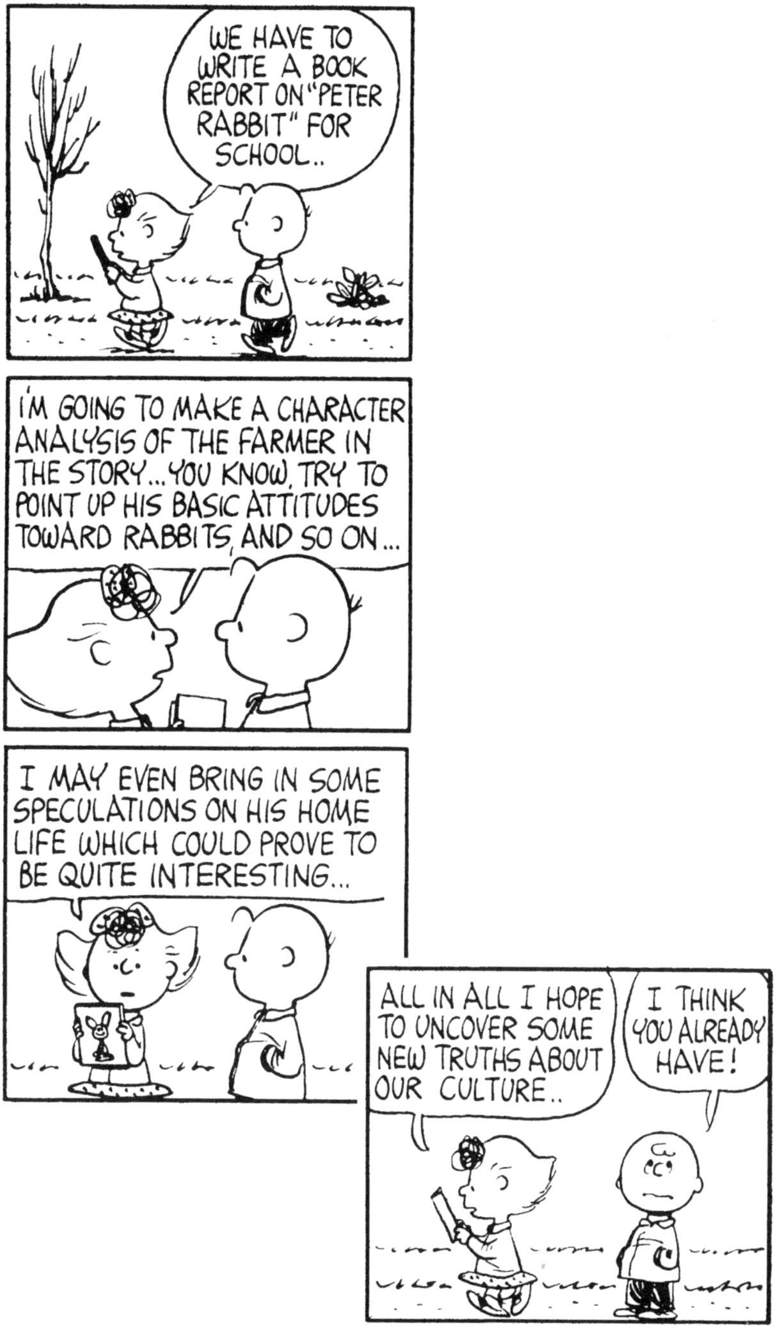
WE HAVE TO WRITE A BOOK REPORT ON "PETER RABBIT" FOR SCHOOL..
I'M GOING TO MAKE A CHARACTER ANALYSIS OF THE FARMER IN THE STORY...YOU KNOW, TRY TO POINT UP HIS BASIC ATTITUDES TOWARD RABBITS, AND SO ON...
I MAY EVEN BRING IN SOME SPECULATIONS ON HIS HOME LIFE WHICH COULD PROVE TO BE QUITE INTERESTING...
ALL IN ALL I HOPE TO UNCOVER SOME NEW TRUTHS ABOUT OUR CULTURE..
I THINK YOU ALREADY HAVE!

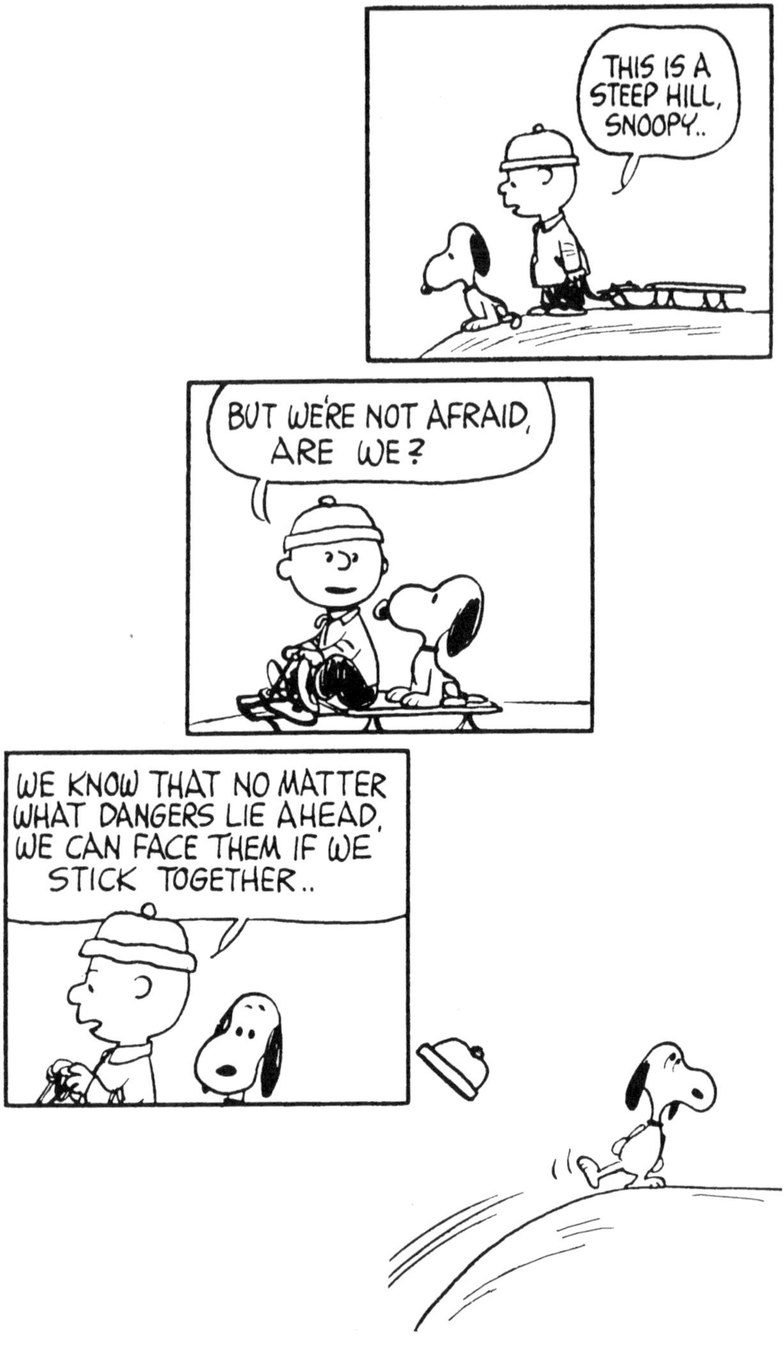
THIS IS A STEEP HILL, SNOOPY..
BUT WE'RE NOT AFRAID, ARE WE?
WE KNOW THAT NO MATTER WHAT DANGERS LIE AHEAD, WE CAN FACE THEM IF WE STICK TOGETHER..

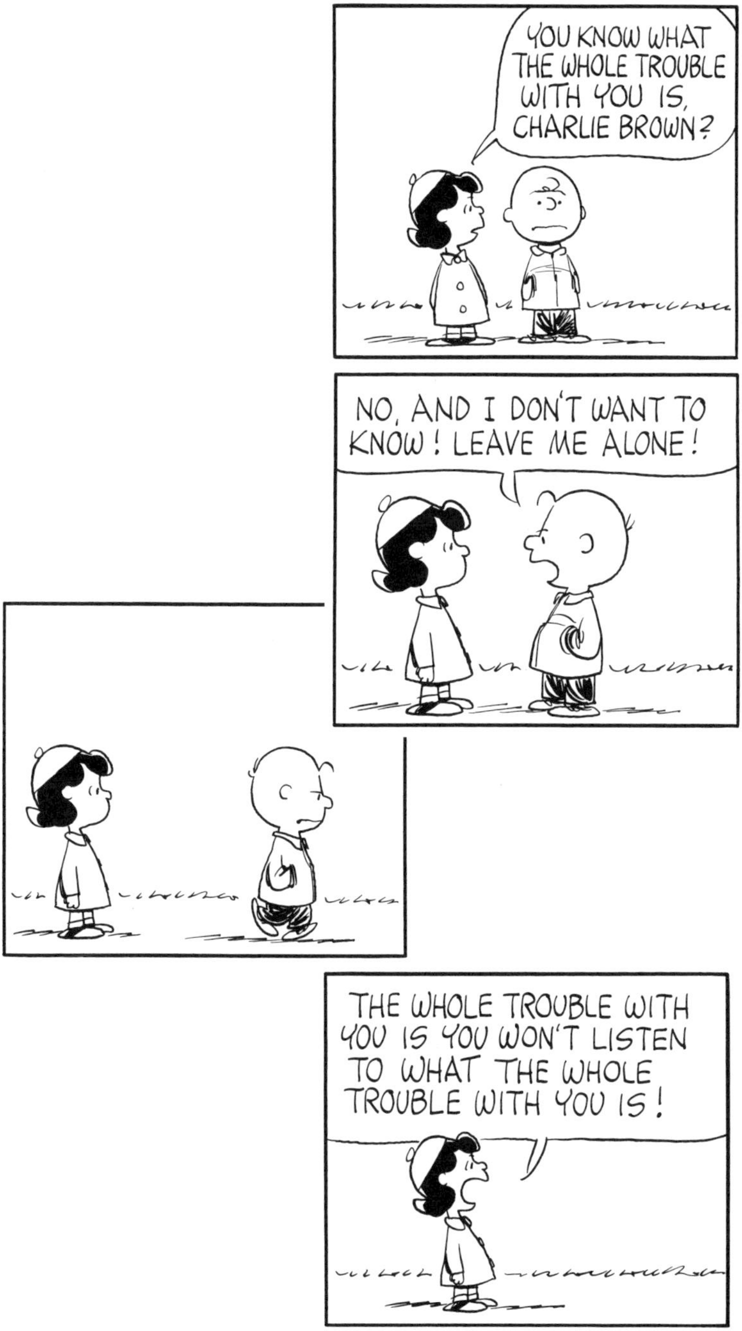
YOU KNOW WHAT THE WHOLE TROUBLE WITH YOU IS, CHARLIE BROWN?
NO, AND I DON'T WANT TO KNOW! LEAVE ME ALONE!
THE WHOLE TROUBLE WITH YOU IS YOU WON'T LISTEN TO WHAT THE WHOLE TROUBLE WITH YOU IS!

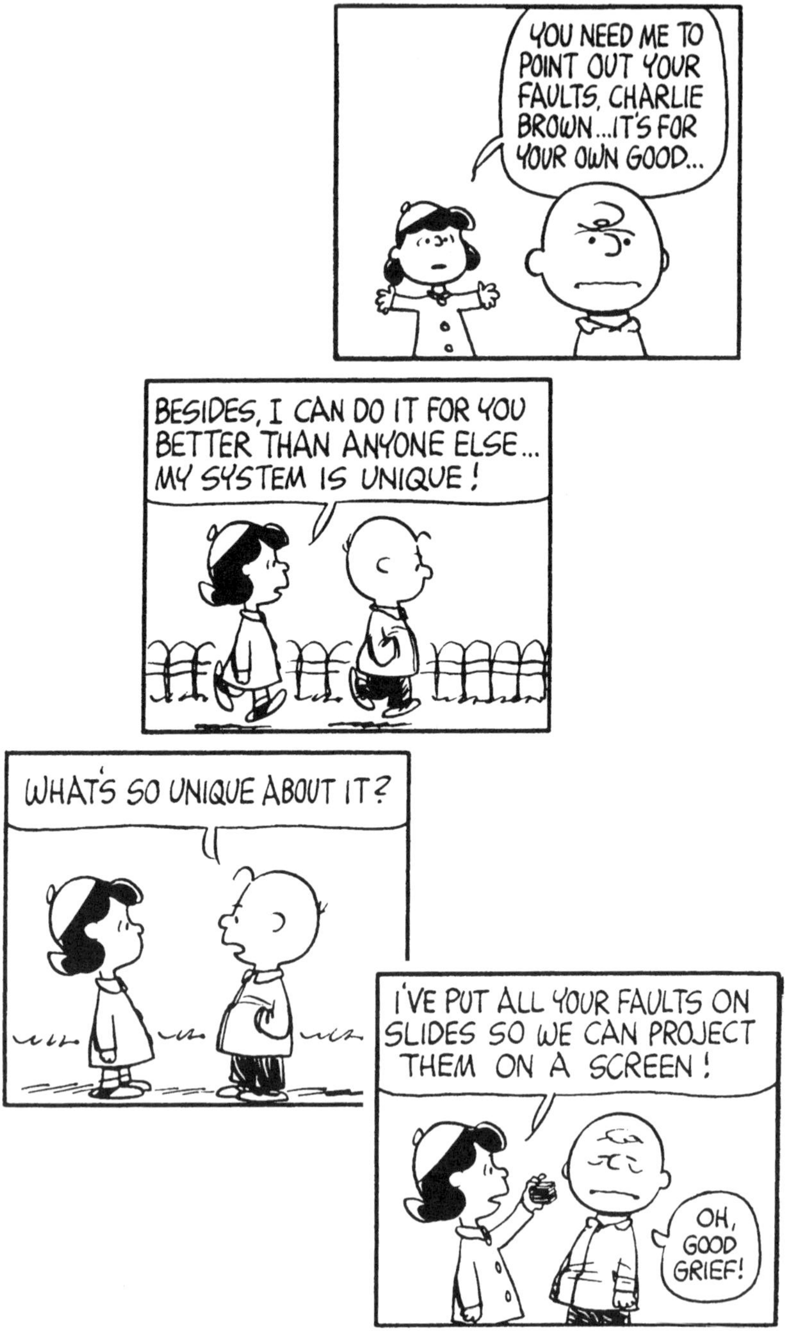
YOU NEED ME TO POINT OUT YOUR FAULTS, CHARLIE BROWN...IT'S FOR YOUR OWN GOOD...
BESIDES, I CAN DO IT FOR YOU BETTER THAN ANYONE ELSE... MY SYSTEM IS UNIQUE!
WHAT'S SO UNIQUE ABOUT IT?
I'VE PUT ALL YOUR FAULTS ON SLIDES SO WE CAN PROJECT THEM ON A SCREEN!
OH, GOOD GRIEF!

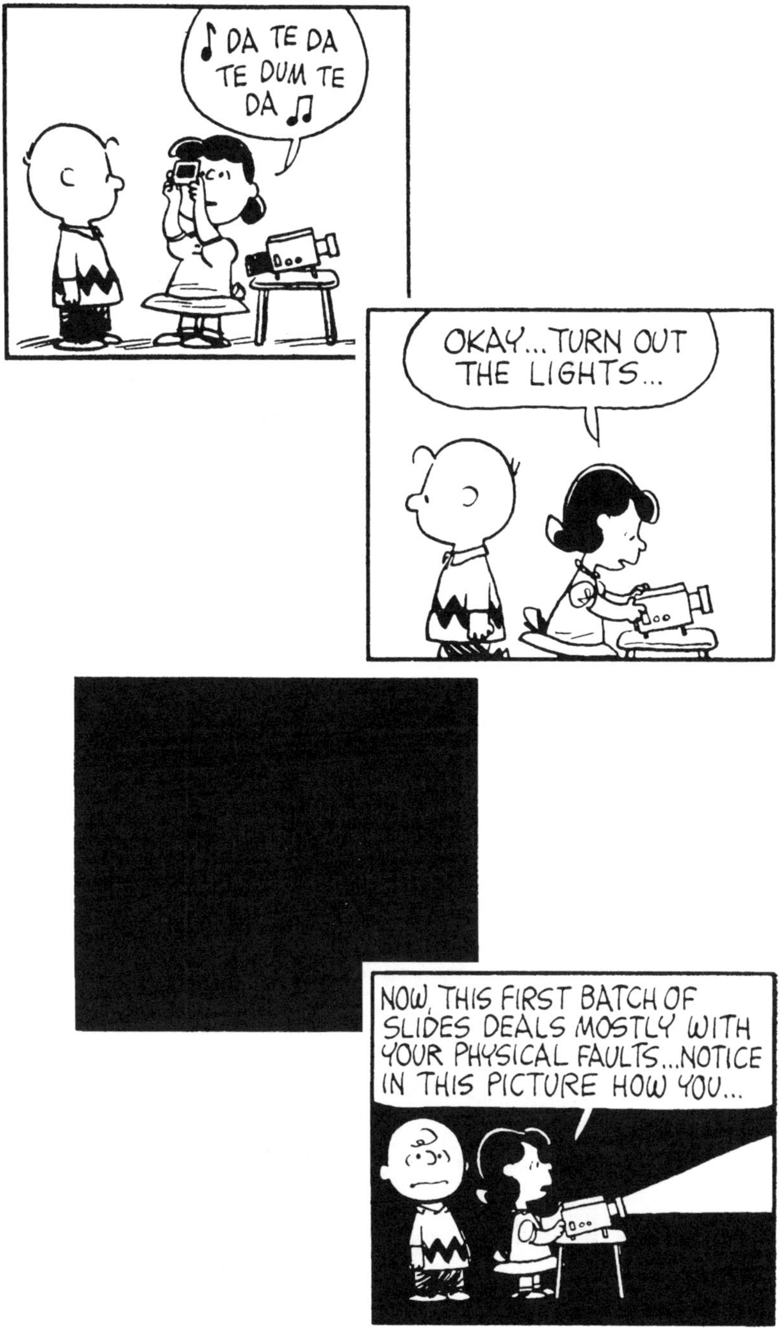

♪ DA TE DA TE DUM TE DA ♫
OKAY... TURN OUT THE LIGHTS...
NOW, THIS FIRST BATCH OF SLIDES DEALS MOSTLY WITH YOUR PHYSICAL FAULTS...NOTICE IN THIS PICTURE HOW YOU...

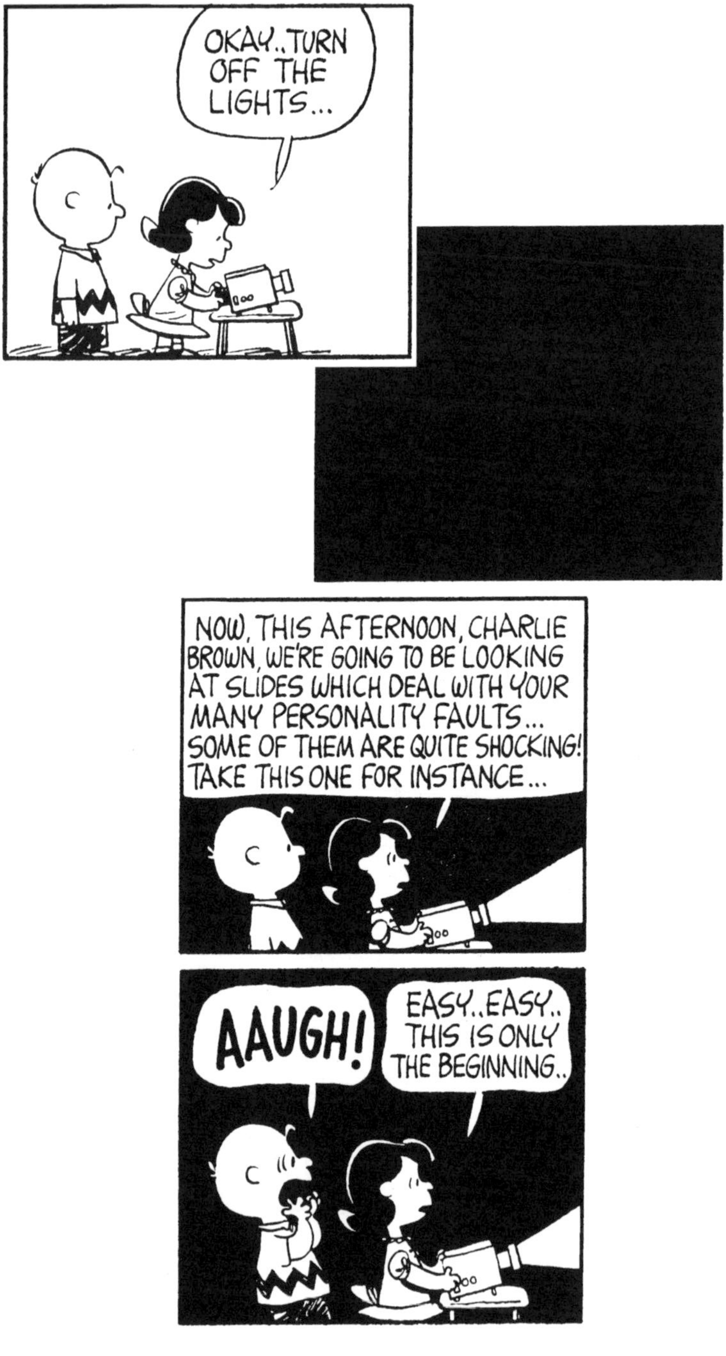
OKAY..TURN OFF THE LIGHTS...
NOW, THIS AFTERNOON, CHARLIE BROWN, WE'RE GOING TO BE LOOKING AT SLIDES WHICH DEAL WITH YOUR MANY PERSONALITY FAULTS... SOME OF THEM ARE QUITE SHOCKING! TAKE THIS ONE FOR INSTANCE...
AAUGH!
EASY..EASY.. THIS IS ONLY THE BEGINNING..

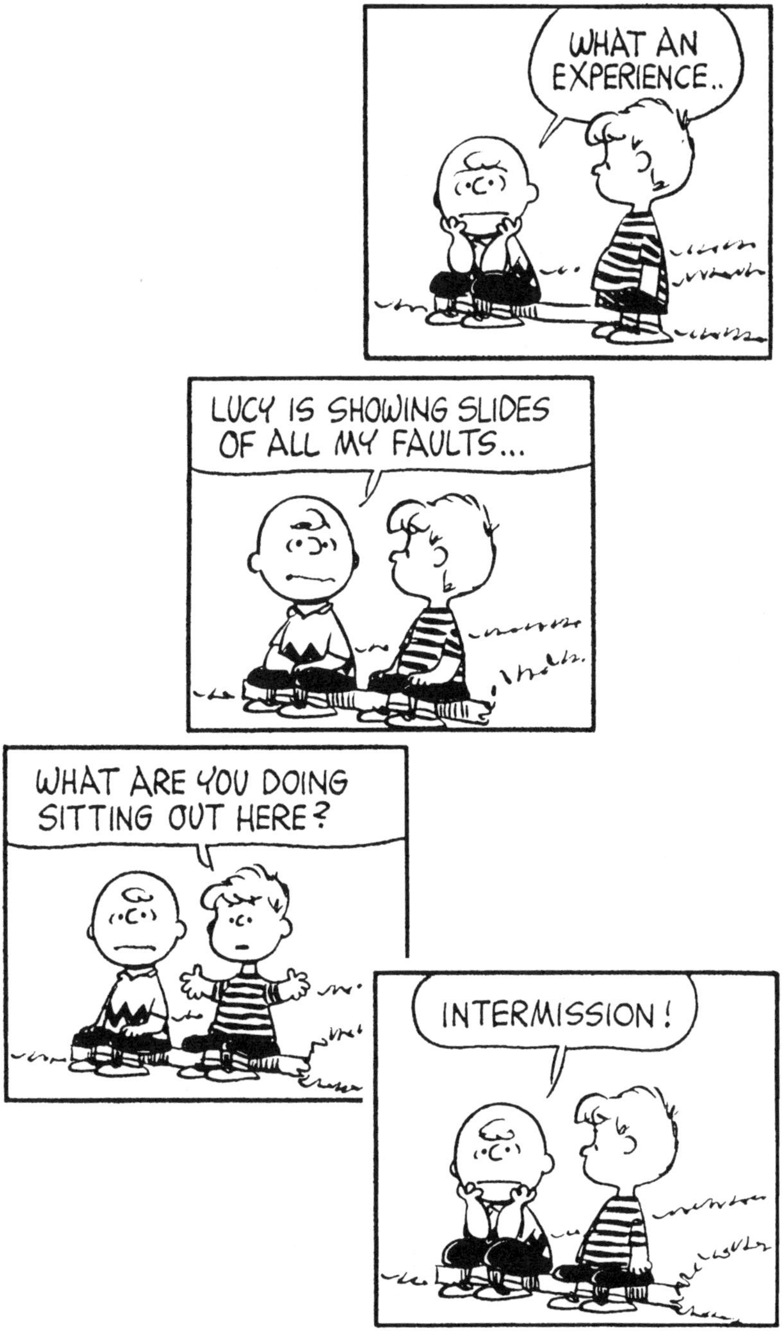
WHAT ARE YOU DOING SITTING OUT HERE?
LUCY IS SHOWING SLIDES OF ALL MY FAULTS...
WHAT AN EXPERIENCE..
INTERMISSION!

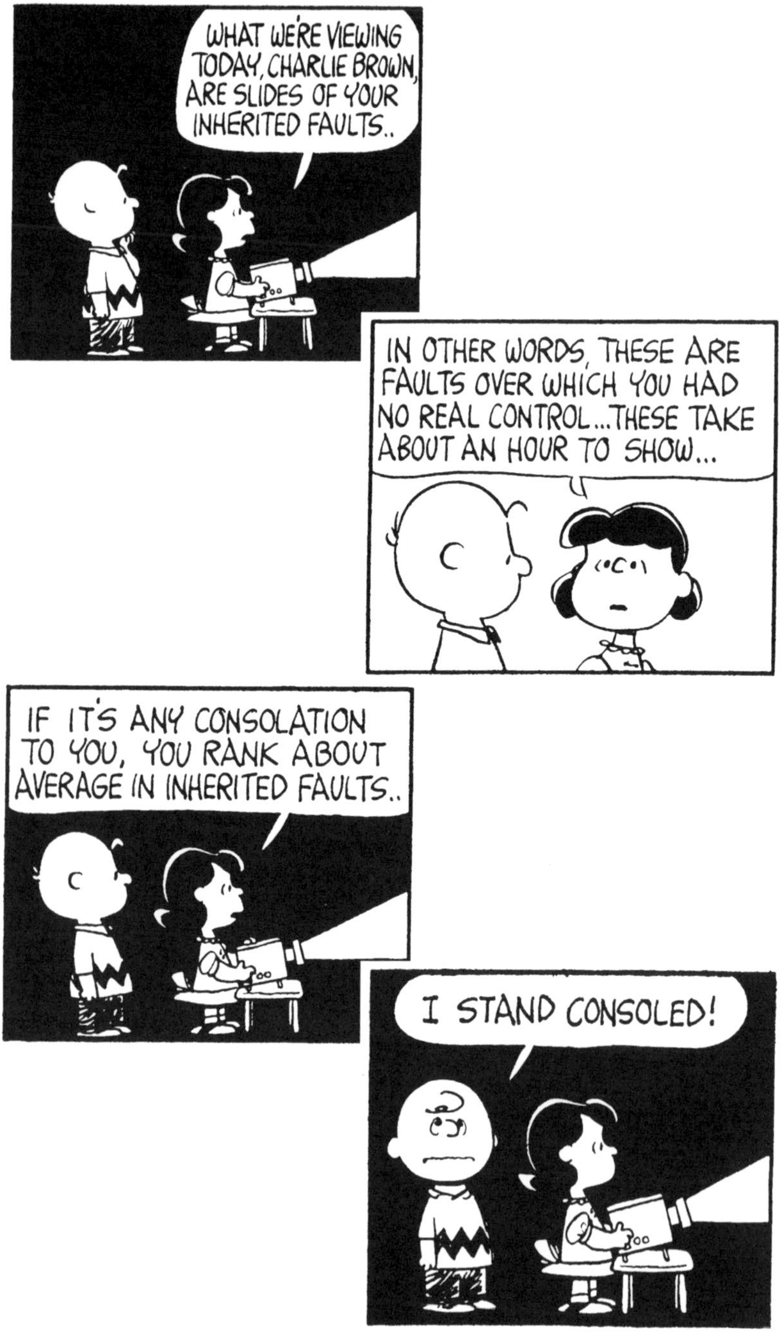
WHAT WE'RE VIEWING TODAY, CHARLIE BROWN, ARE SLIDES OF YOUR INHERITED FAULTS..
IN OTHER WORDS, THESE ARE FAULTS OVER WHICH YOU HAD NO REAL CONTROL...THESE TAKE ABOUT AN HOUR TO SHOW...
IF IT'S ANY CONSOLATION TO YOU, YOU RANK ABOUT AVERAGE IN INHERITED FAULTS..
I STAND CONSOLED!

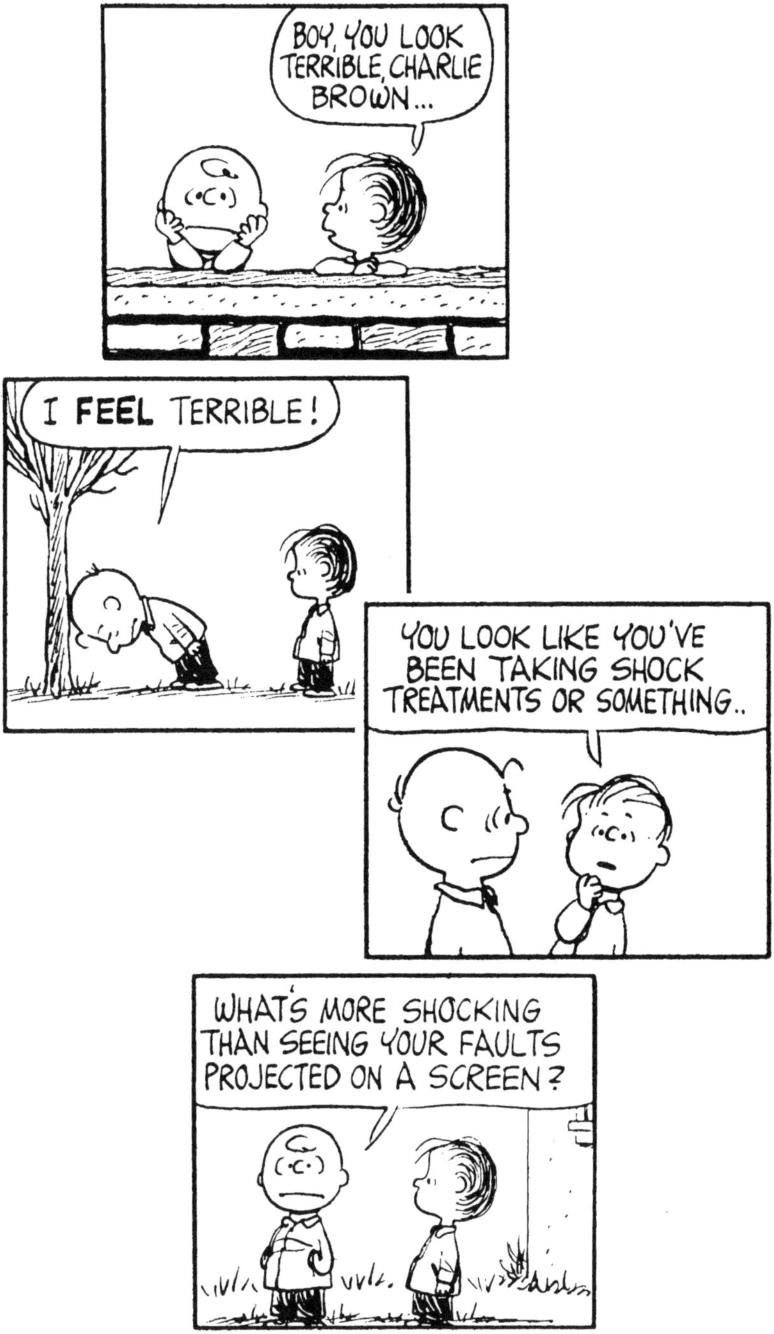
BOY, YOU LOOK TERRIBLE, CHARLIE BROWN...
I FEEL TERRIBLE!
YOU LOOK LIKE YOU'VE BEEN TAKING SHOCK TREATMENTS OR SOMETHING..
WHAT'S MORE SHOCKING THAN SEEING YOUR FAULTS PROJECTED ON A SCREEN?

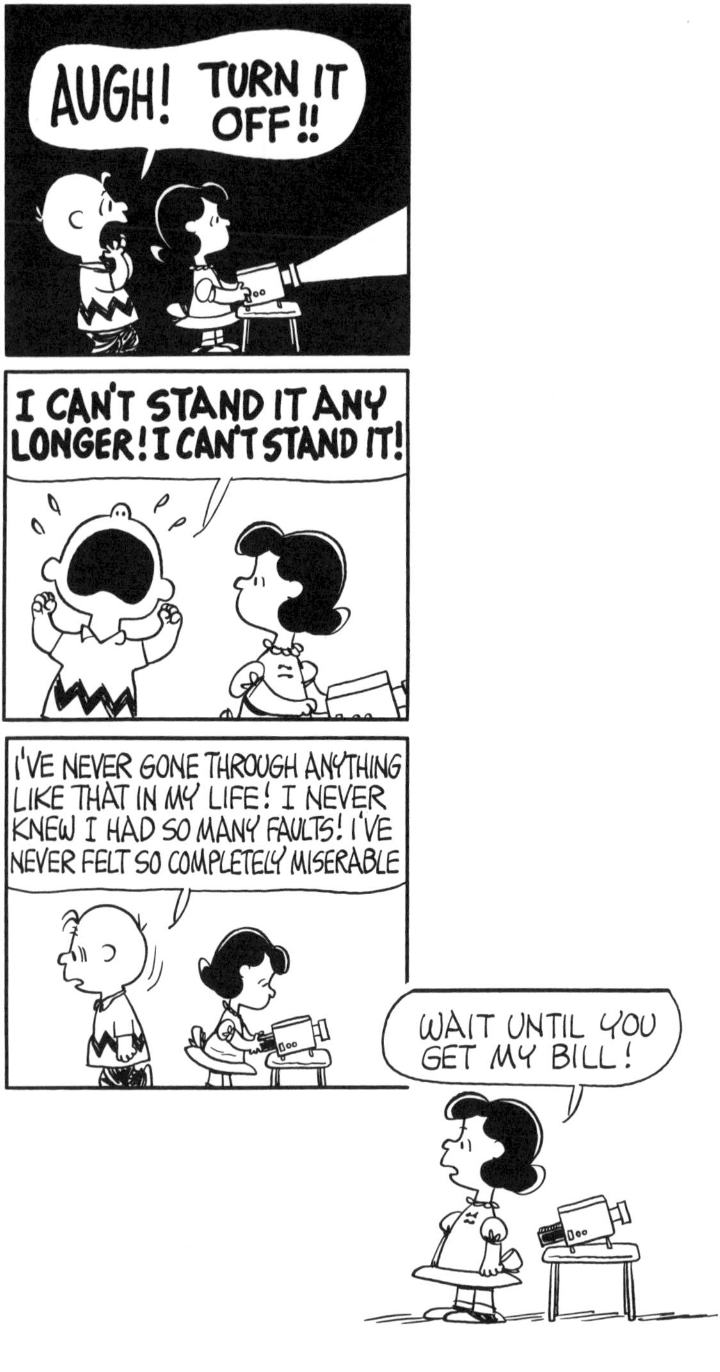
AUGH! TURN IT OFF!!
I CAN'T STAND IT ANY LONGER! I CAN'T STAND IT!
I'VE NEVER GONE THROUGH ANYTHING LIKE THAT IN MY LIFE! I NEVER KNEW I HAD SO MANY FAULTS! I'VE NEVER FELT SO COMPLETELY MISERABLE
WAIT UNTIL YOU GET MY BILL!

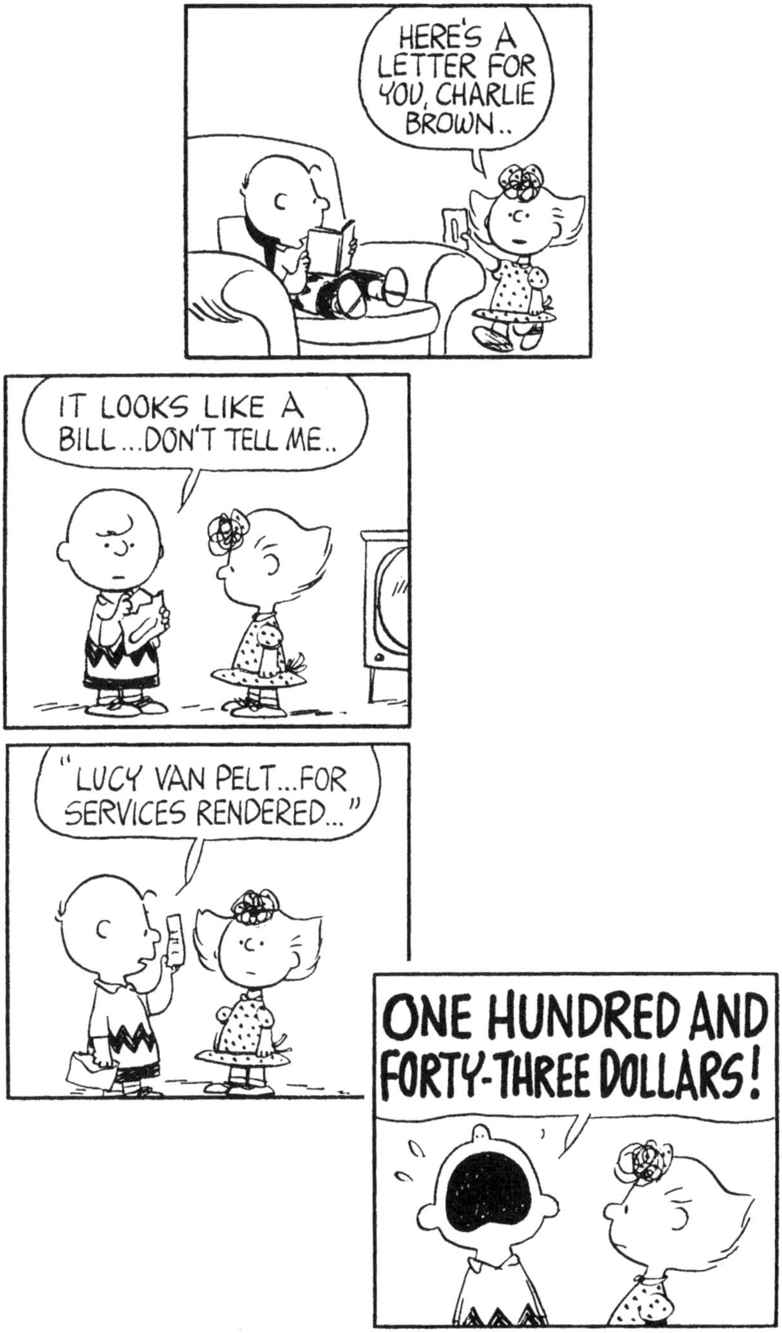
HERE'S A LETTER FOR YOU, CHARLIE BROWN..
IT LOOKS LIKE A BILL...DON'T TELL ME..
"LUCY VAN PELT...FOR SERVICES RENDERED..."
ONE HUNDRED AND FORTY-THREE DOLLARS!

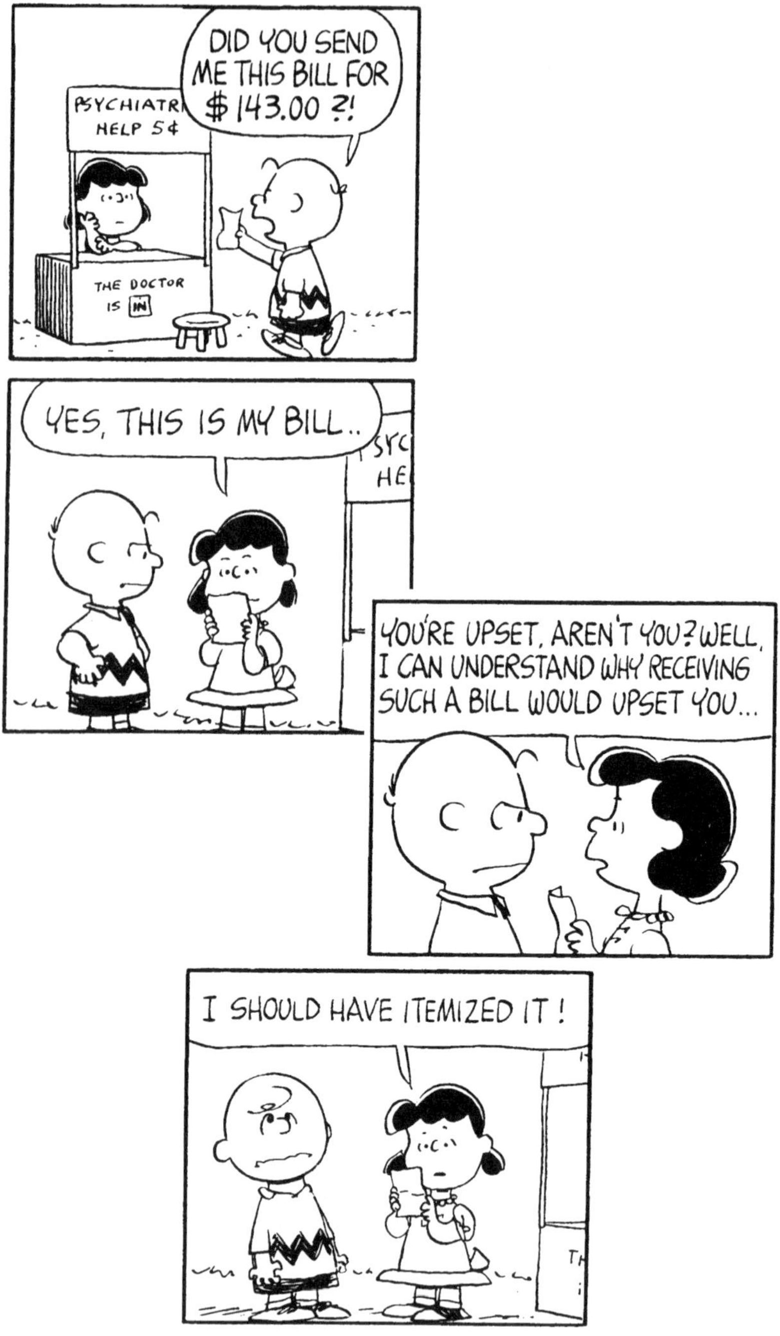
DID YOU SEND ME THIS BILL FOR $143.00 ?!
PSYCHIATRI
HELP 5¢
THE DOCTOR IS IN
YES, THIS IS MY BILL..
YOU'RE UPSET, AREN'T YOU? WELL, I CAN UNDERSTAND WHY RECEIVING SUCH A BILL WOULD UPSET YOU...
I SHOULD HAVE ITEMIZED IT !

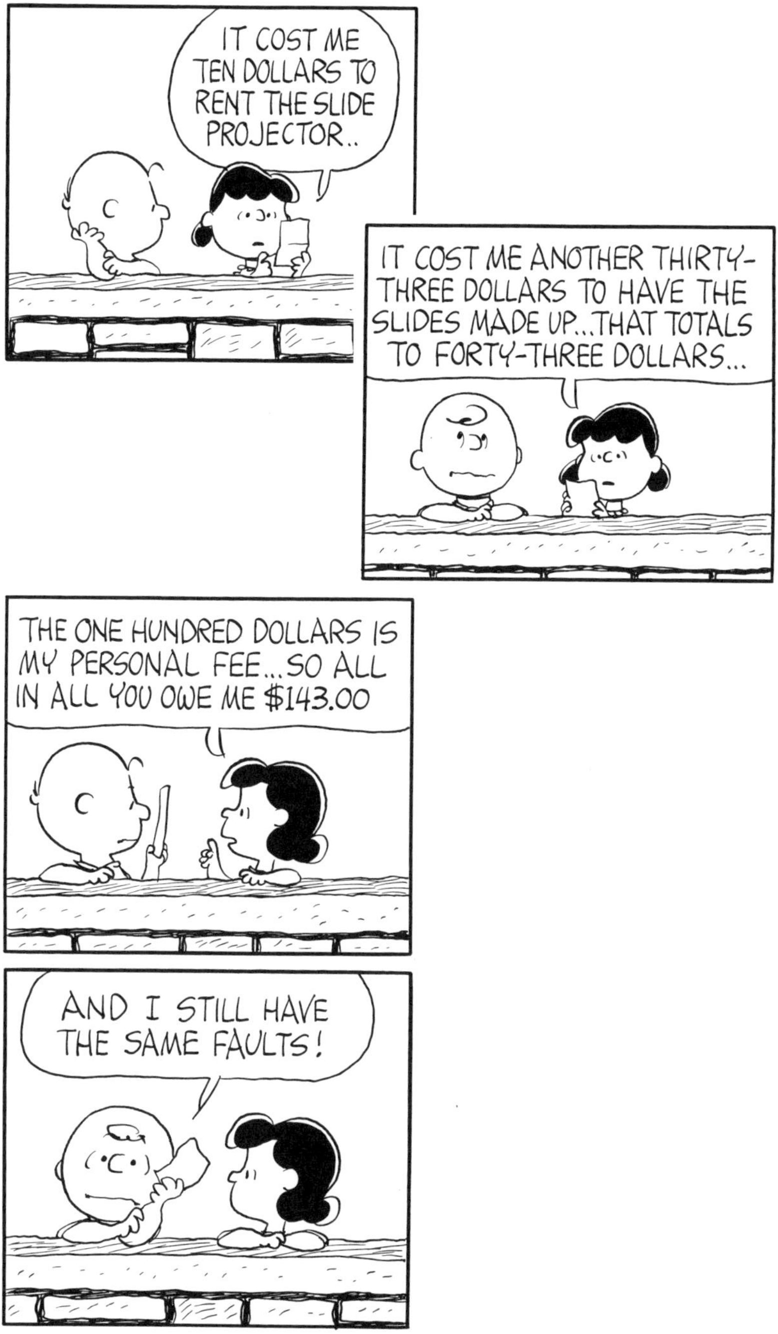
IT COST ME TEN DOLLARS TO RENT THE SLIDE PROJECTOR..
IT COST ME ANOTHER THIRTY-THREE DOLLARS TO HAVE THE SLIDES MADE UP...THAT TOTALS TO FORTY-THREE DOLLARS...
THE ONE HUNDRED DOLLARS IS MY PERSONAL FEE...SO ALL IN ALL YOU OWE ME $143.00
AND I STILL HAVE THE SAME FAULTS!

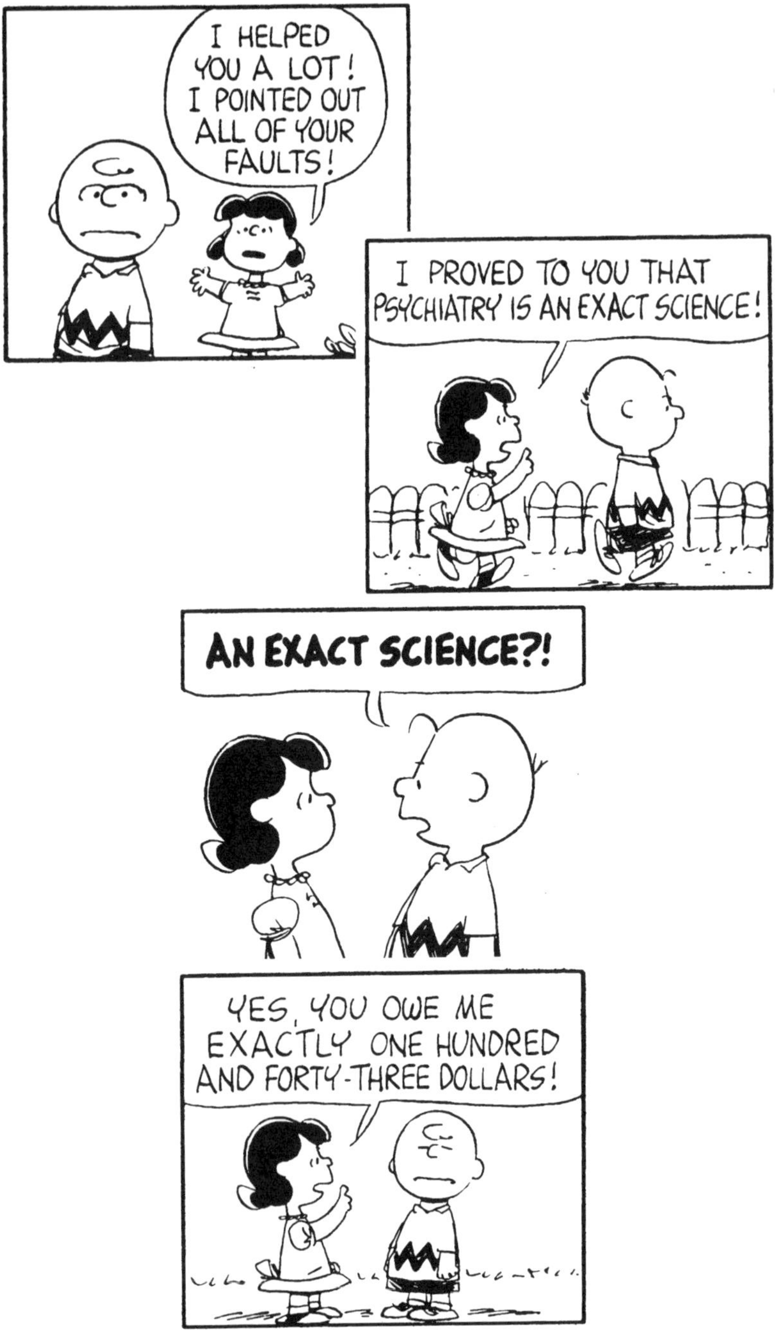
I HELPED YOU A LOT! I POINTED OUT ALL OF YOUR FAULTS!
I PROVED TO YOU THAT PSYCHIATRY IS AN EXACT SCIENCE!
AN EXACT SCIENCE?!
YES, YOU OWE ME EXACTLY ONE HUNDRED AND FORTY-THREE DOLLARS!

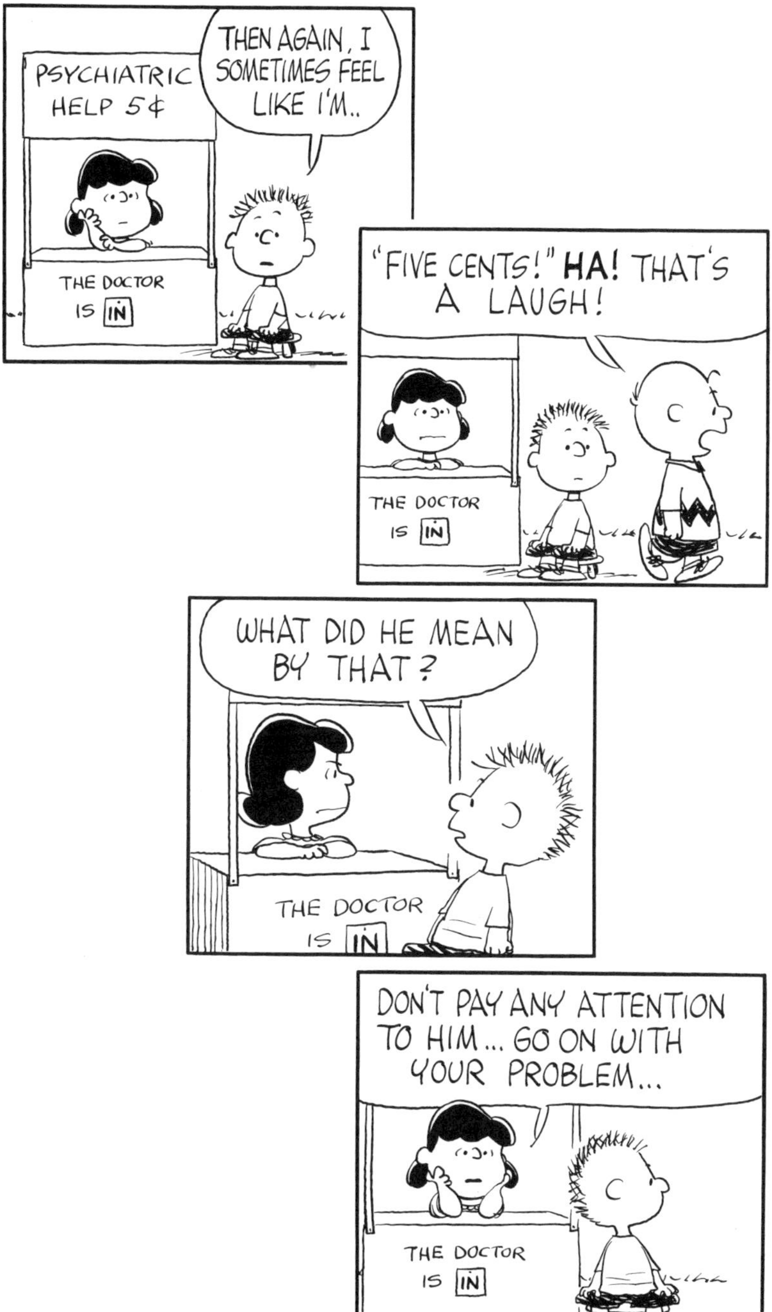
PSYCHIATRIC HELP 5¢
THEN AGAIN, I SOMETIMES FEEL LIKE I'M..
THE DOCTOR IS IN
"FIVE CENTS!" HA! THAT'S A LAUGH!
THE DOCTOR IS IN
WHAT DID HE MEAN BY THAT?
THE DOCTOR IS IN
DON'T PAY ANY ATTENTION TO HIM... GO ON WITH YOUR PROBLEM...
THE DOCTOR IS IN

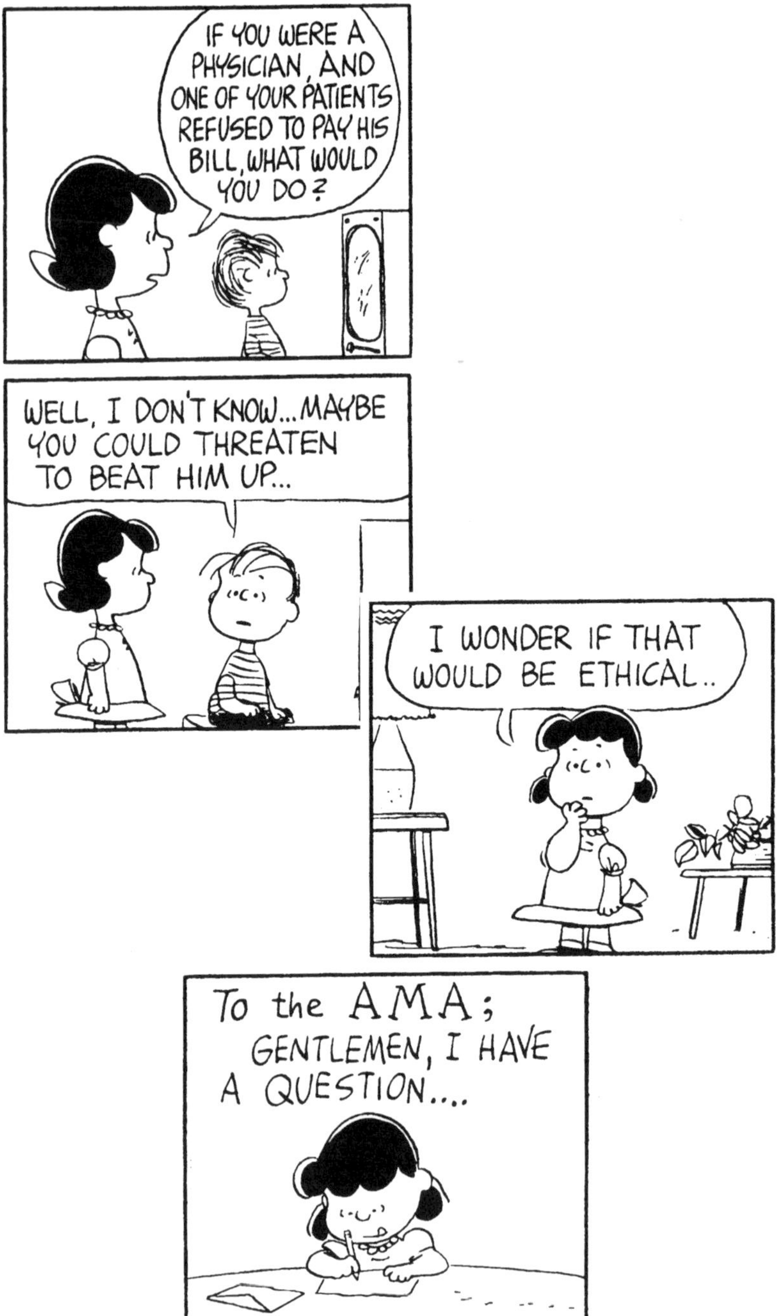
IF YOU WERE A PHYSICIAN, AND ONE OF YOUR PATIENTS REFUSED TO PAY HIS BILL, WHAT WOULD YOU DO?
WELL, I DON'T KNOW...MAYBE YOU COULD THREATEN TO BEAT HIM UP...
I WONDER IF THAT WOULD BE ETHICAL..
To the AMA;
GENTLEMEN, I HAVE A QUESTION....

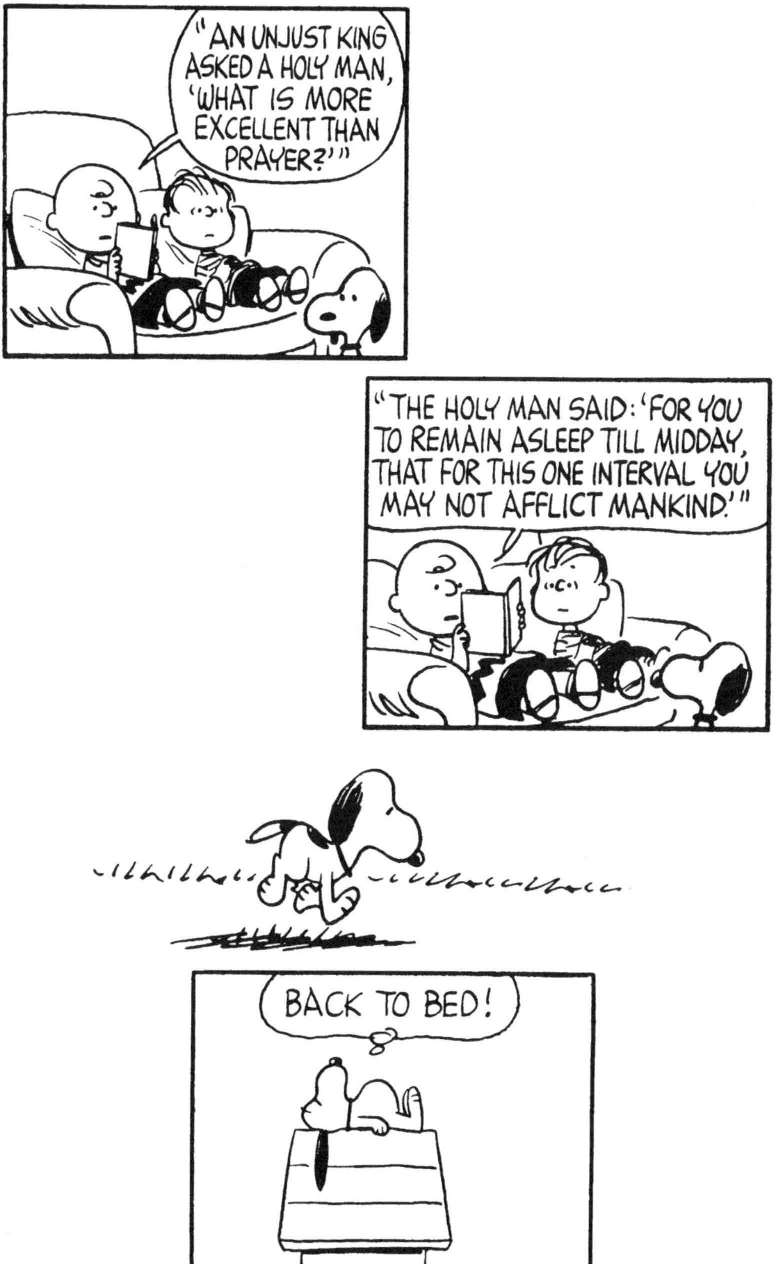
"AN UNJUST KING ASKED A HOLY MAN, 'WHAT IS MORE EXCELLENT THAN PRAYER?'"
"THE HOLY MAN SAID: 'FOR YOU TO REMAIN ASLEEP TILL MIDDAY, THAT FOR THIS ONE INTERVAL YOU MAY NOT AFFLICT MANKIND.'"
BACK TO BED!

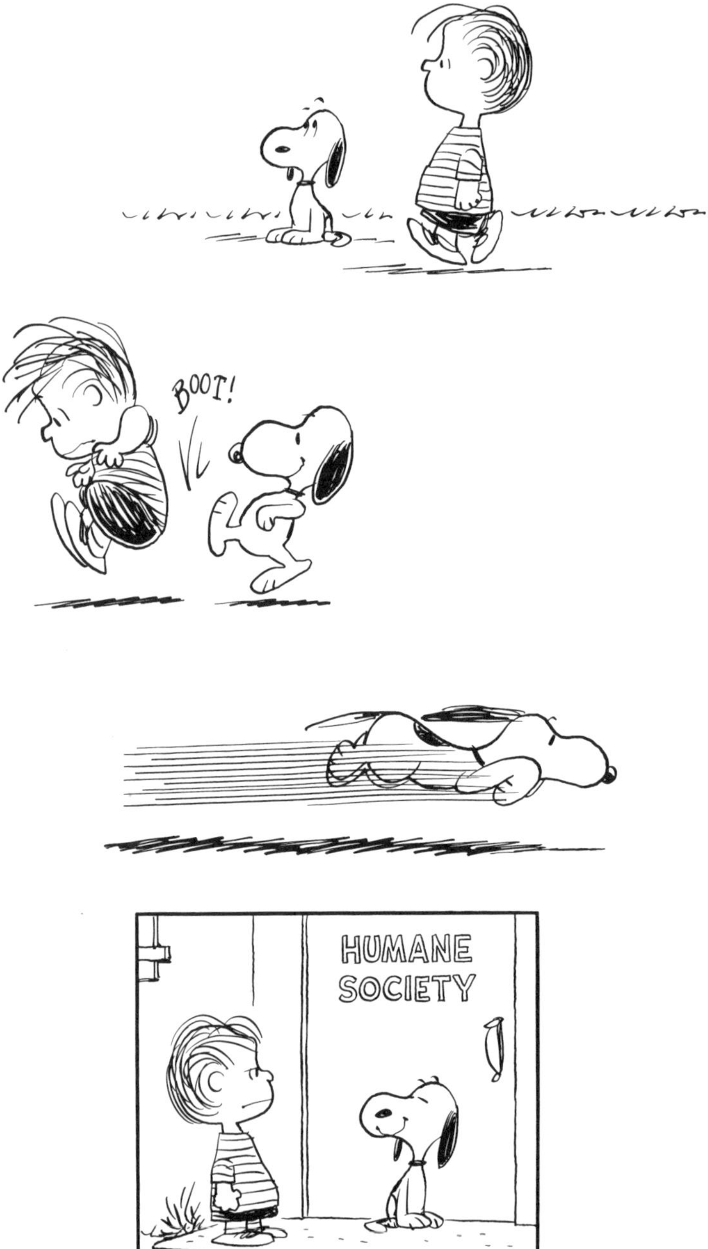
BOOT!
HUMANE SOCIETY

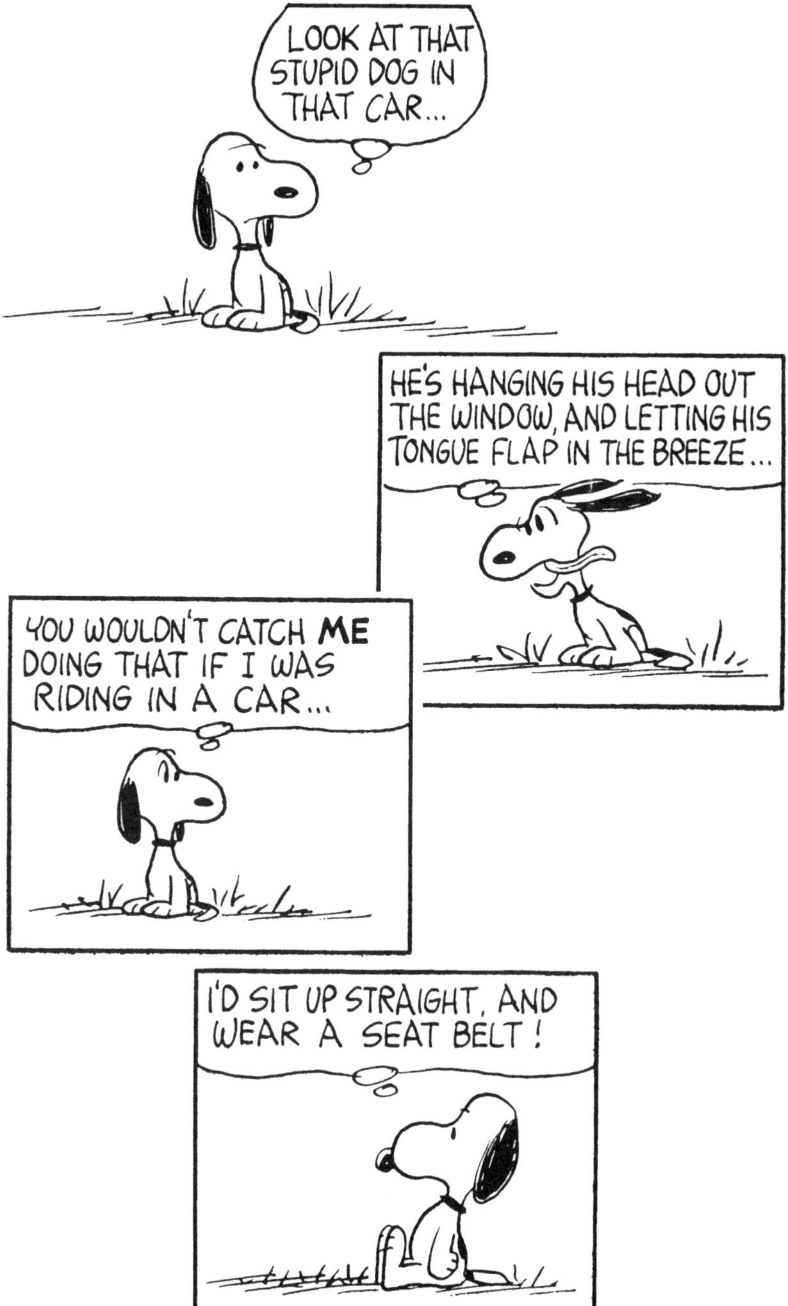
LOOK AT THAT STUPID DOG IN THAT CAR...
HE'S HANGING HIS HEAD OUT THE WINDOW, AND LETTING HIS TONGUE FLAP IN THE BREEZE...
YOU WOULDN'T CATCH **ME** DOING THAT IF I WAS RIDING IN A CAR...
I'D SIT UP STRAIGHT, AND WEAR A SEAT BELT!

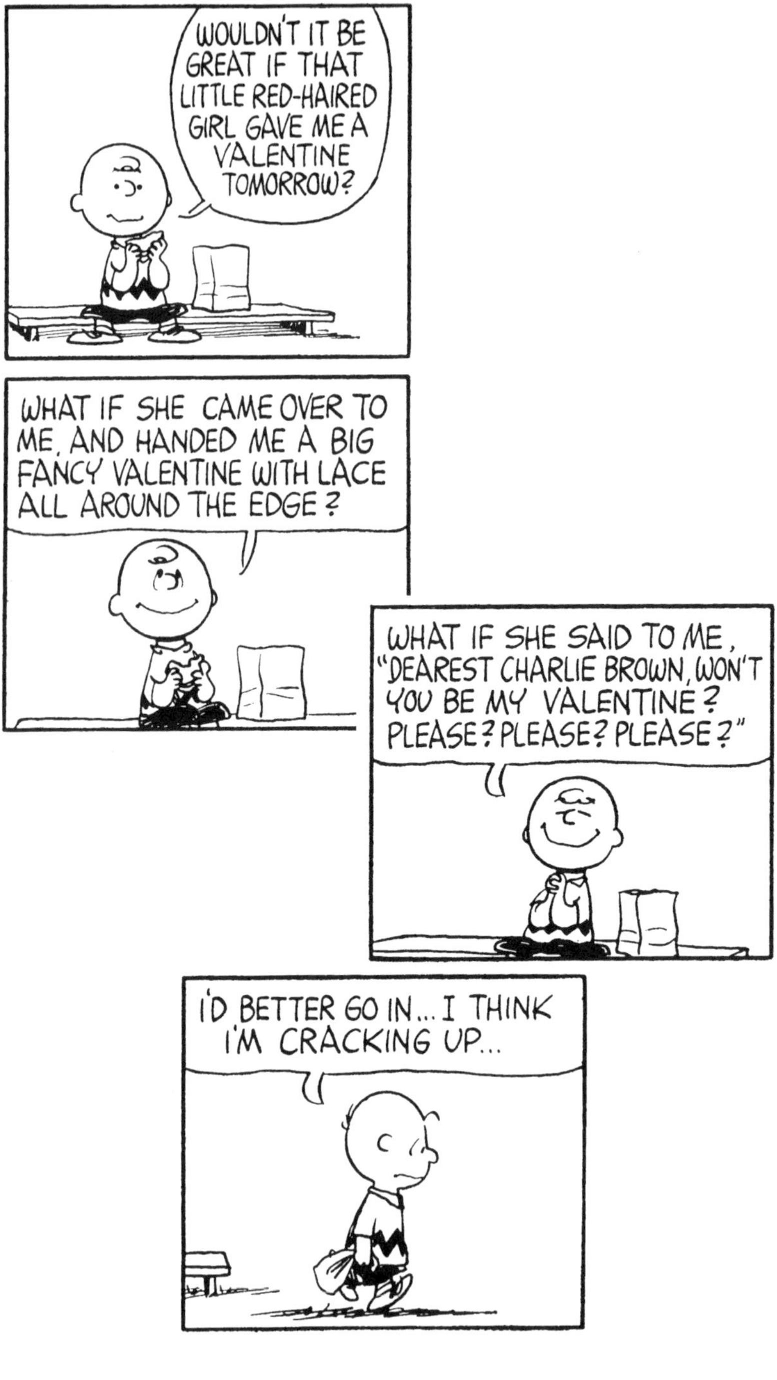
WOULDN'T IT BE GREAT IF THAT LITTLE RED-HAIRED GIRL GAVE ME A VALENTINE TOMORROW?
WHAT IF SHE CAME OVER TO ME, AND HANDED ME A BIG FANCY VALENTINE WITH LACE ALL AROUND THE EDGE?
WHAT IF SHE SAID TO ME, "DEAREST CHARLIE BROWN, WON'T YOU BE MY VALENTINE? PLEASE? PLEASE? PLEASE?"
I'D BETTER GO IN... I THINK I'M CRACKING UP...

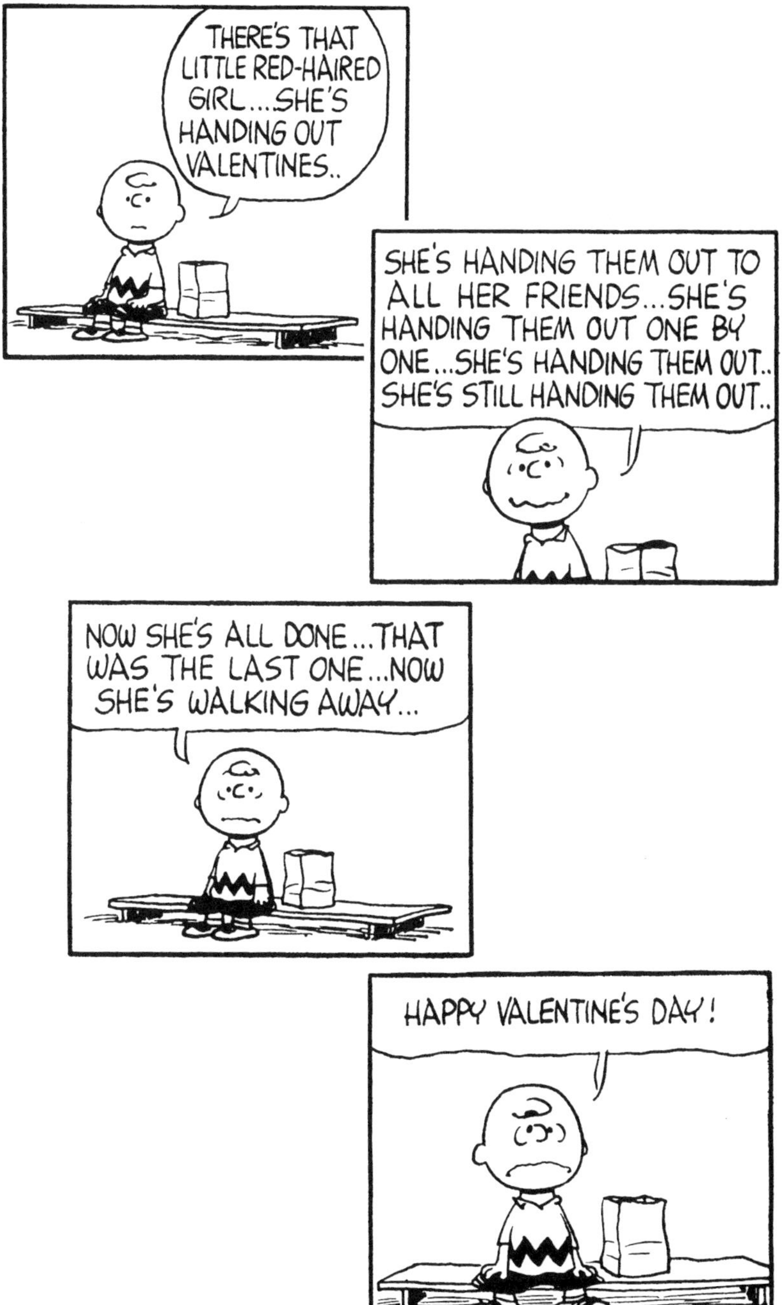
THERE'S THAT LITTLE RED-HAIRED GIRL....SHE'S HANDING OUT VALENTINES..
SHE'S HANDING THEM OUT TO ALL HER FRIENDS...SHE'S HANDING THEM OUT ONE BY ONE...SHE'S HANDING THEM OUT.. SHE'S STILL HANDING THEM OUT..
NOW SHE'S ALL DONE...THAT WAS THE LAST ONE...NOW SHE'S WALKING AWAY...
HAPPY VALENTINE'S DAY!

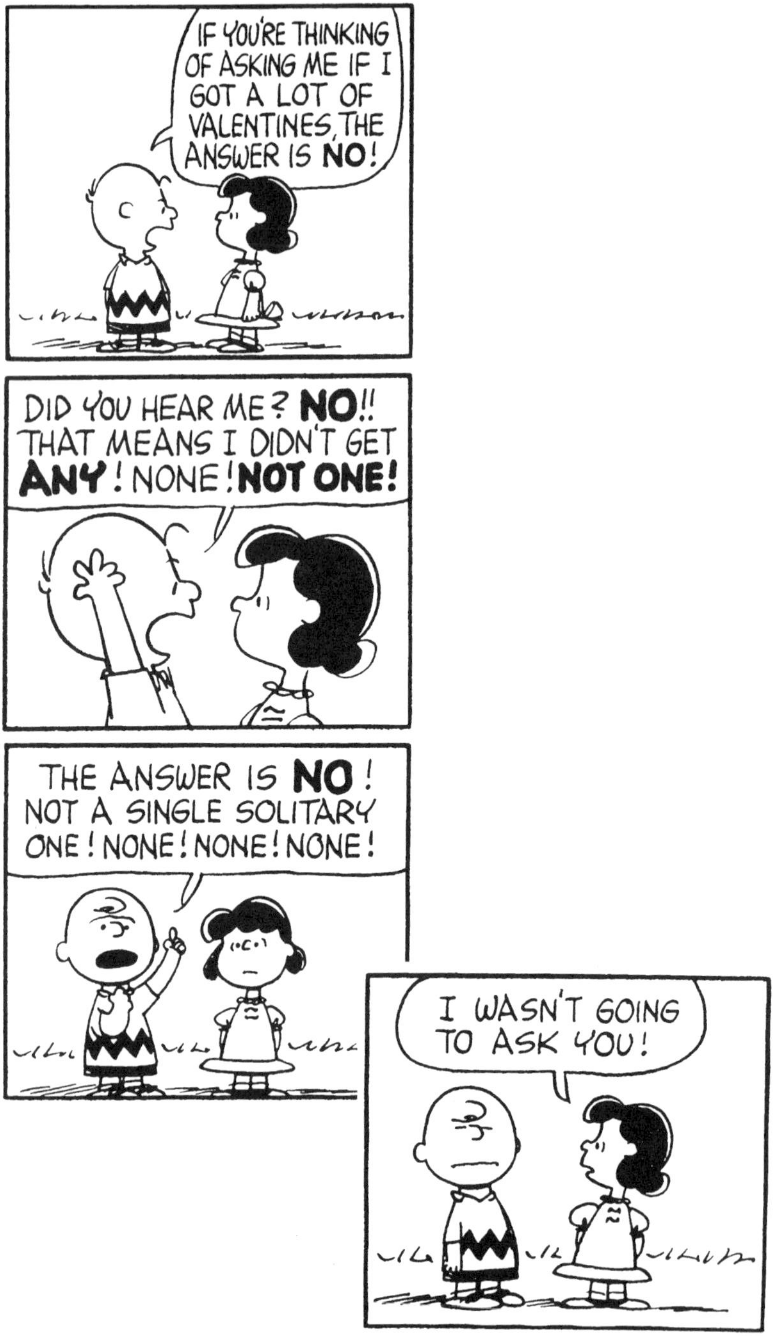
IF YOU'RE THINKING OF ASKING ME IF I GOT A LOT OF VALENTINES, THE ANSWER IS **NO**!
DID YOU HEAR ME? **NO**!! THAT MEANS I DIDN'T GET **ANY**! NONE! **NOT ONE!**
THE ANSWER IS **NO**! NOT A SINGLE SOLITARY ONE! NONE! NONE! NONE!
I WASN'T GOING TO ASK YOU!

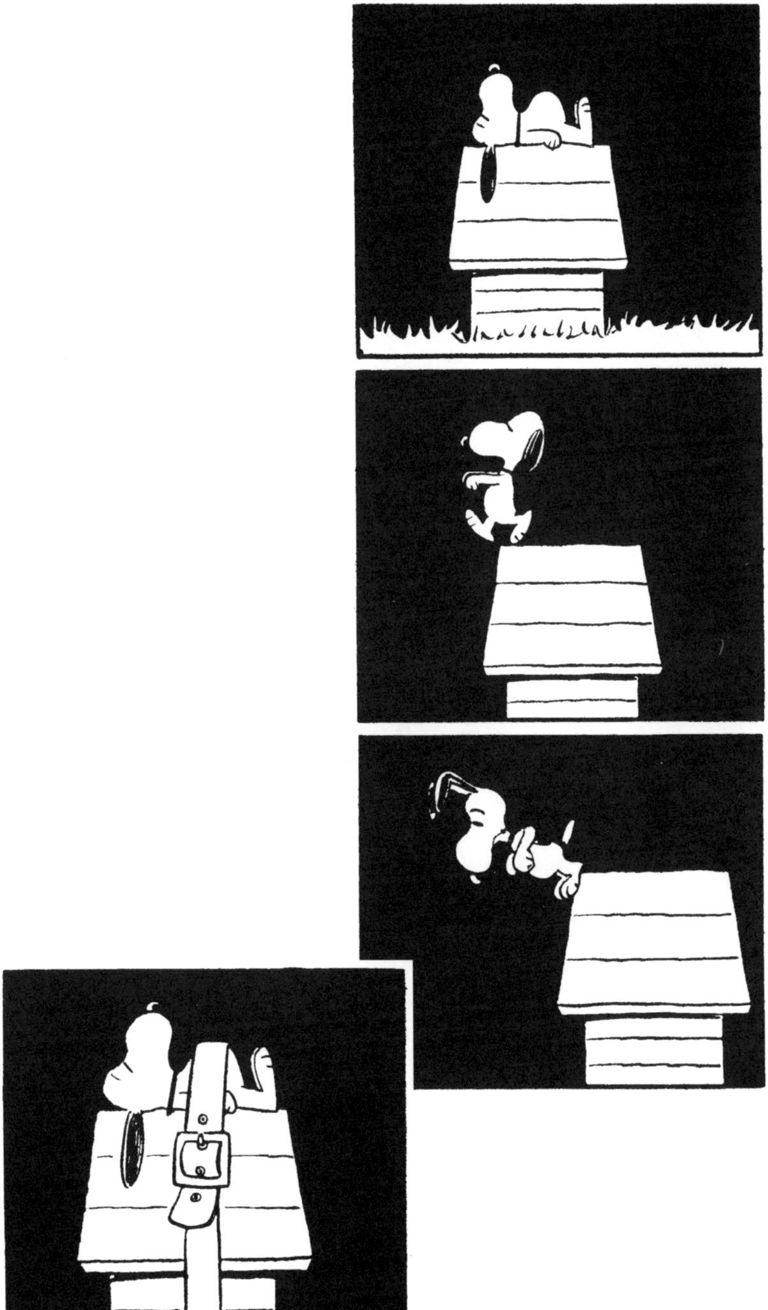

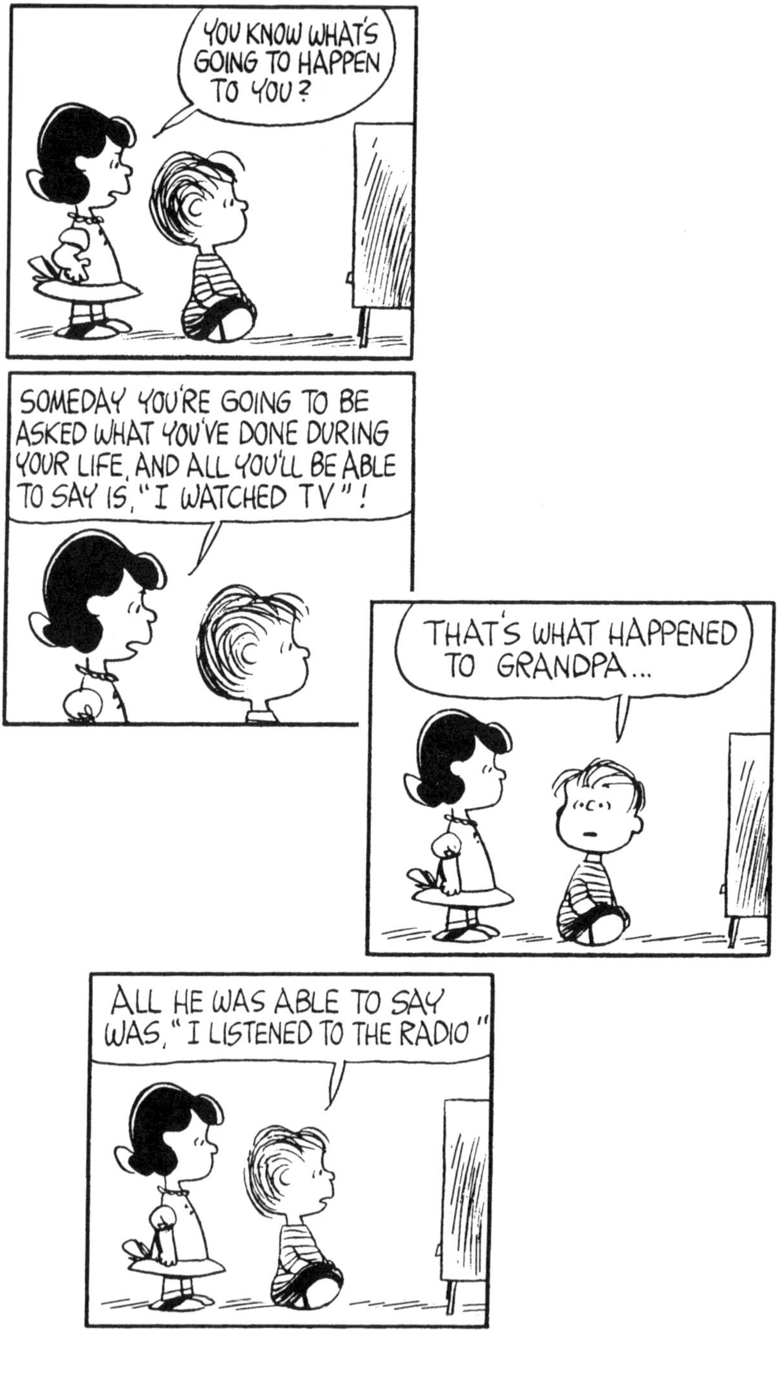
YOU KNOW WHAT'S GOING TO HAPPEN TO YOU?
SOMEDAY YOU'RE GOING TO BE ASKED WHAT YOU'VE DONE DURING YOUR LIFE, AND ALL YOU'LL BE ABLE TO SAY IS, "I WATCHED TV"!
THAT'S WHAT HAPPENED TO GRANDPA...
ALL HE WAS ABLE TO SAY WAS, "I LISTENED TO THE RADIO"

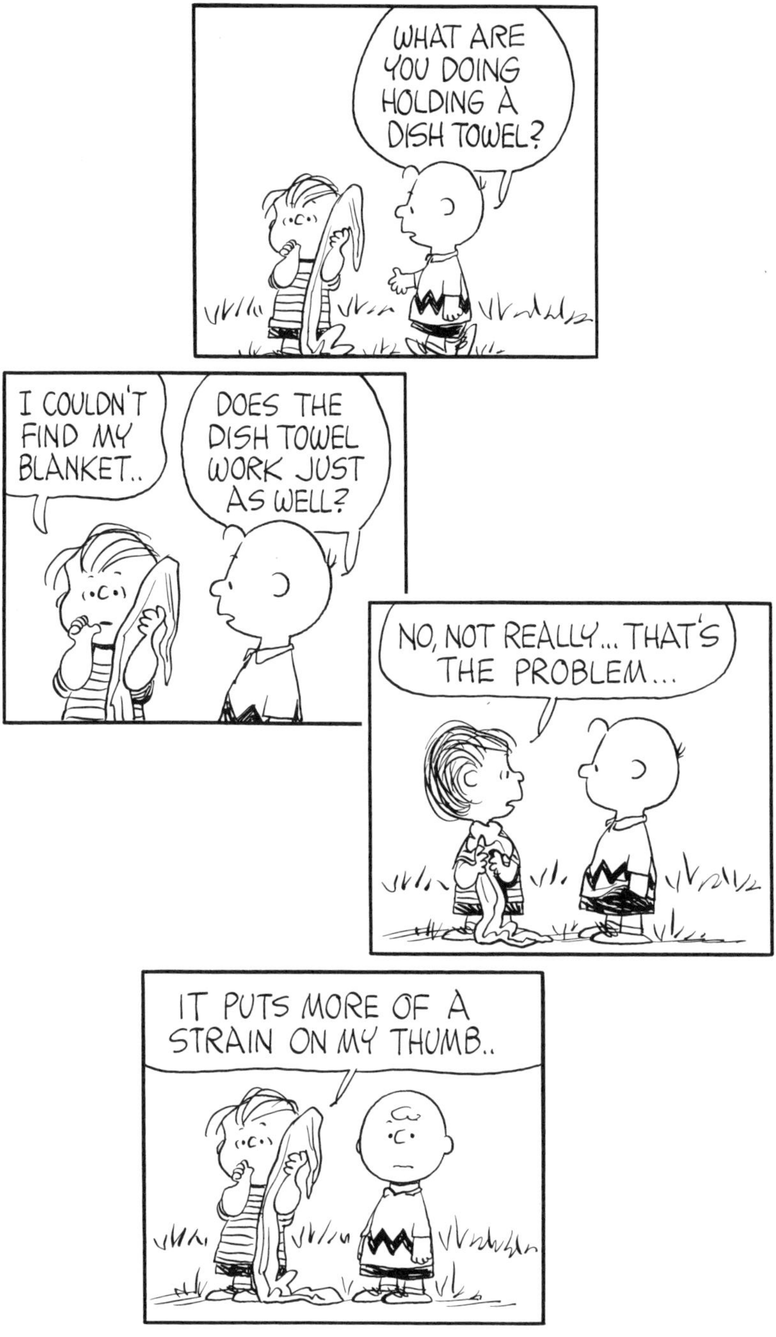
WHAT ARE YOU DOING HOLDING A DISH TOWEL?
I COULDN'T FIND MY BLANKET..
DOES THE DISH TOWEL WORK JUST AS WELL?
NO, NOT REALLY... THAT'S THE PROBLEM...
IT PUTS MORE OF A STRAIN ON MY THUMB..

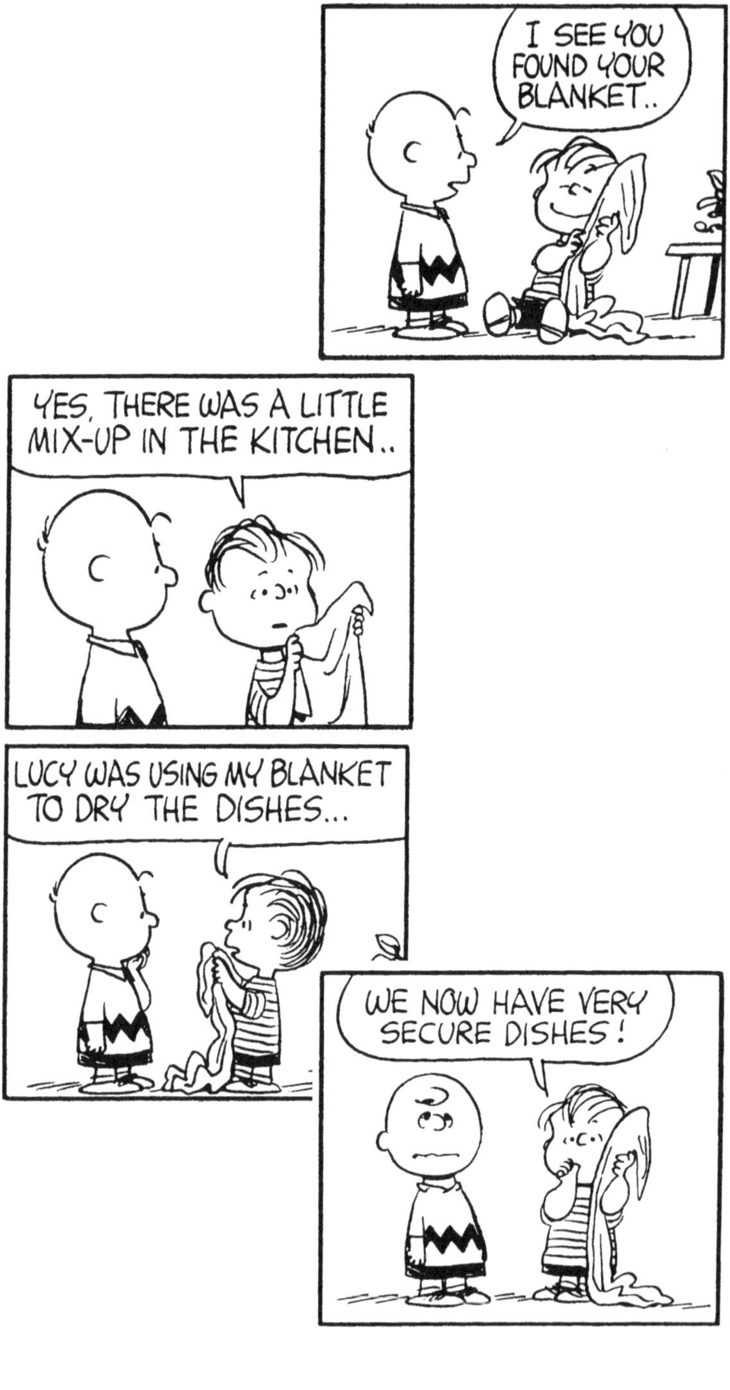
I SEE YOU FOUND YOUR BLANKET..
YES, THERE WAS A LITTLE MIX-UP IN THE KITCHEN..
LUCY WAS USING MY BLANKET TO DRY THE DISHES...
WE NOW HAVE VERY SECURE DISHES!

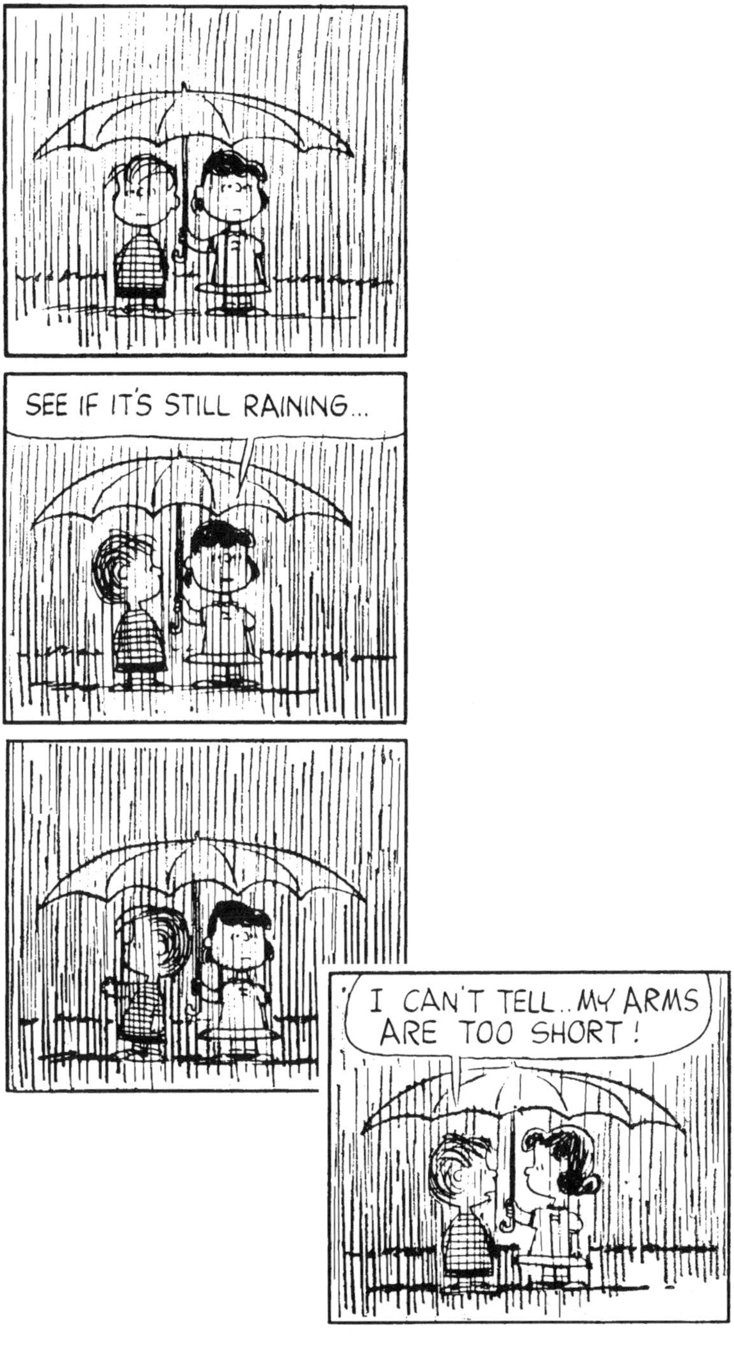
SEE IF IT'S STILL RAINING...
I CAN'T TELL..MY ARMS ARE TOO SHORT!

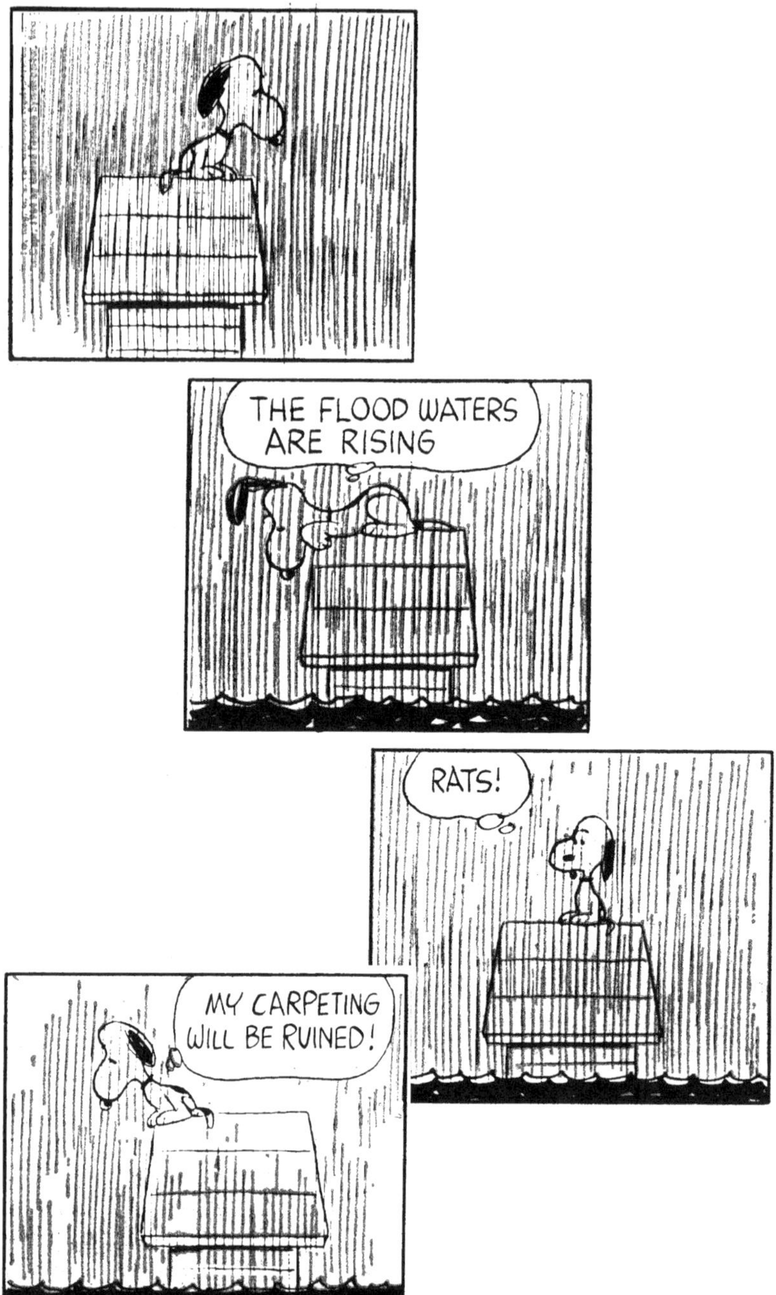
THE FLOOD WATERS ARE RISING
RATS!
MY CARPETING WILL BE RUINED!

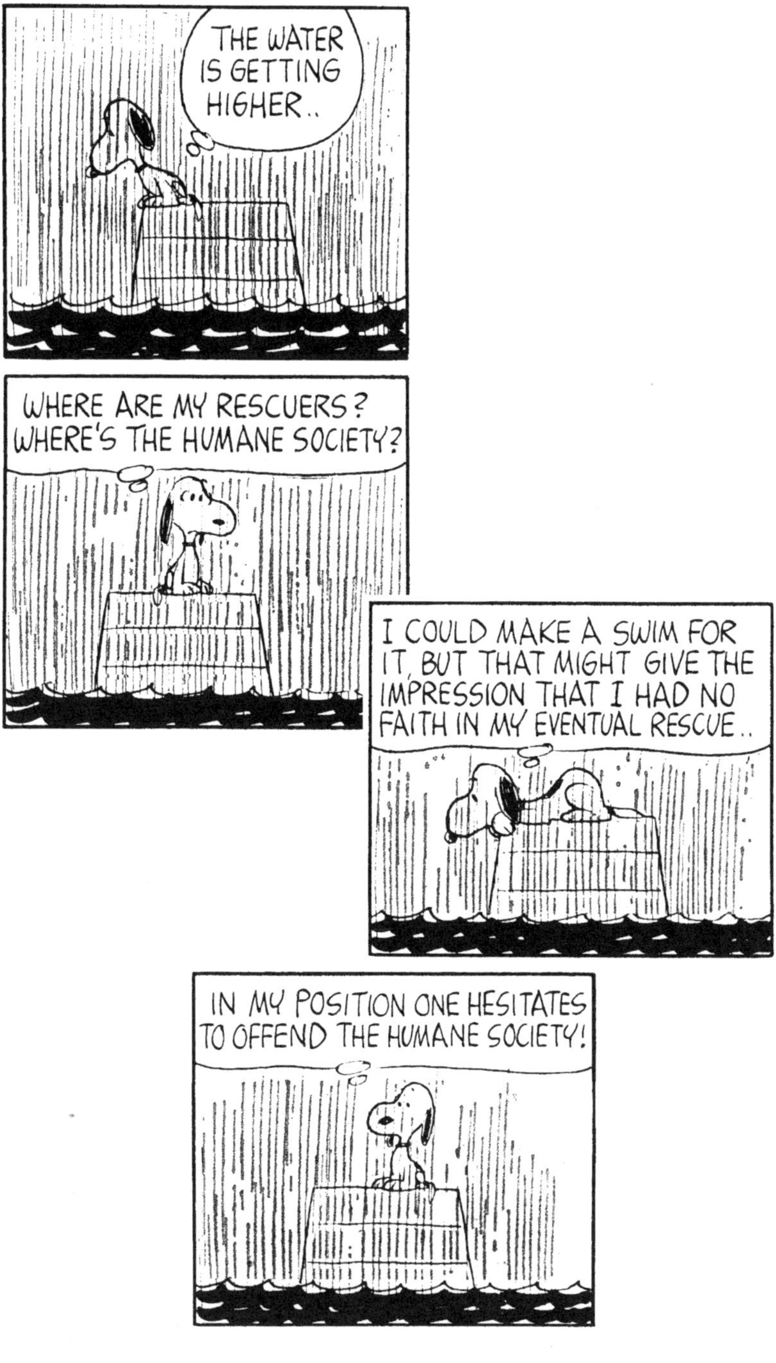
THE WATER IS GETTING HIGHER..
WHERE ARE MY RESCUERS? WHERE'S THE HUMANE SOCIETY?
I COULD MAKE A SWIM FOR IT, BUT THAT MIGHT GIVE THE IMPRESSION THAT I HAD NO FAITH IN MY EVENTUAL RESCUE..
IN MY POSITION ONE HESITATES TO OFFEND THE HUMANE SOCIETY!

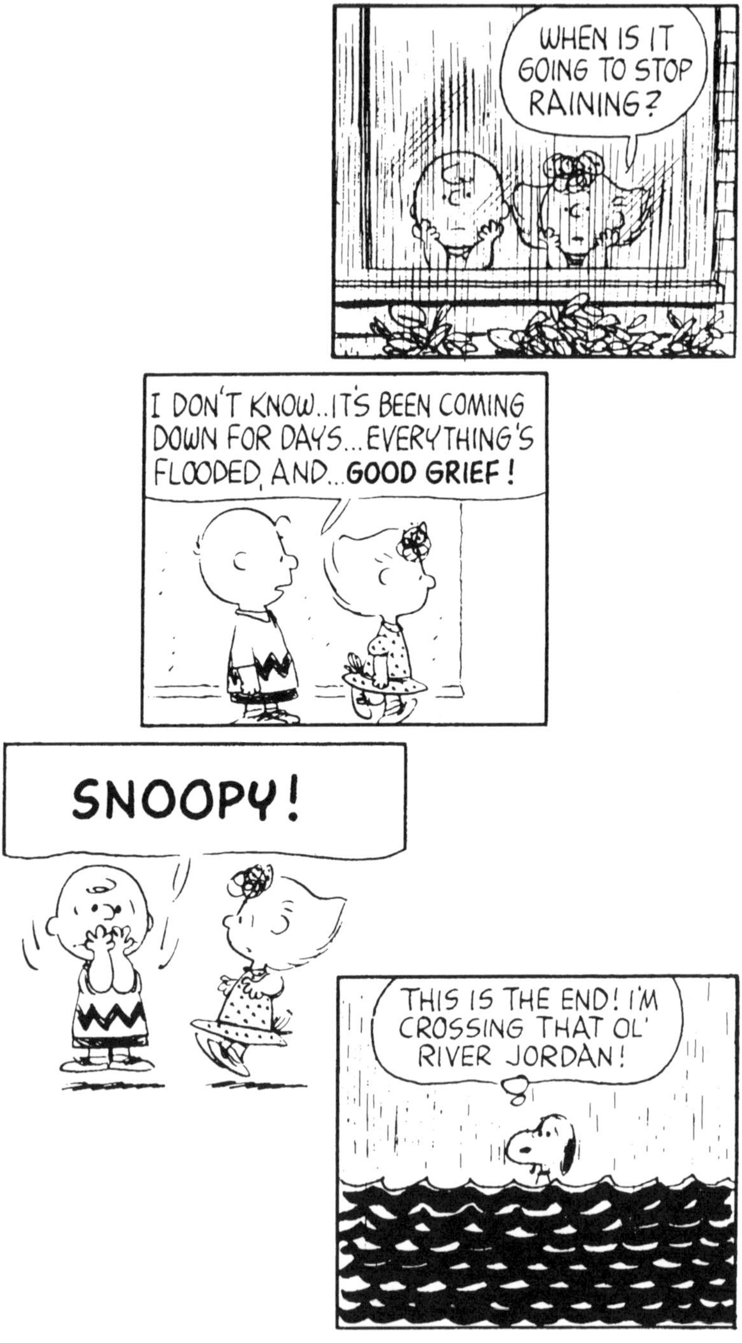
WHEN IS IT GOING TO STOP RAINING?
I DON'T KNOW..IT'S BEEN COMING DOWN FOR DAYS...EVERYTHING'S FLOODED, AND...GOOD GRIEF!
SNOOPY!
THIS IS THE END! I'M CROSSING THAT OL' RIVER JORDAN!

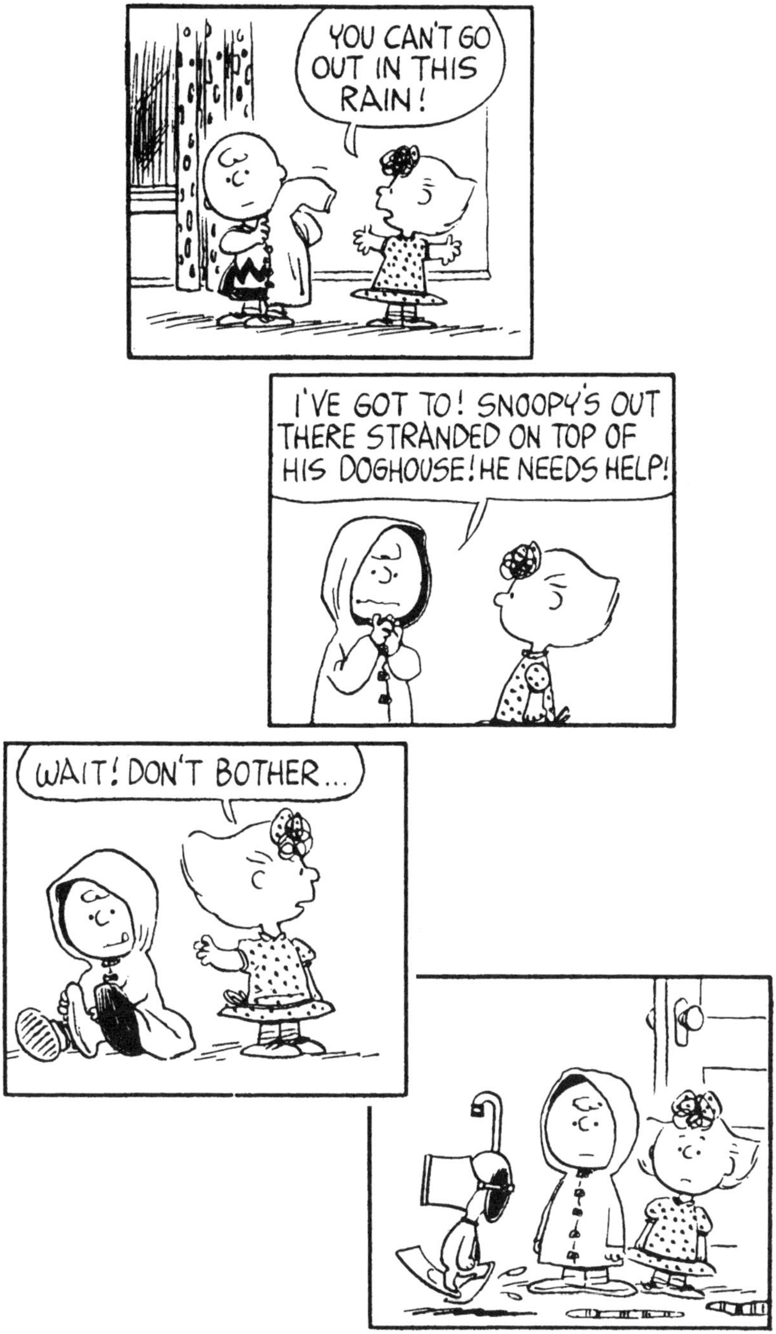
YOU CAN'T GO OUT IN THIS RAIN!
I'VE GOT TO! SNOOPY'S OUT THERE STRANDED ON TOP OF HIS DOGHOUSE! HE NEEDS HELP!
WAIT! DON'T BOTHER...

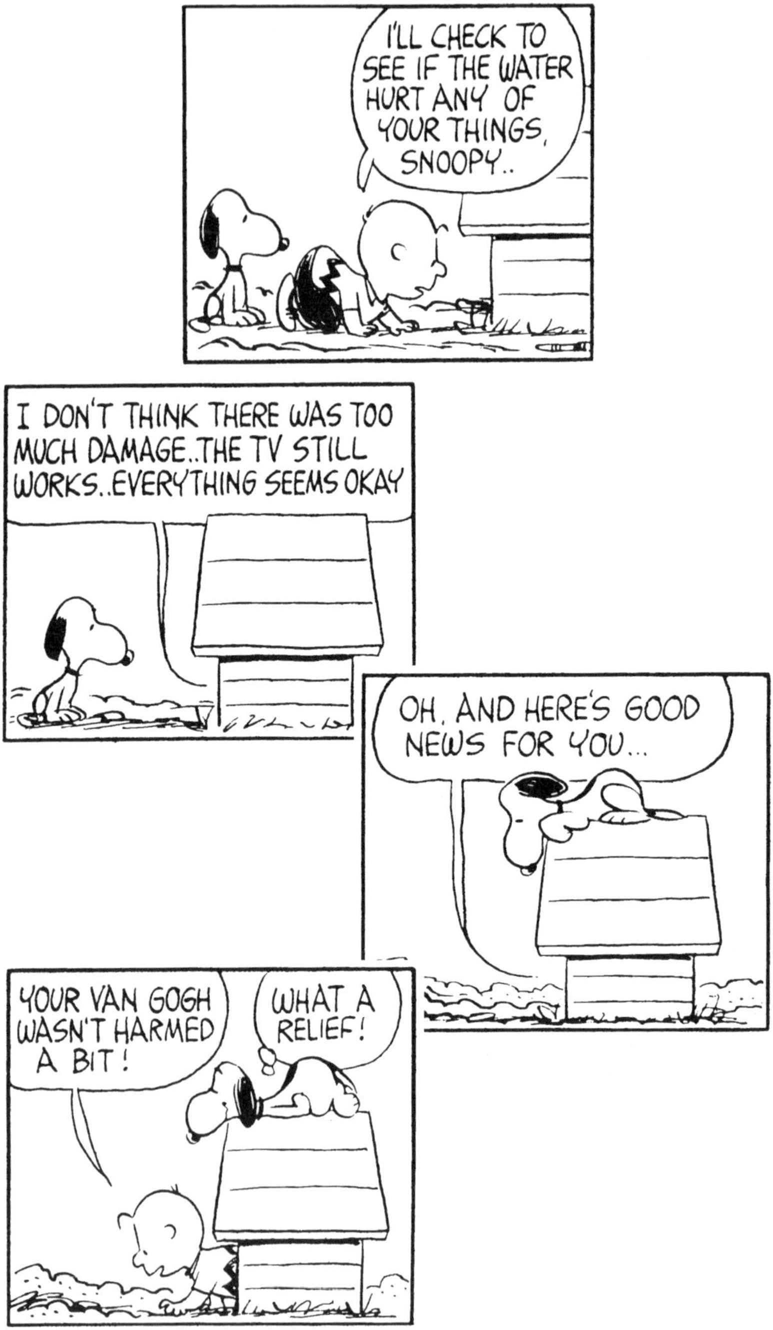
I'LL CHECK TO SEE IF THE WATER HURT ANY OF YOUR THINGS, SNOOPY..
I DON'T THINK THERE WAS TOO MUCH DAMAGE..THE TV STILL WORKS..EVERYTHING SEEMS OKAY
OH, AND HERE'S GOOD NEWS FOR YOU...
YOUR VAN GOGH WASN'T HARMED A BIT!
WHAT A RELIEF!

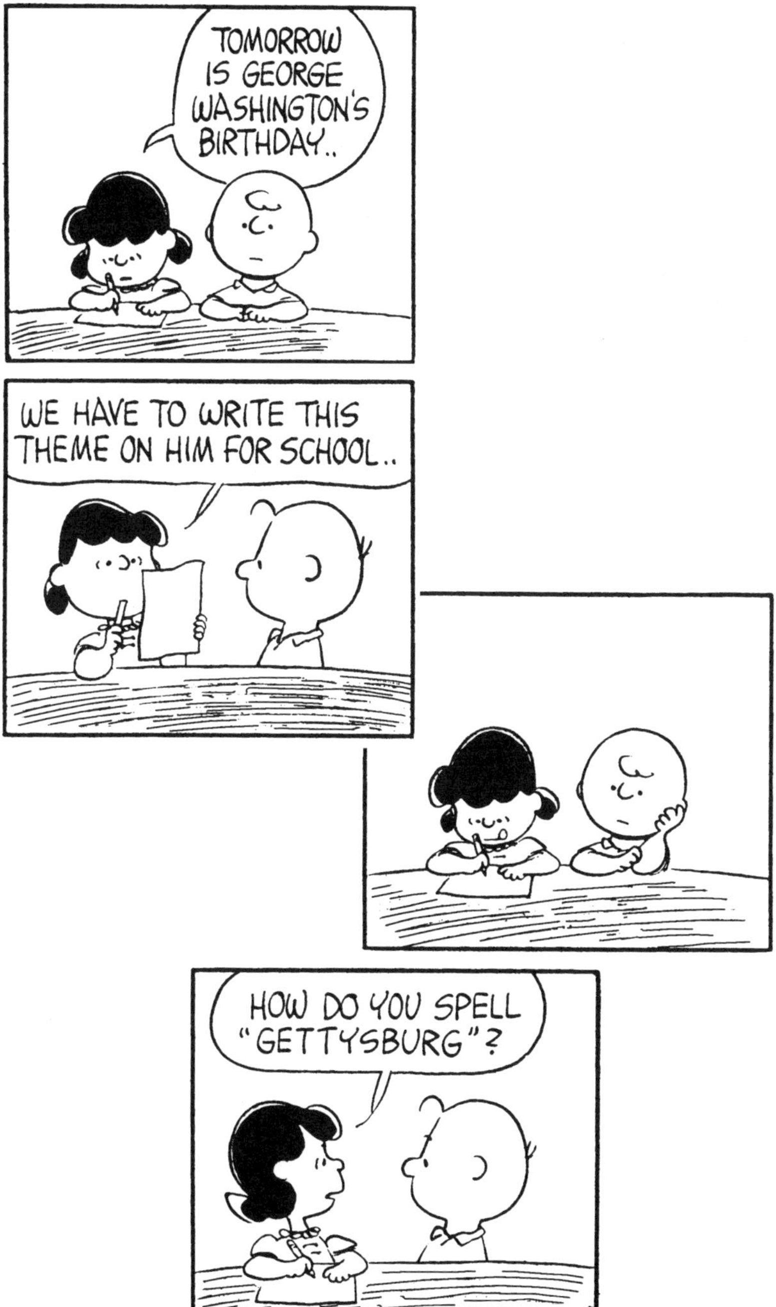
TOMORROW IS GEORGE WASHINGTON'S BIRTHDAY..
WE HAVE TO WRITE THIS THEME ON HIM FOR SCHOOL..
HOW DO YOU SPELL "GETTYSBURG"?

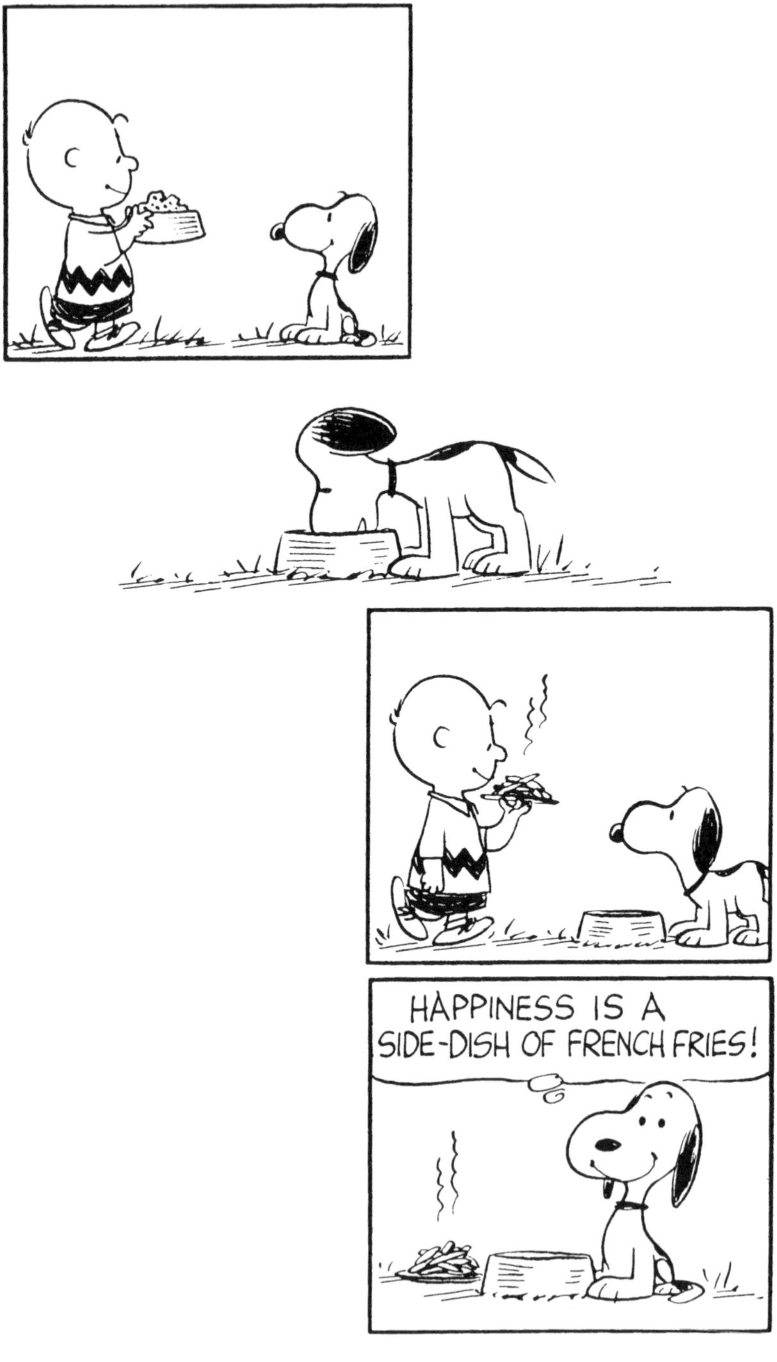
HAPPINESS IS A SIDE-DISH OF FRENCH FRIES!

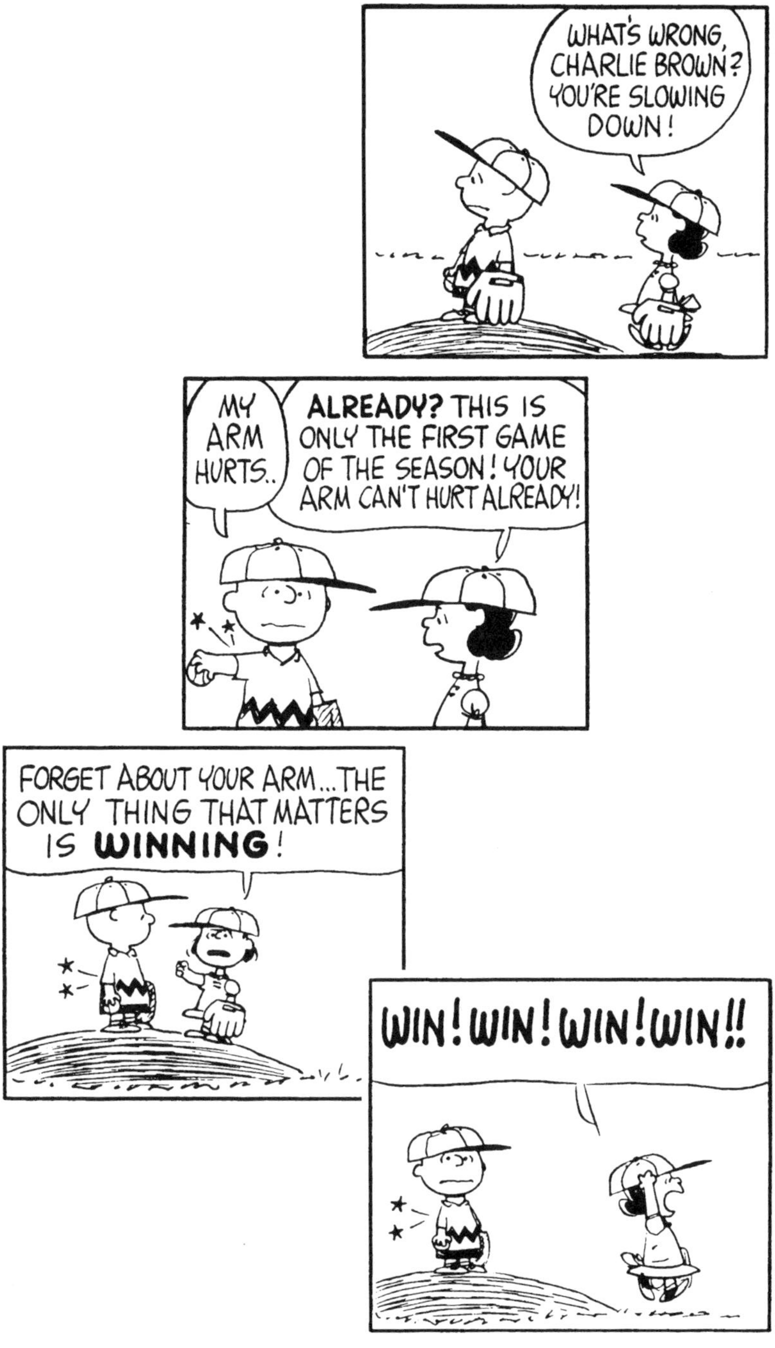
WHAT'S WRONG, CHARLIE BROWN? YOU'RE SLOWING DOWN!
MY ARM HURTS..
ALREADY? THIS IS ONLY THE FIRST GAME OF THE SEASON! YOUR ARM CAN'T HURT ALREADY!
FORGET ABOUT YOUR ARM...THE ONLY THING THAT MATTERS IS **WINNING**!
WIN! WIN! WIN! WIN!!

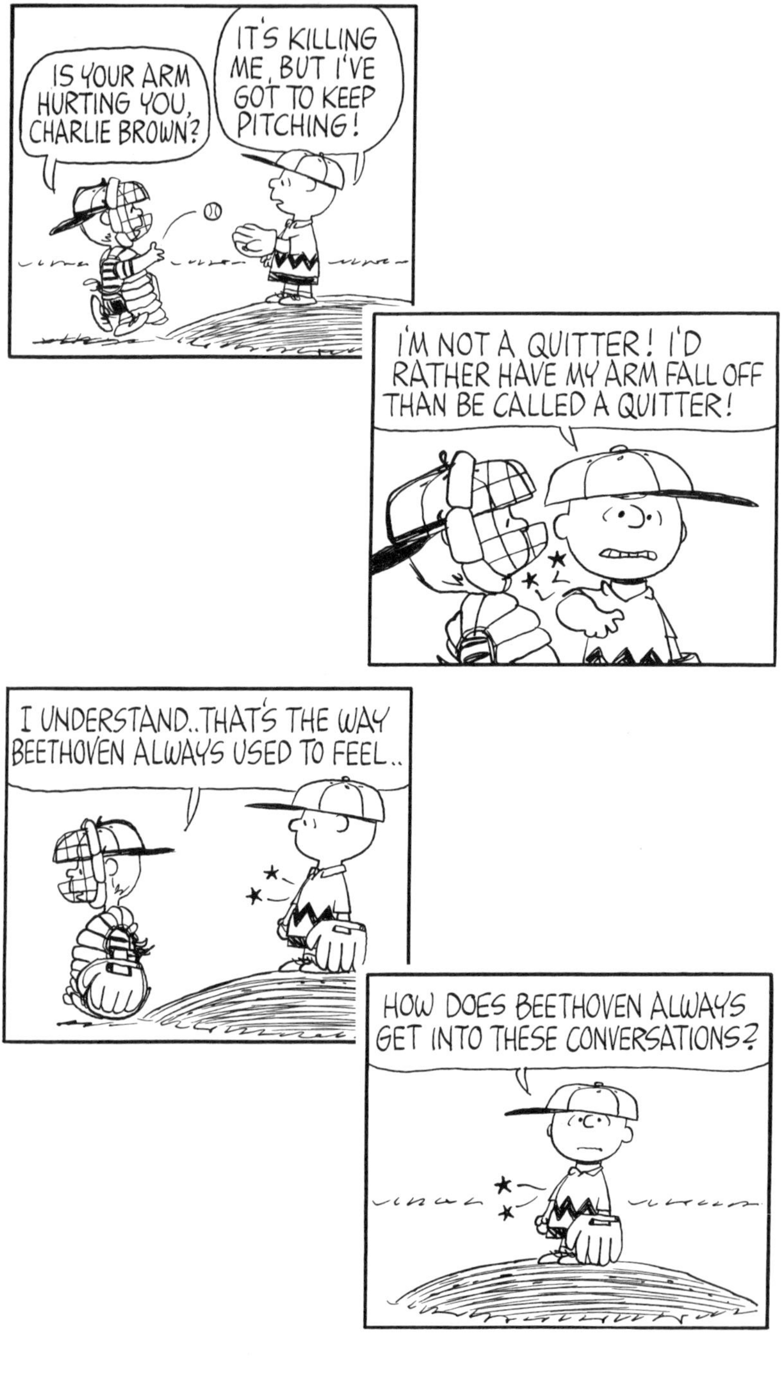
IS YOUR ARM HURTING YOU, CHARLIE BROWN?
IT'S KILLING ME, BUT I'VE GOT TO KEEP PITCHING!
I'M NOT A QUITTER! I'D RATHER HAVE MY ARM FALL OFF THAN BE CALLED A QUITTER!
I UNDERSTAND..THAT'S THE WAY BEETHOVEN ALWAYS USED TO FEEL..
HOW DOES BEETHOVEN ALWAYS GET INTO THESE CONVERSATIONS?

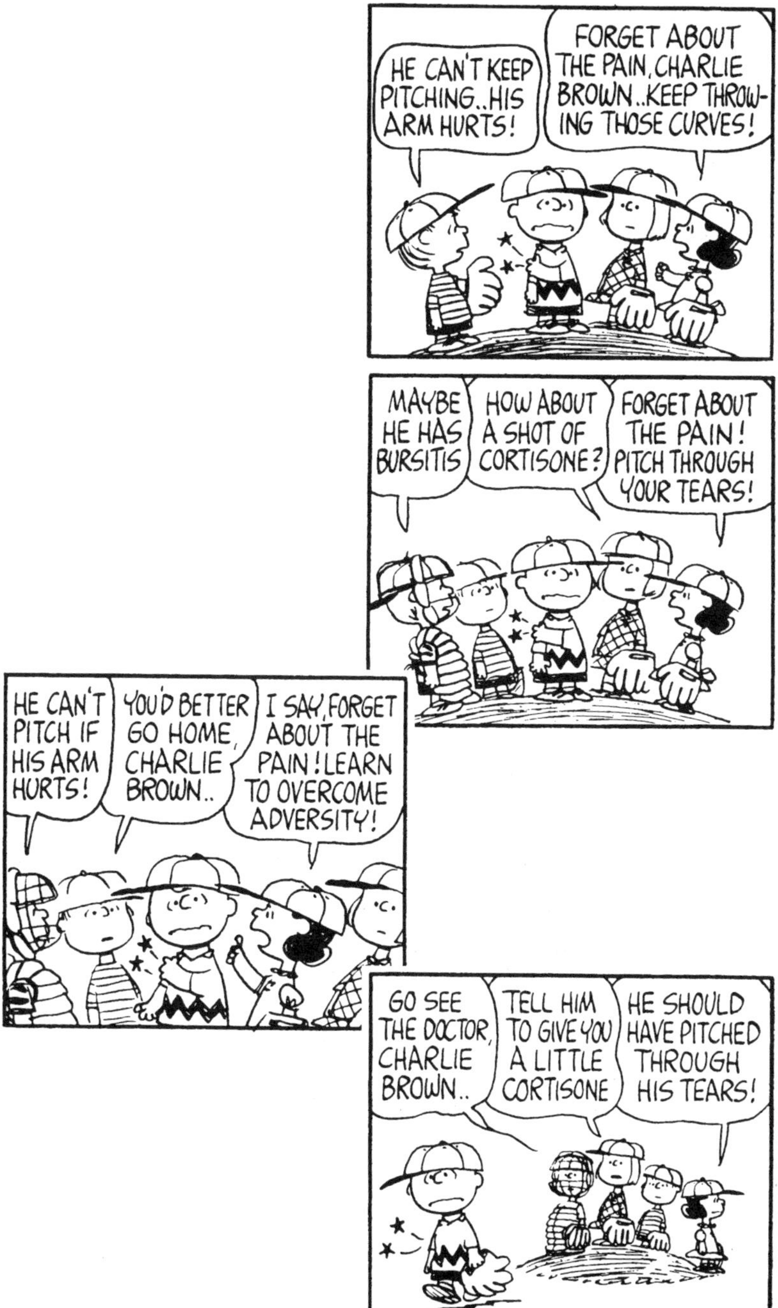
HE CAN'T KEEP PITCHING..HIS ARM HURTS!
FORGET ABOUT THE PAIN, CHARLIE BROWN..KEEP THROWING THOSE CURVES!
MAYBE HE HAS BURSITIS
HOW ABOUT A SHOT OF CORTISONE?
FORGET ABOUT THE PAIN! PITCH THROUGH YOUR TEARS!
HE CAN'T PITCH IF HIS ARM HURTS!
YOU'D BETTER GO HOME, CHARLIE BROWN..
I SAY, FORGET ABOUT THE PAIN! LEARN TO OVERCOME ADVERSITY!
GO SEE THE DOCTOR, CHARLIE BROWN..
TELL HIM TO GIVE YOU A LITTLE CORTISONE
HE SHOULD HAVE PITCHED THROUGH HIS TEARS!

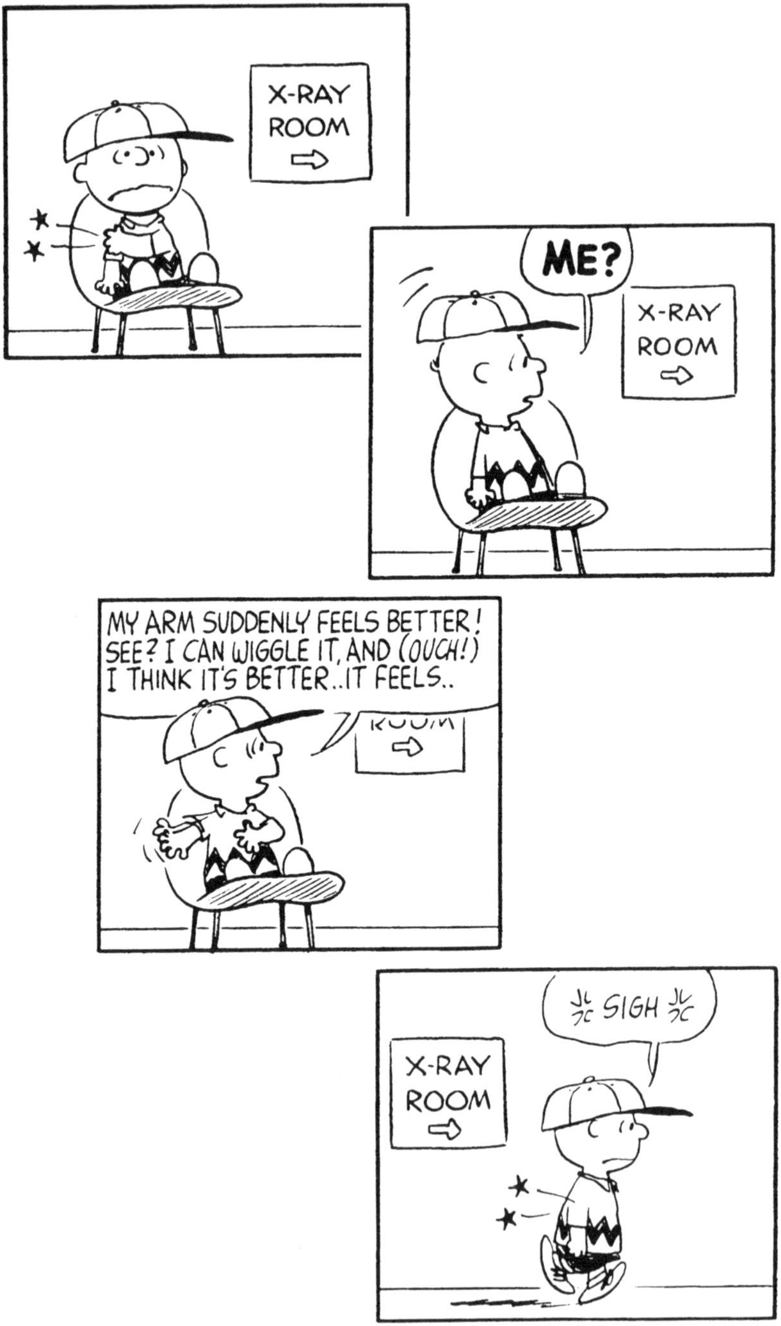
X-RAY ROOM
ME?
X-RAY ROOM
MY ARM SUDDENLY FEELS BETTER! SEE? I CAN WIGGLE IT, AND (OUCH!) I THINK IT'S BETTER..IT FEELS..
X-RAY ROOM
SIGH

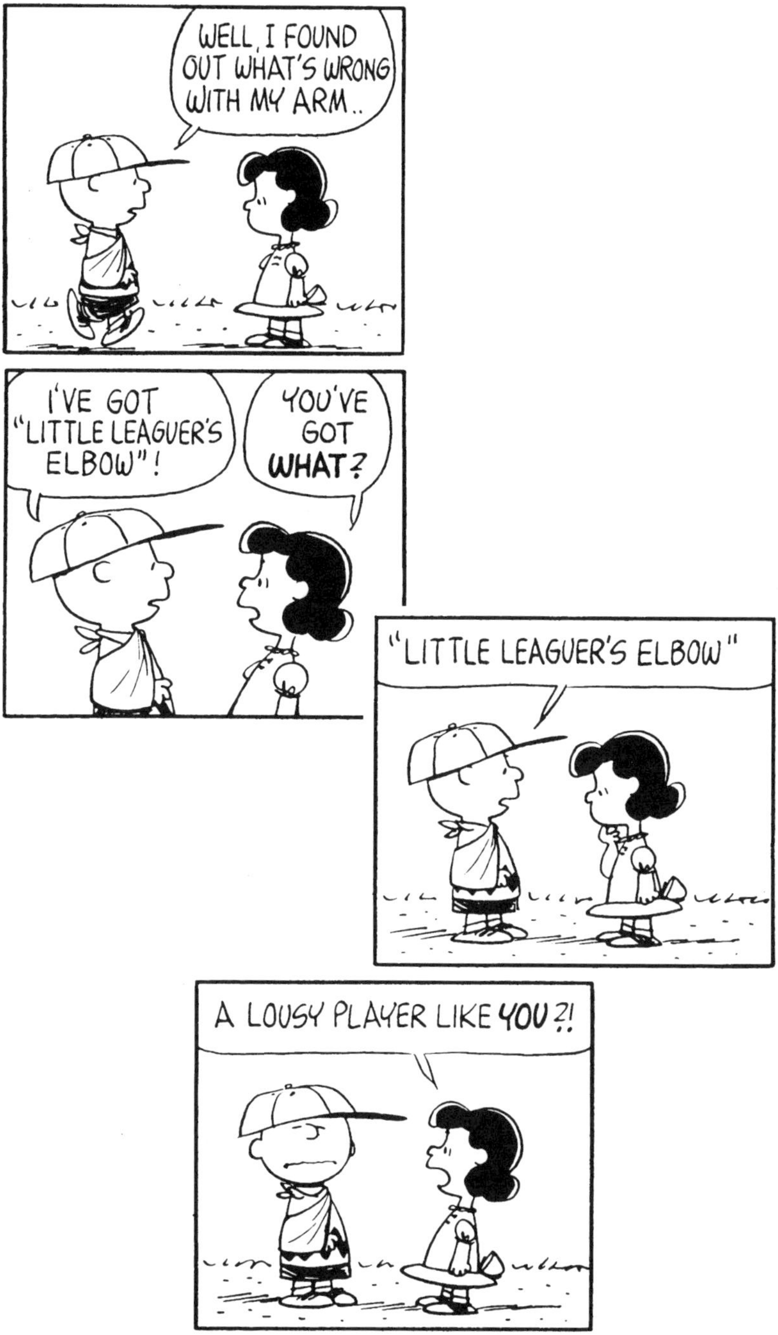
WELL, I FOUND OUT WHAT'S WRONG WITH MY ARM..
I'VE GOT "LITTLE LEAGUER'S ELBOW"!
YOU'VE GOT WHAT?
"LITTLE LEAGUER'S ELBOW"
A LOUSY PLAYER LIKE YOU?!

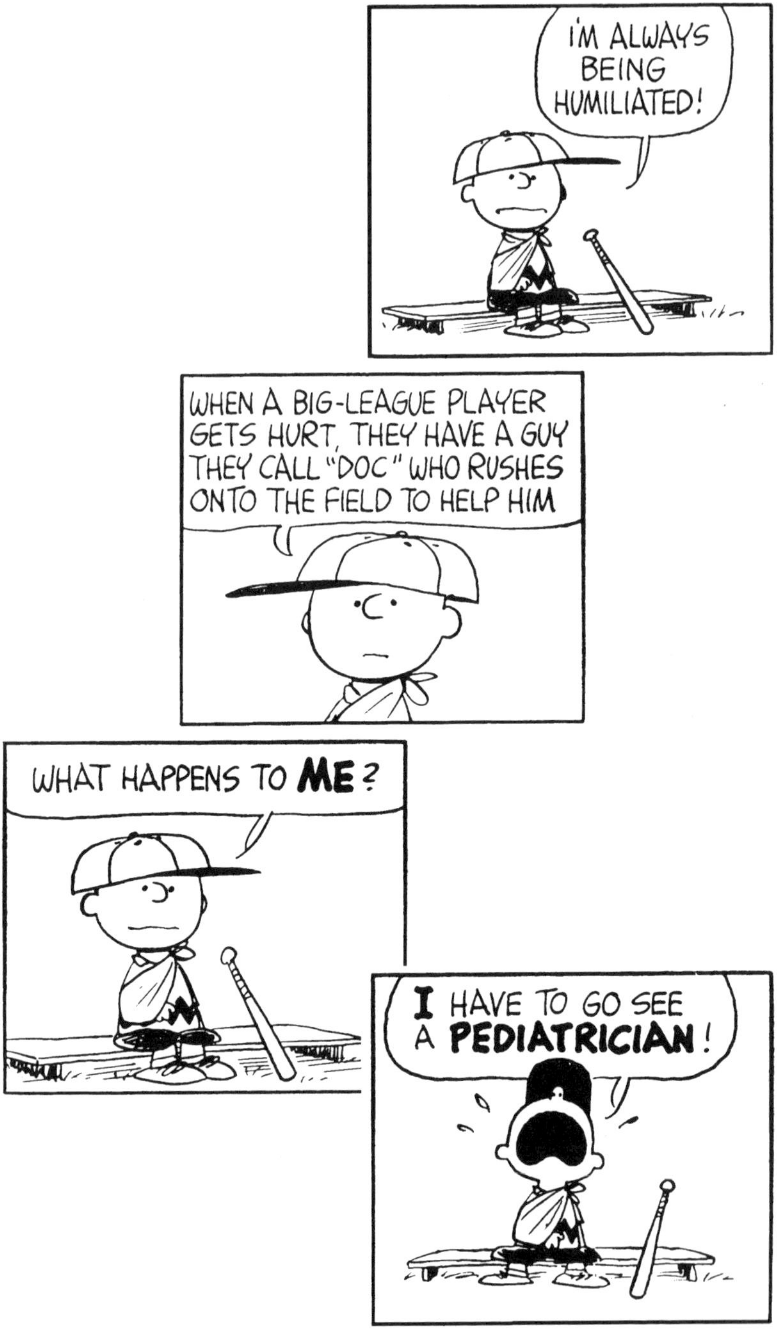
I'M ALWAYS BEING HUMILIATED!
WHEN A BIG-LEAGUE PLAYER GETS HURT, THEY HAVE A GUY THEY CALL "DOC" WHO RUSHES ONTO THE FIELD TO HELP HIM
WHAT HAPPENS TO **ME**?
I HAVE TO GO SEE A **PEDIATRICIAN**!

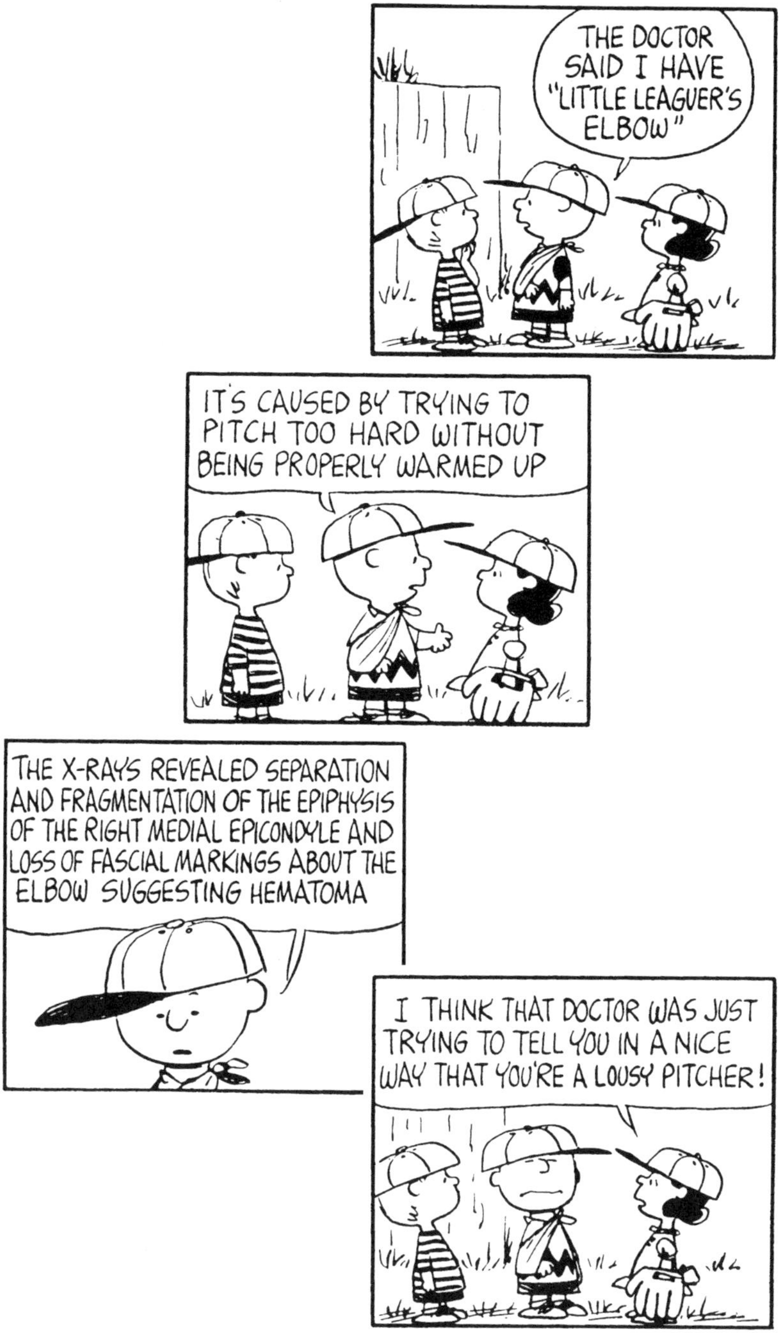
THE DOCTOR SAID I HAVE "LITTLE LEAGUER'S ELBOW"
IT'S CAUSED BY TRYING TO PITCH TOO HARD WITHOUT BEING PROPERLY WARMED UP
THE X-RAYS REVEALED SEPARATION AND FRAGMENTATION OF THE EPIPHYSIS OF THE RIGHT MEDIAL EPICONDYLE AND LOSS OF FASCIAL MARKINGS ABOUT THE ELBOW SUGGESTING HEMATOMA
I THINK THAT DOCTOR WAS JUST TRYING TO TELL YOU IN A NICE WAY THAT YOU'RE A LOUSY PITCHER!

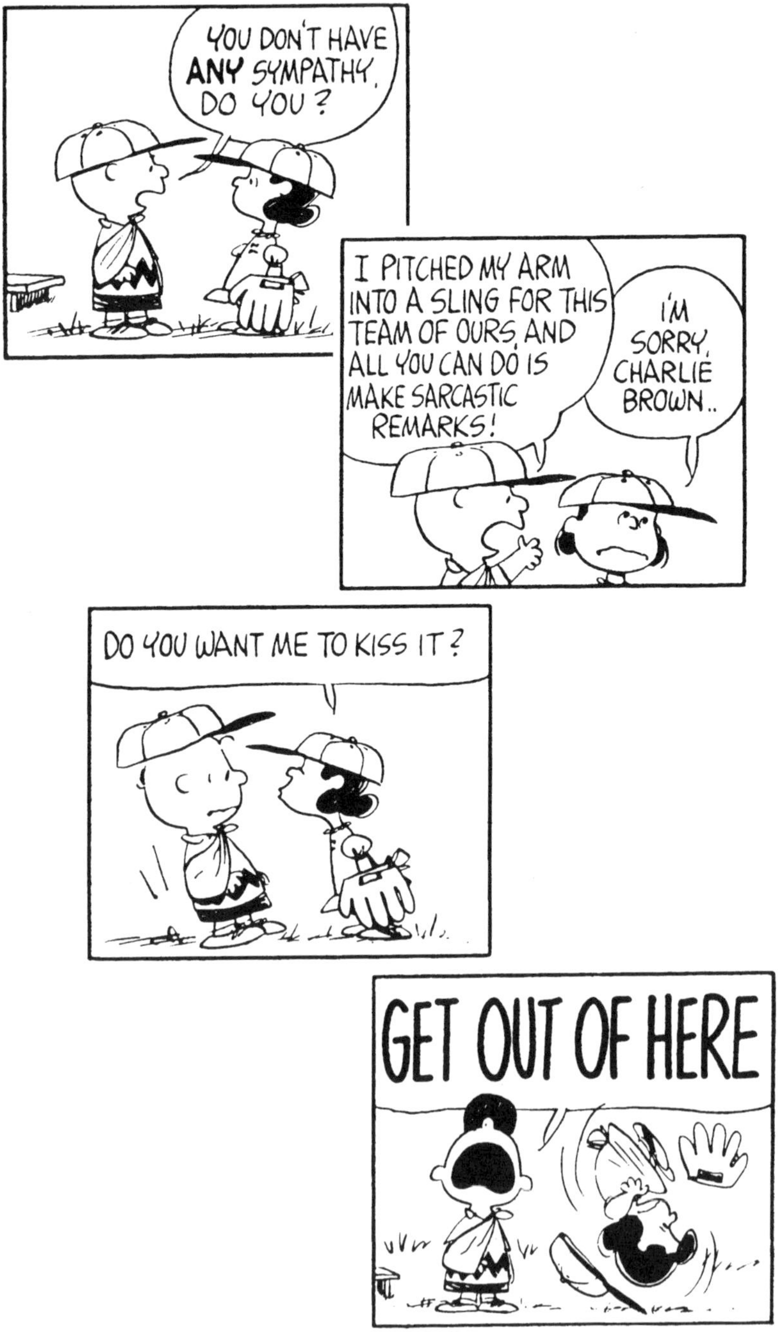
YOU DON'T HAVE **ANY** SYMPATHY, DO YOU?
I PITCHED MY ARM INTO A SLING FOR THIS TEAM OF OURS, AND ALL YOU CAN DO IS MAKE SARCASTIC REMARKS!
I'M SORRY, CHARLIE BROWN..
DO YOU WANT ME TO KISS IT?
GET OUT OF HERE

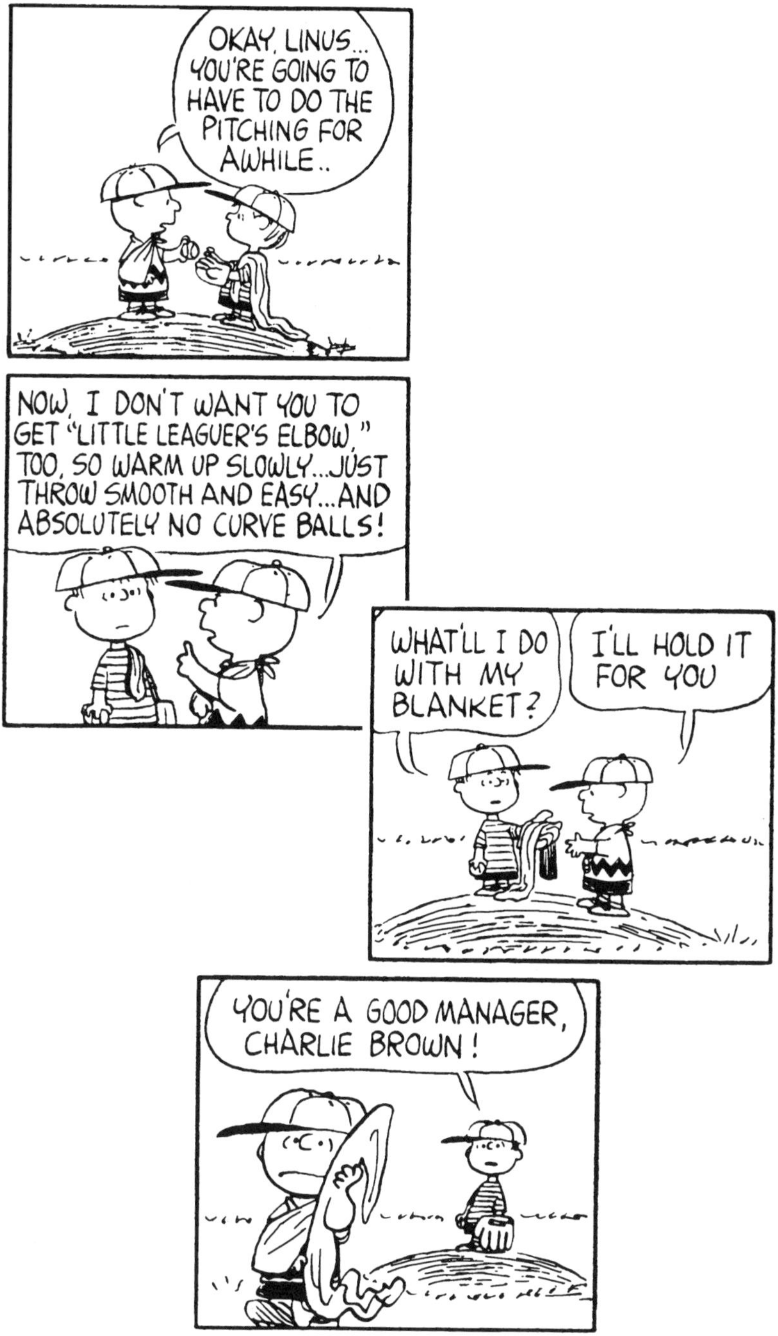
OKAY, LINUS... YOU'RE GOING TO HAVE TO DO THE PITCHING FOR AWHILE..
NOW, I DON'T WANT YOU TO GET "LITTLE LEAGUER'S ELBOW," TOO, SO WARM UP SLOWLY...JUST THROW SMOOTH AND EASY...AND ABSOLUTELY NO CURVE BALLS!
WHAT'LL I DO WITH MY BLANKET?
I'LL HOLD IT FOR YOU
YOU'RE A GOOD MANAGER, CHARLIE BROWN!

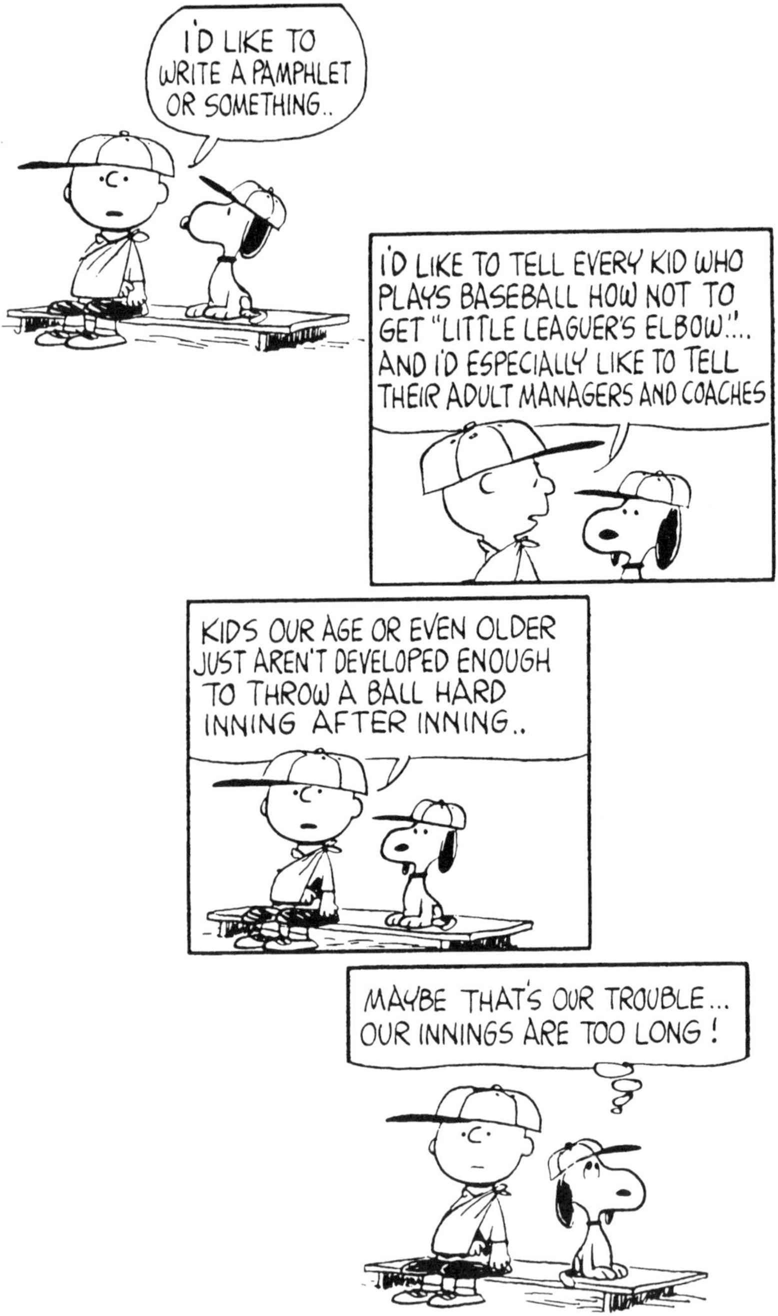
I'D LIKE TO WRITE A PAMPHLET OR SOMETHING..
I'D LIKE TO TELL EVERY KID WHO PLAYS BASEBALL HOW NOT TO GET "LITTLE LEAGUER'S ELBOW."... AND I'D ESPECIALLY LIKE TO TELL THEIR ADULT MANAGERS AND COACHES
KIDS OUR AGE OR EVEN OLDER JUST AREN'T DEVELOPED ENOUGH TO THROW A BALL HARD INNING AFTER INNING..
MAYBE THAT'S OUR TROUBLE... OUR INNINGS ARE TOO LONG!

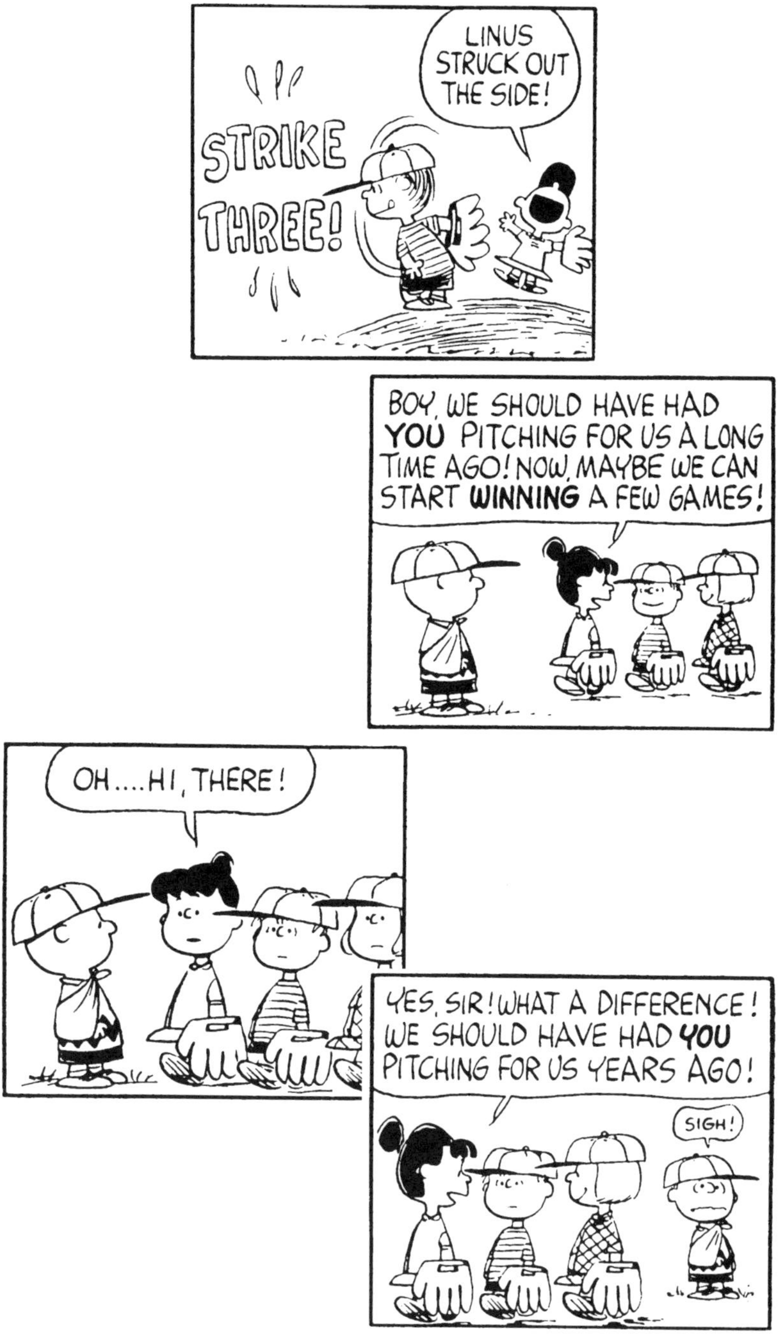
STRIKE THREE!
LINUS STRUCK OUT THE SIDE!
BOY, WE SHOULD HAVE HAD **YOU** PITCHING FOR US A LONG TIME AGO! NOW, MAYBE WE CAN START **WINNING** A FEW GAMES!
OH....HI, THERE!
YES, SIR! WHAT A DIFFERENCE! WE SHOULD HAVE HAD **YOU** PITCHING FOR US YEARS AGO!
SIGH!

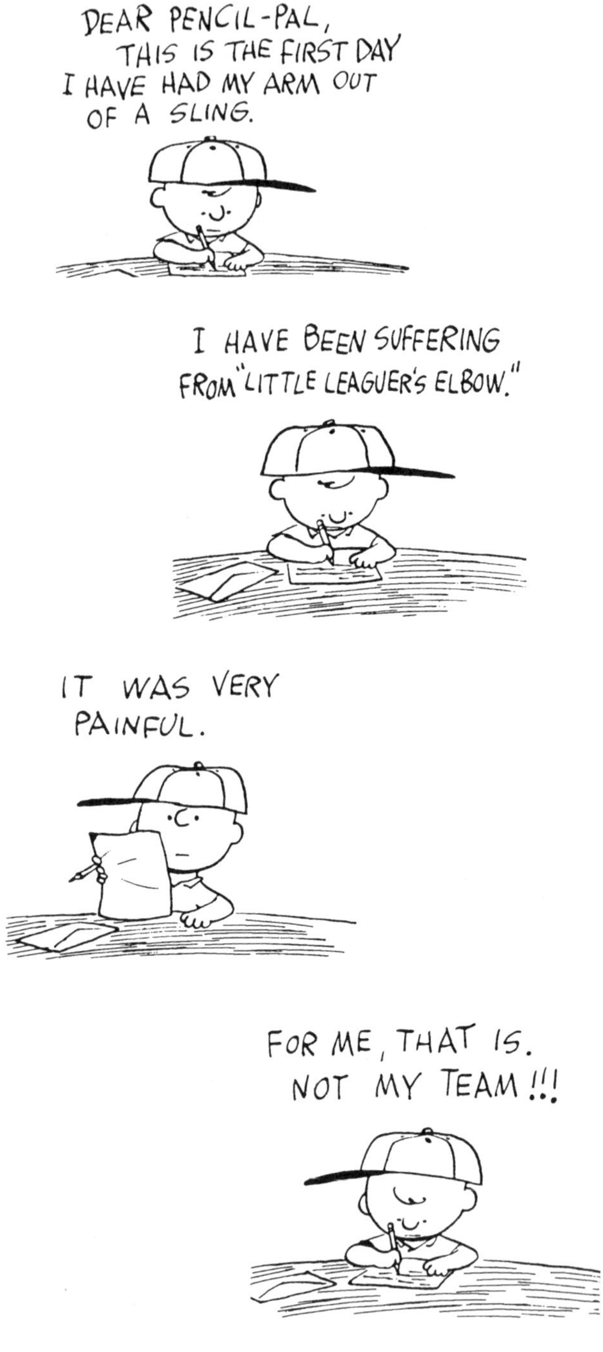
DEAR PENCIL-PAL,
THIS IS THE FIRST DAY I HAVE HAD MY ARM OUT OF A SLING.
I HAVE BEEN SUFFERING FROM "LITTLE LEAGUER'S ELBOW."
IT WAS VERY PAINFUL.
FOR ME, THAT IS. NOT MY TEAM!!!

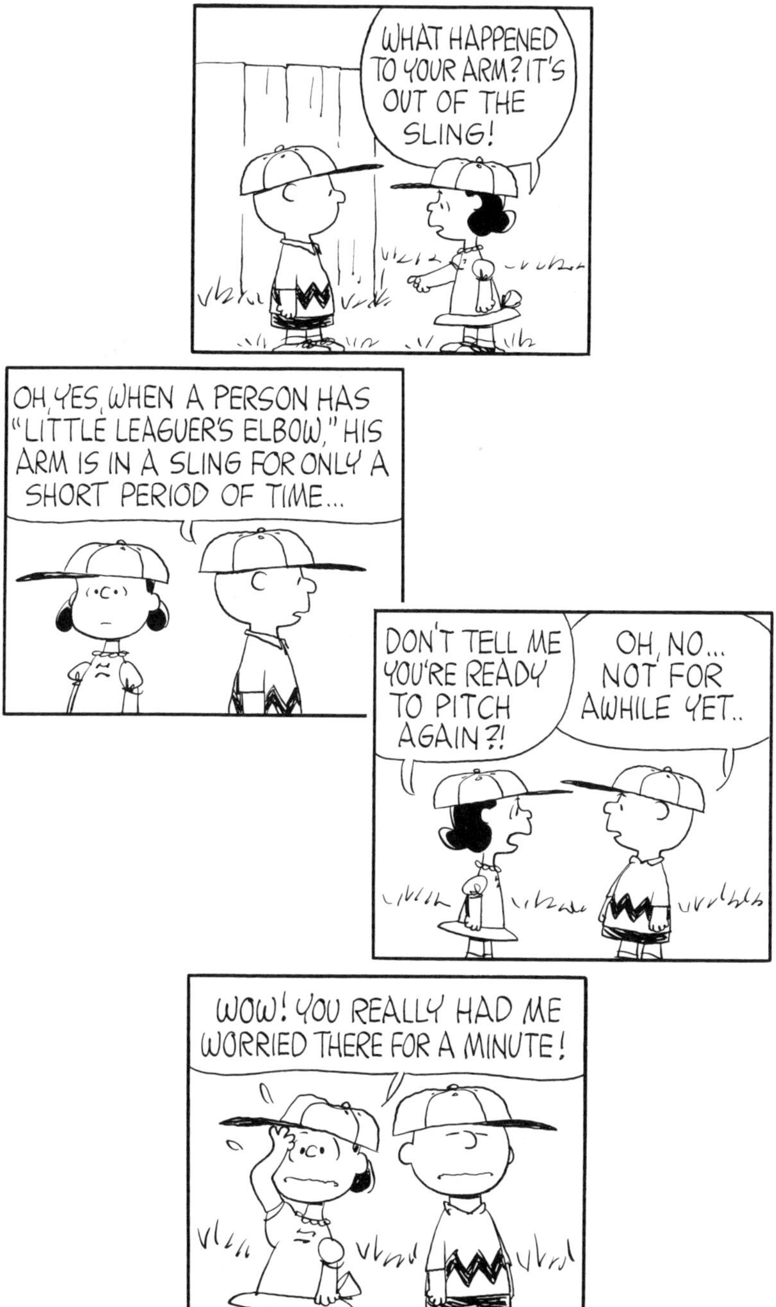
WHAT HAPPENED TO YOUR ARM? IT'S OUT OF THE SLING!
OH, YES, WHEN A PERSON HAS "LITTLE LEAGUER'S ELBOW," HIS ARM IS IN A SLING FOR ONLY A SHORT PERIOD OF TIME...
DON'T TELL ME YOU'RE READY TO PITCH AGAIN?!
OH, NO... NOT FOR AWHILE YET..
WOW! YOU REALLY HAD ME WORRIED THERE FOR A MINUTE!

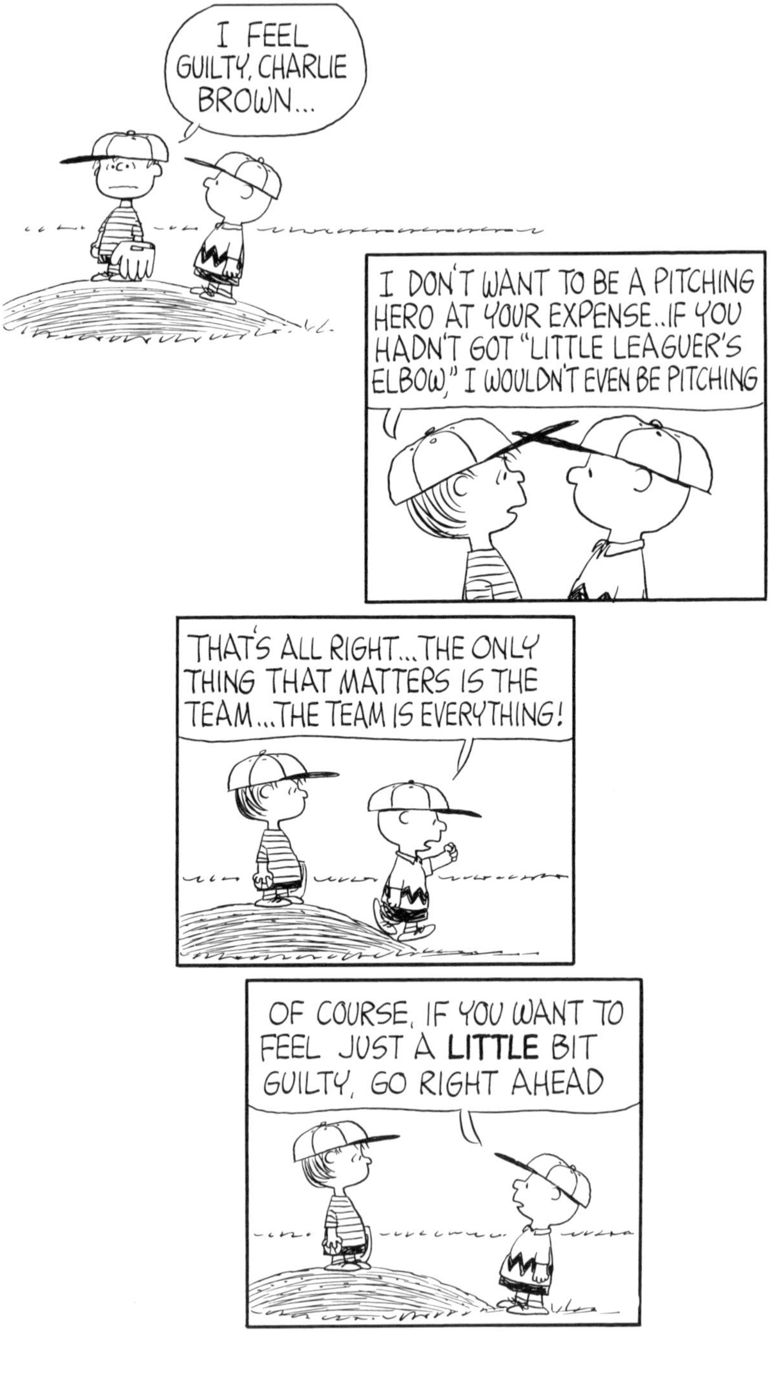
I FEEL GUILTY, CHARLIE BROWN...
I DON'T WANT TO BE A PITCHING HERO AT YOUR EXPENSE..IF YOU HADN'T GOT "LITTLE LEAGUER'S ELBOW," I WOULDN'T EVEN BE PITCHING
THAT'S ALL RIGHT...THE ONLY THING THAT MATTERS IS THE TEAM...THE TEAM IS EVERYTHING!
OF COURSE, IF YOU WANT TO FEEL JUST A **LITTLE** BIT GUILTY, GO RIGHT AHEAD

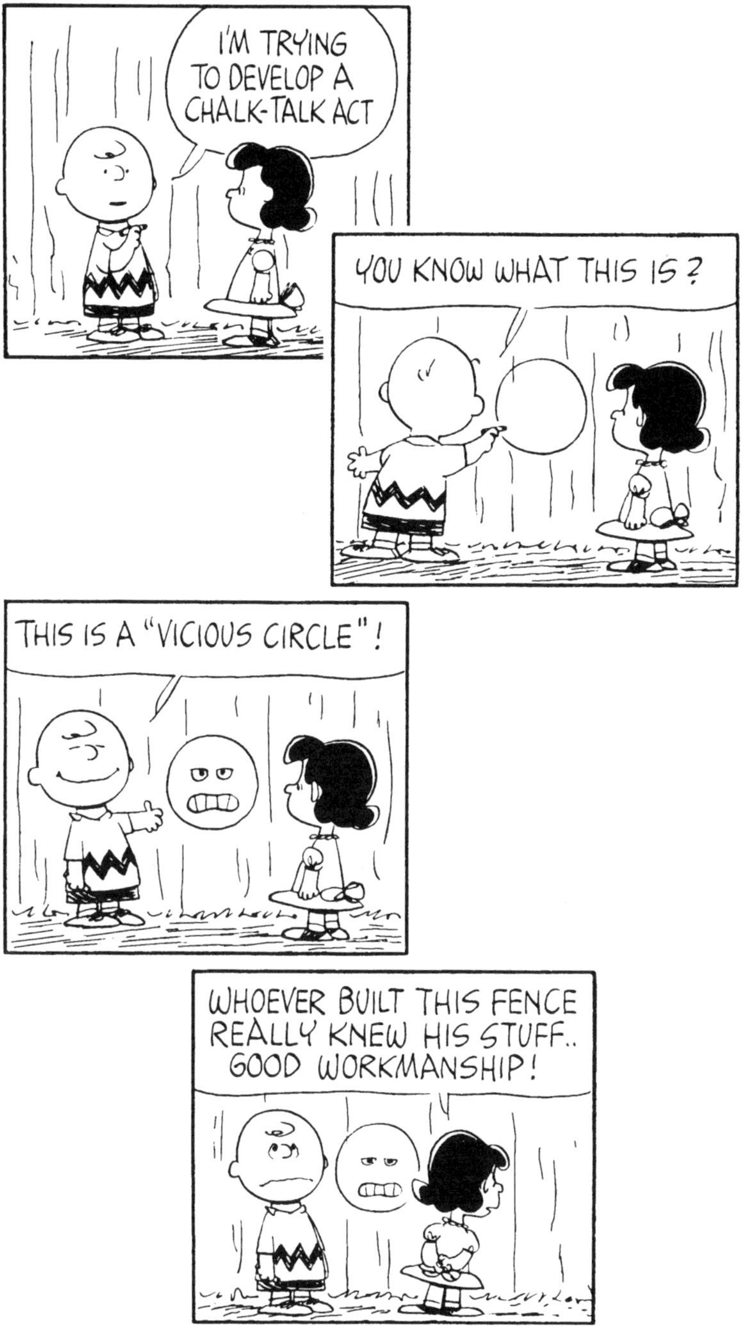
I'M TRYING TO DEVELOP A CHALK-TALK ACT
YOU KNOW WHAT THIS IS?
THIS IS A "VICIOUS CIRCLE"!
WHOEVER BUILT THIS FENCE REALLY KNEW HIS STUFF.. GOOD WORKMANSHIP!

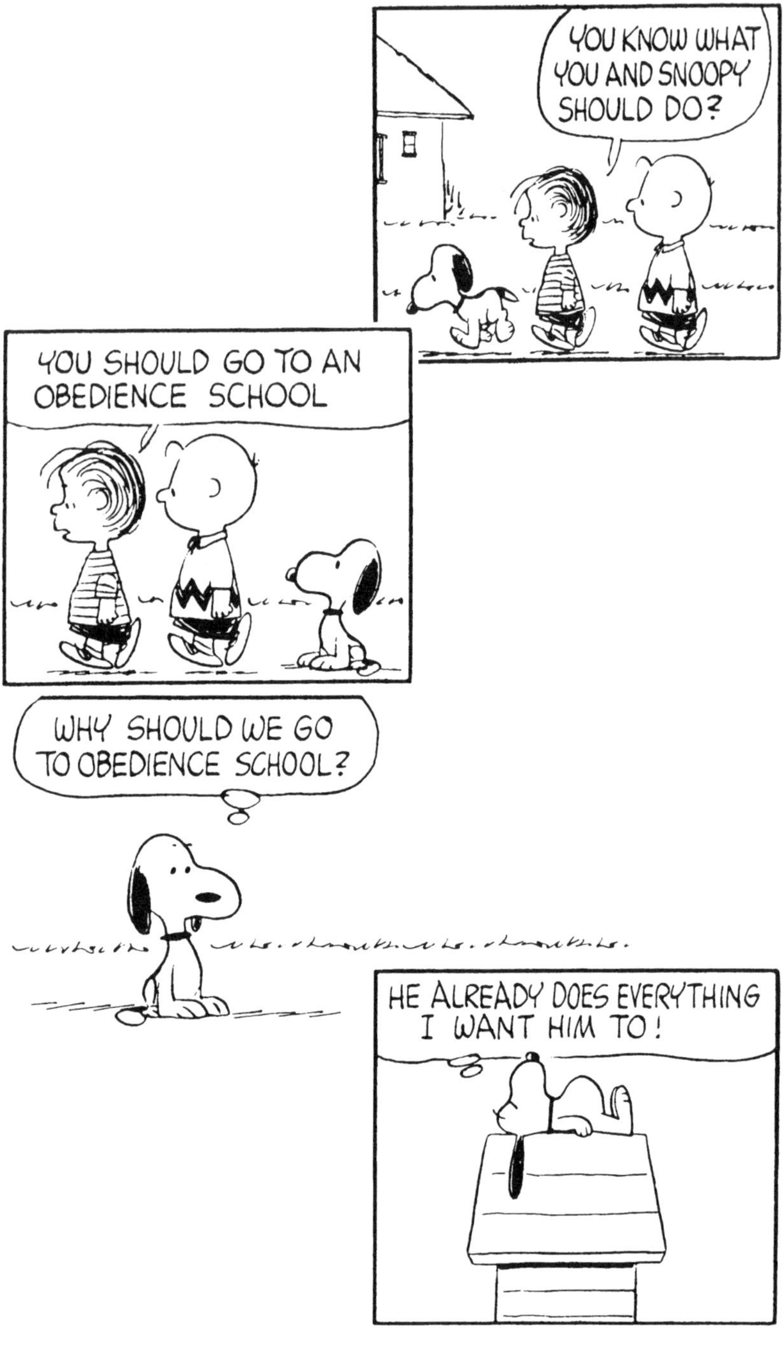

YOU KNOW WHAT YOU AND SNOOPY SHOULD DO?
YOU SHOULD GO TO AN OBEDIENCE SCHOOL
WHY SHOULD WE GO TO OBEDIENCE SCHOOL?
HE ALREADY DOES EVERYTHING I WANT HIM TO!

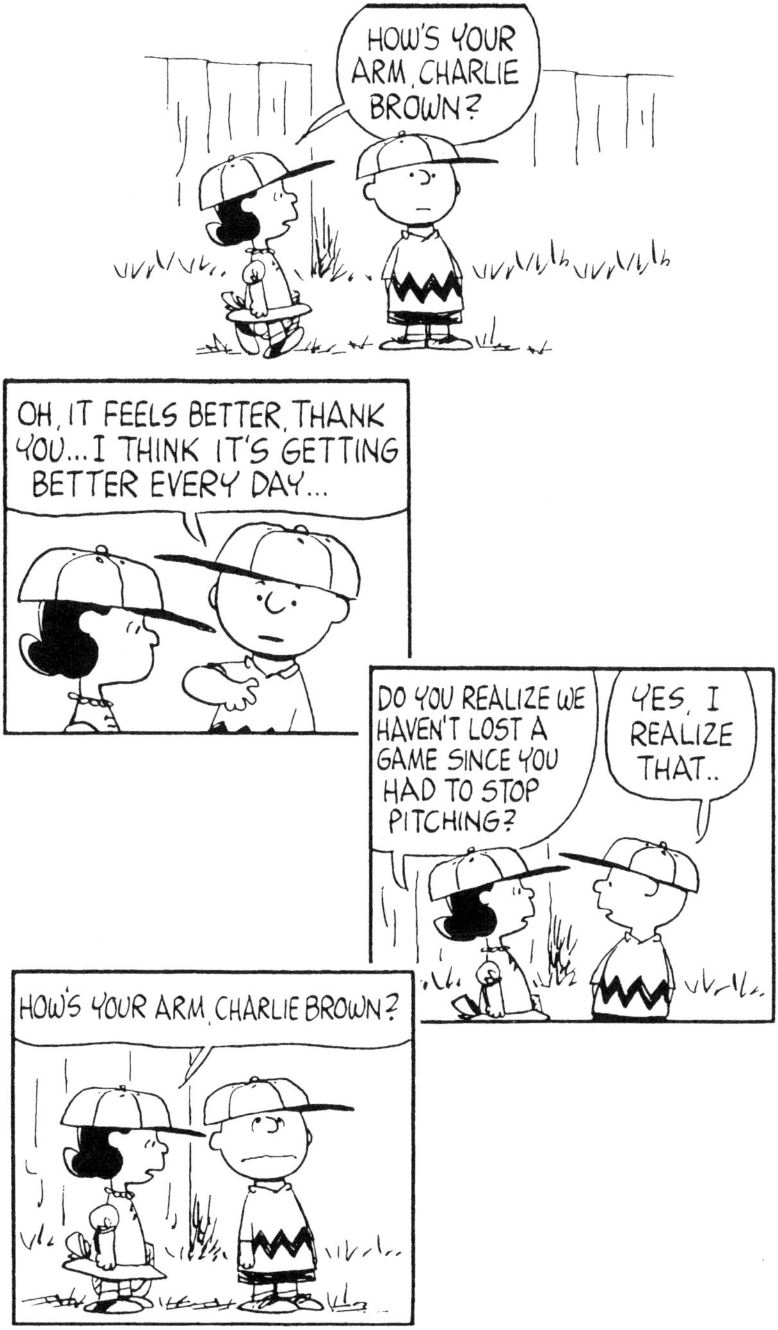
HOW'S YOUR ARM, CHARLIE BROWN?
OH, IT FEELS BETTER, THANK YOU...I THINK IT'S GETTING BETTER EVERY DAY...
DO YOU REALIZE WE HAVEN'T LOST A GAME SINCE YOU HAD TO STOP PITCHING?
YES, I REALIZE THAT..
HOW'S YOUR ARM, CHARLIE BROWN?

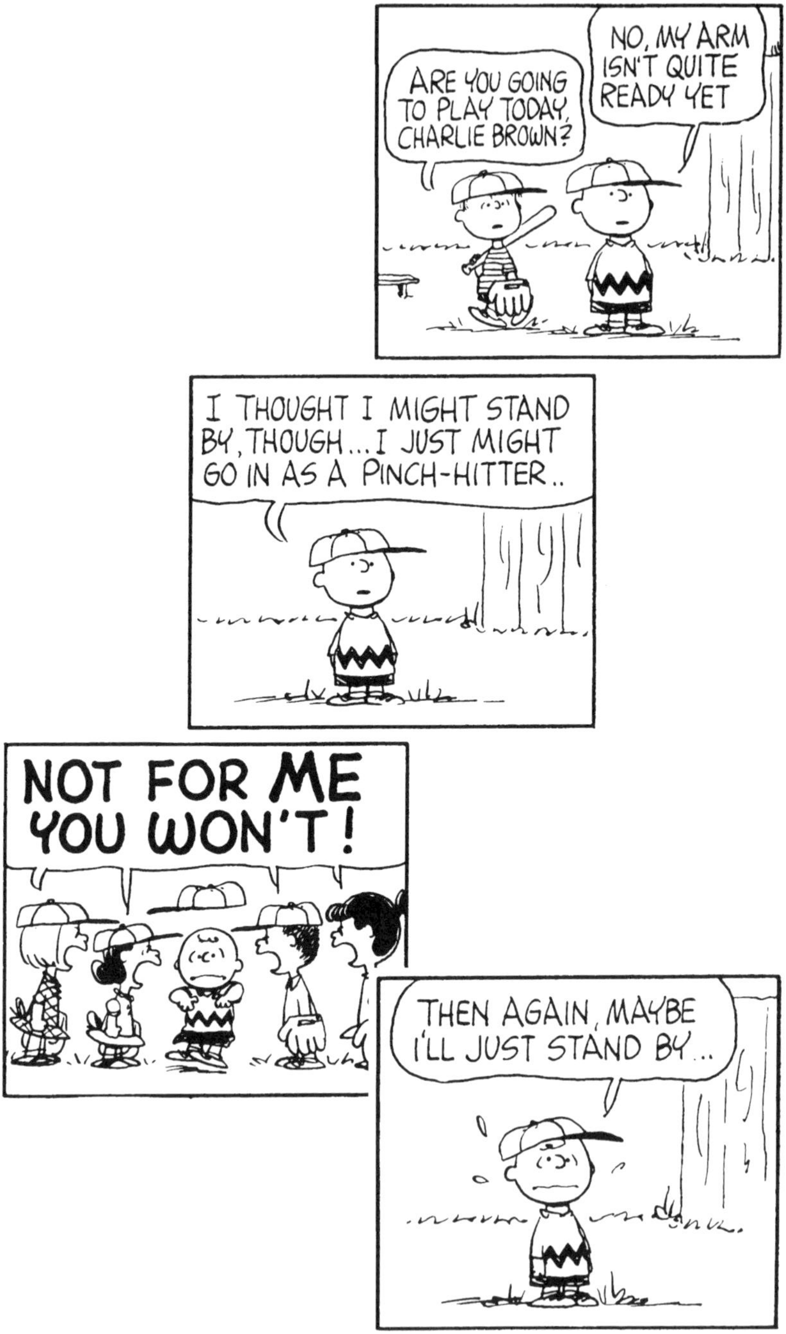
ARE YOU GOING TO PLAY TODAY, CHARLIE BROWN?
NO, MY ARM ISN'T QUITE READY YET
I THOUGHT I MIGHT STAND BY, THOUGH... I JUST MIGHT GO IN AS A PINCH-HITTER..
NOT FOR ME YOU WON'T!
THEN AGAIN, MAYBE I'LL JUST STAND BY...

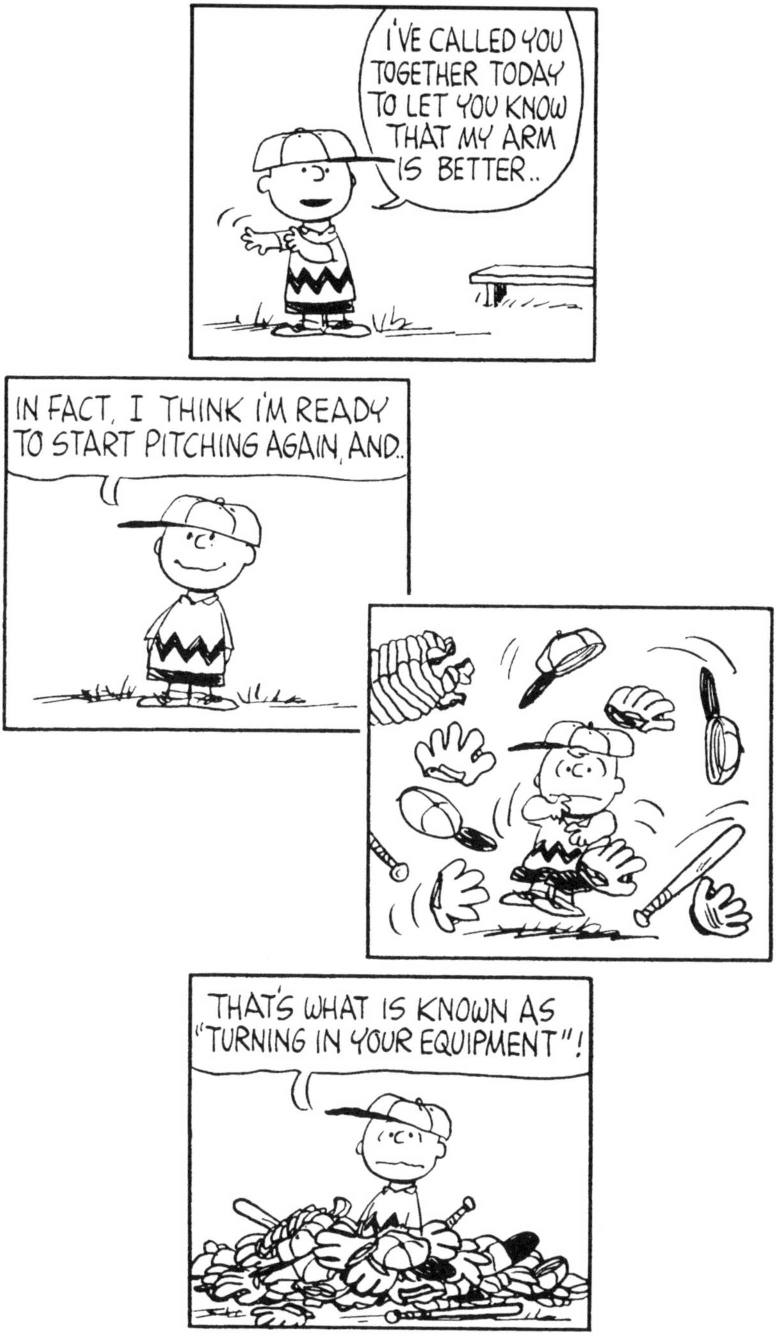
I'VE CALLED YOU TOGETHER TODAY TO LET YOU KNOW THAT MY ARM IS BETTER..
IN FACT, I THINK I'M READY TO START PITCHING AGAIN, AND..
THAT'S WHAT IS KNOWN AS "TURNING IN YOUR EQUIPMENT"!

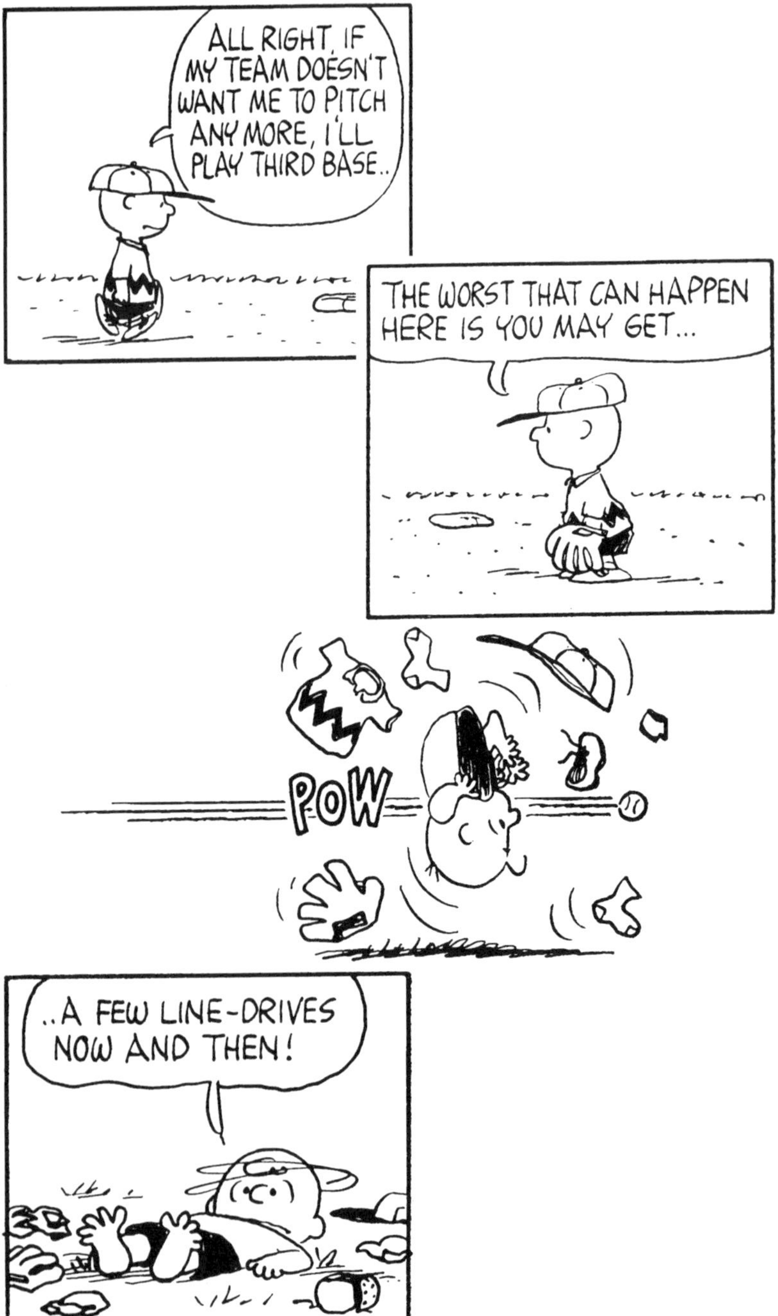
ALL RIGHT, IF MY TEAM DOESN'T WANT ME TO PITCH ANY MORE, I'LL PLAY THIRD BASE..
THE WORST THAT CAN HAPPEN HERE IS YOU MAY GET...
POW
..A FEW LINE-DRIVES NOW AND THEN!

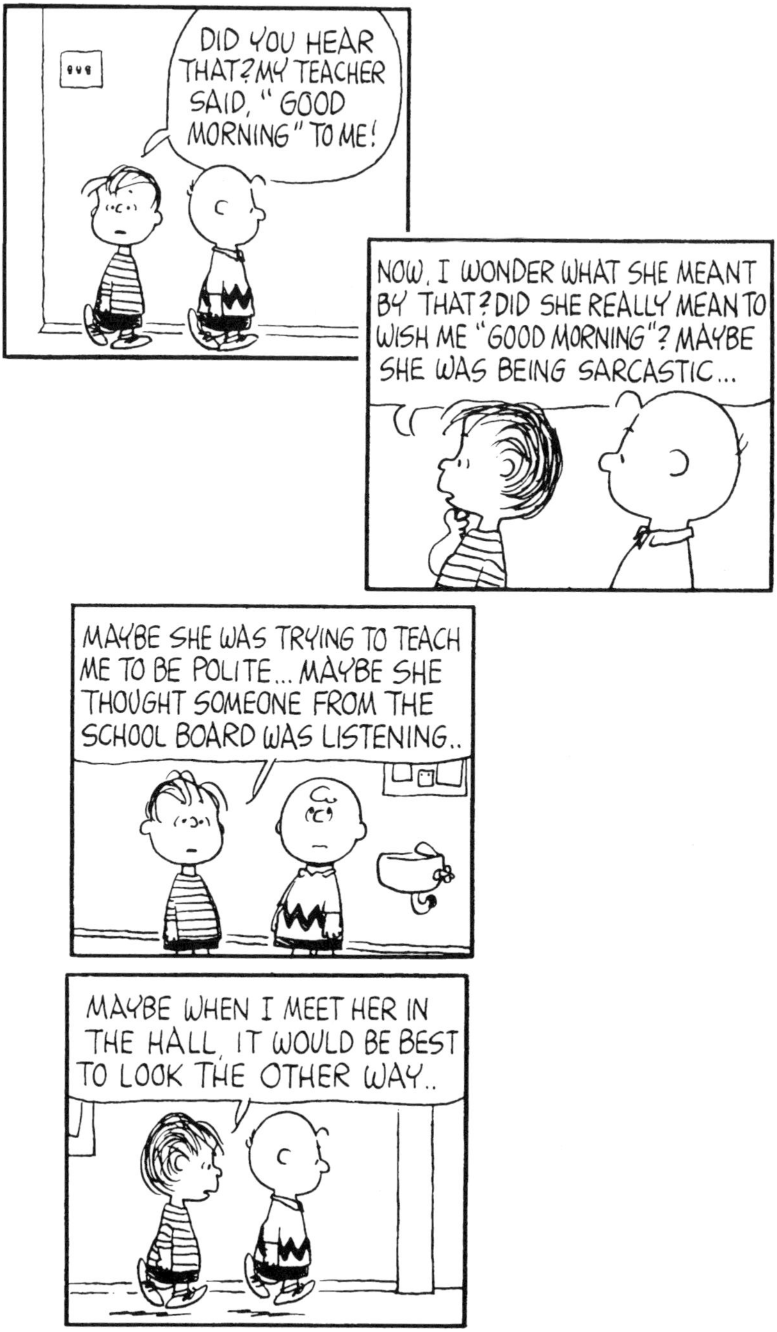
DID YOU HEAR THAT? MY TEACHER SAID, "GOOD MORNING" TO ME!
NOW, I WONDER WHAT SHE MEANT BY THAT? DID SHE REALLY MEAN TO WISH ME "GOOD MORNING"? MAYBE SHE WAS BEING SARCASTIC...
MAYBE SHE WAS TRYING TO TEACH ME TO BE POLITE... MAYBE SHE THOUGHT SOMEONE FROM THE SCHOOL BOARD WAS LISTENING..
MAYBE WHEN I MEET HER IN THE HALL, IT WOULD BE BEST TO LOOK THE OTHER WAY..

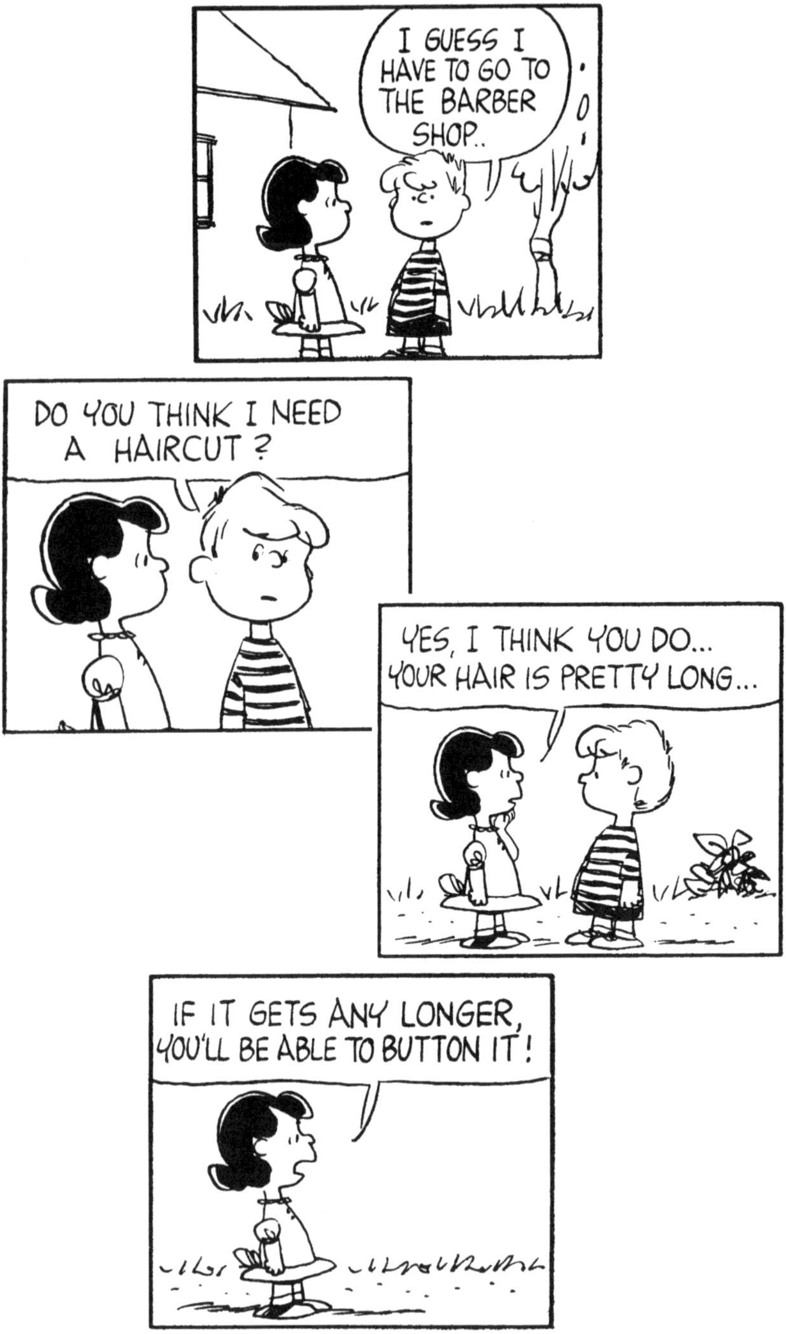
I GUESS I HAVE TO GO TO THE BARBER SHOP..
DO YOU THINK I NEED A HAIRCUT ?
YES, I THINK YOU DO... YOUR HAIR IS PRETTY LONG...
IF IT GETS ANY LONGER, YOU'LL BE ABLE TO BUTTON IT !

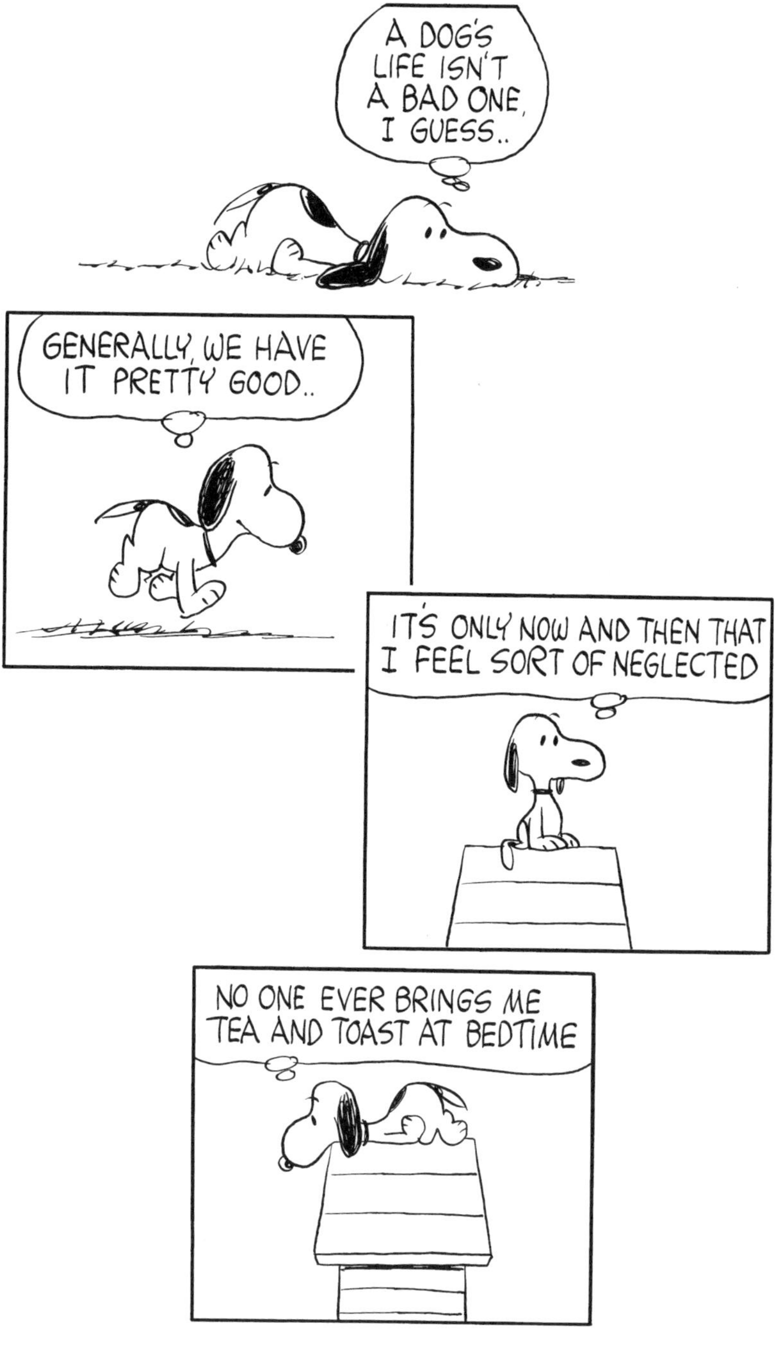
A DOG'S LIFE ISN'T A BAD ONE, I GUESS..
GENERALLY, WE HAVE IT PRETTY GOOD..
IT'S ONLY NOW AND THEN THAT I FEEL SORT OF NEGLECTED
NO ONE EVER BRINGS ME TEA AND TOAST AT BEDTIME

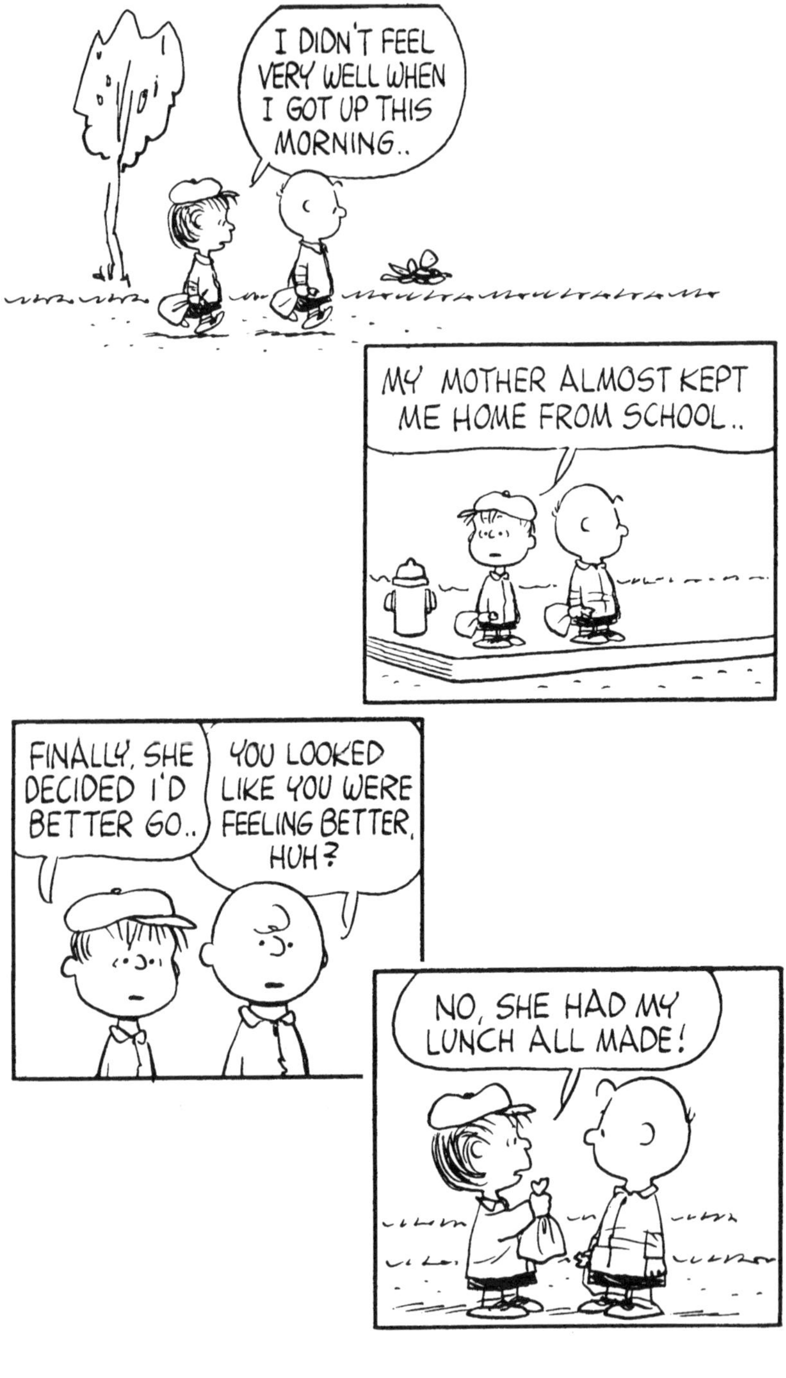
I DIDN'T FEEL VERY WELL WHEN I GOT UP THIS MORNING..
MY MOTHER ALMOST KEPT ME HOME FROM SCHOOL..
FINALLY, SHE DECIDED I'D BETTER GO..
YOU LOOKED LIKE YOU WERE FEELING BETTER, HUH?
NO, SHE HAD MY LUNCH ALL MADE!

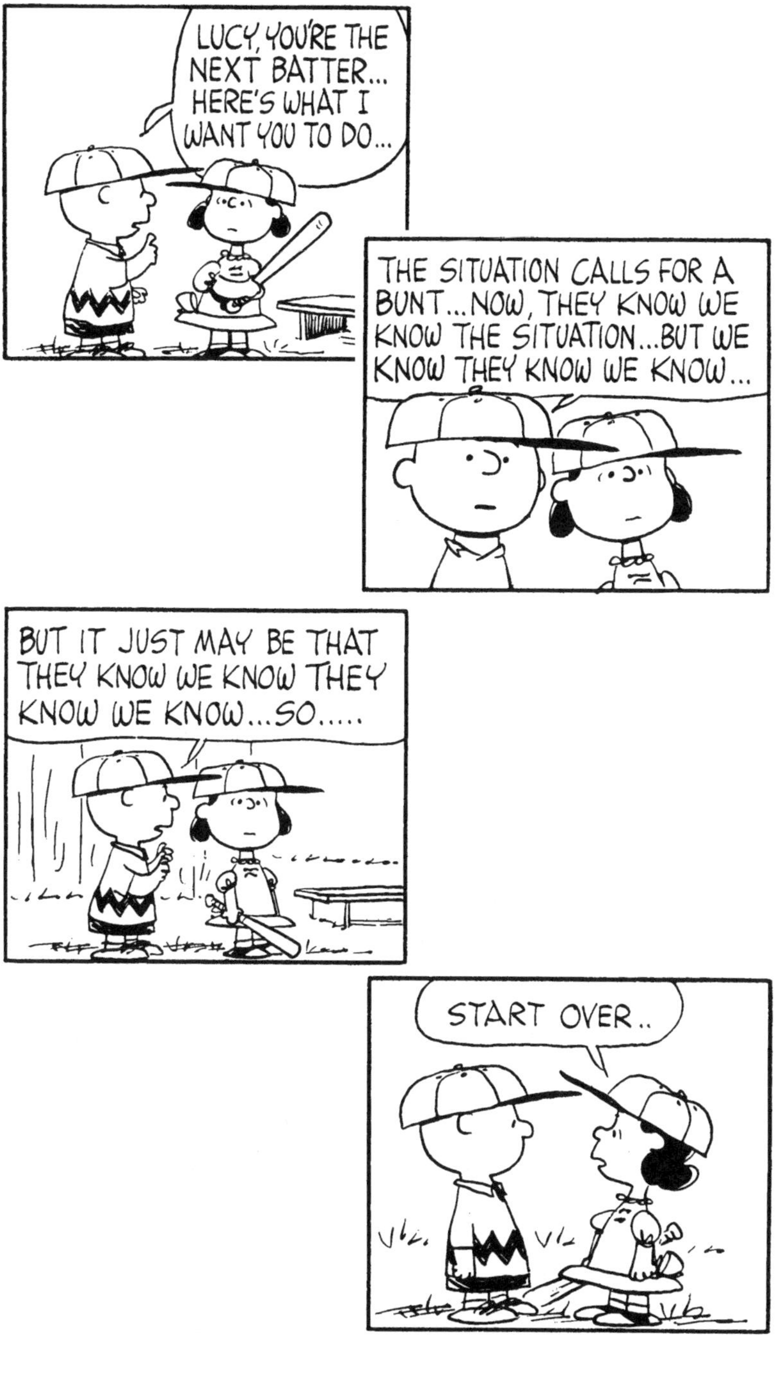
LUCY, YOU'RE THE NEXT BATTER... HERE'S WHAT I WANT YOU TO DO...
THE SITUATION CALLS FOR A BUNT...NOW, THEY KNOW WE KNOW THE SITUATION...BUT WE KNOW THEY KNOW WE KNOW...
BUT IT JUST MAY BE THAT THEY KNOW WE KNOW THEY KNOW WE KNOW...SO.....
START OVER..

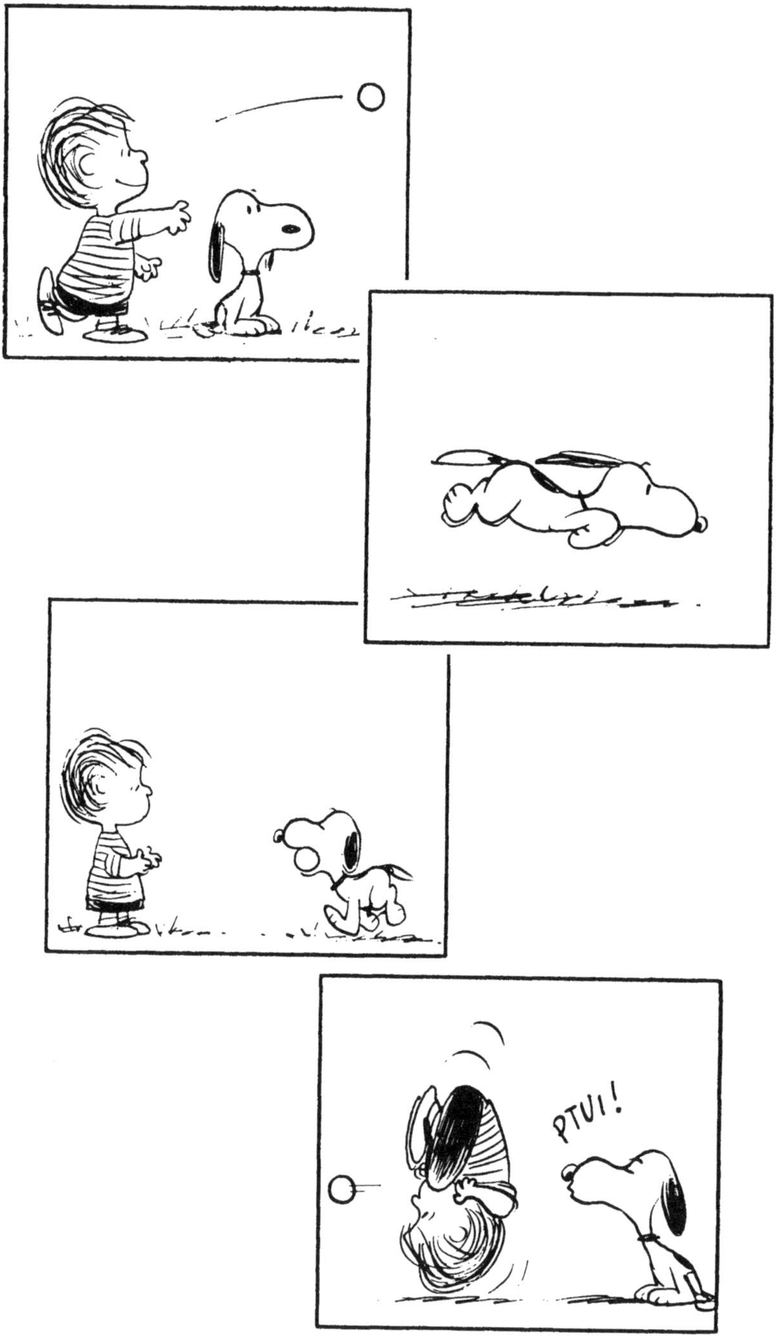
PTUI!

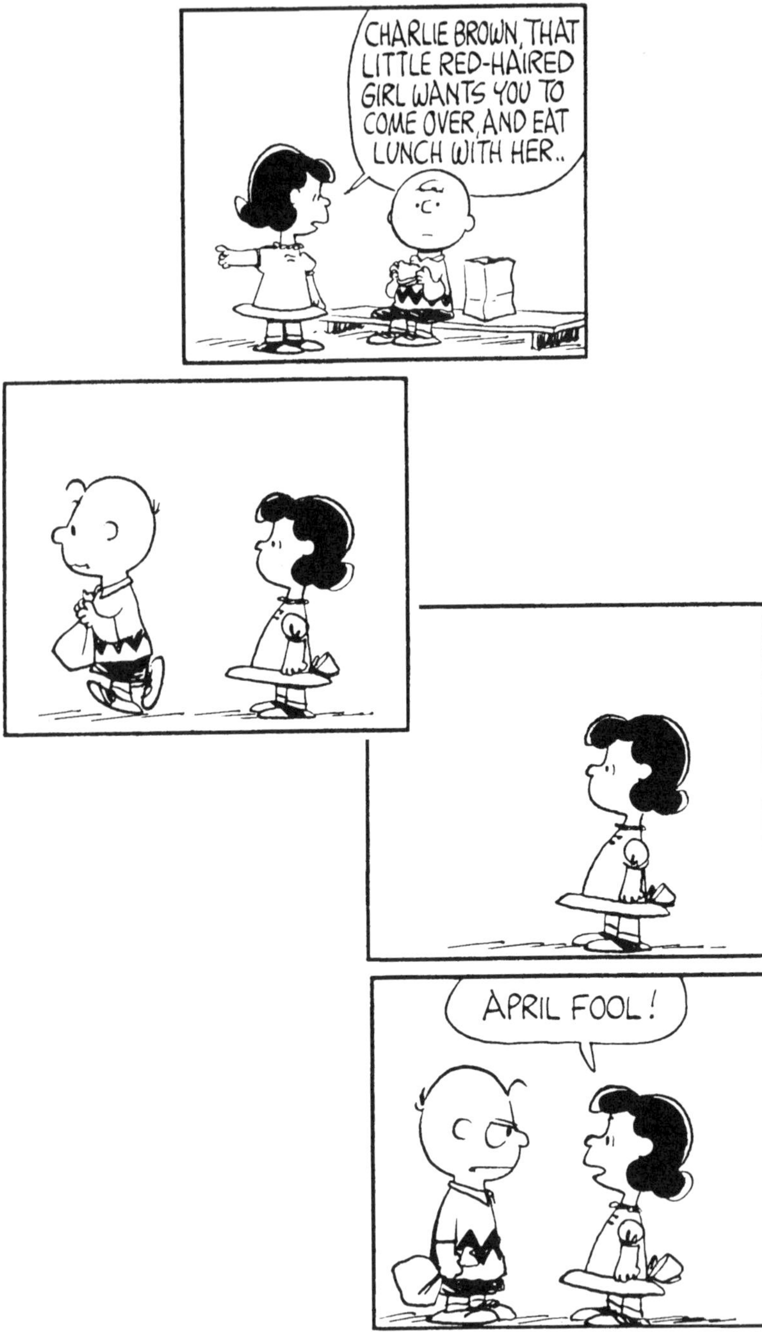
CHARLIE BROWN, THAT LITTLE RED-HAIRED GIRL WANTS YOU TO COME OVER, AND EAT LUNCH WITH HER..
APRIL FOOL!

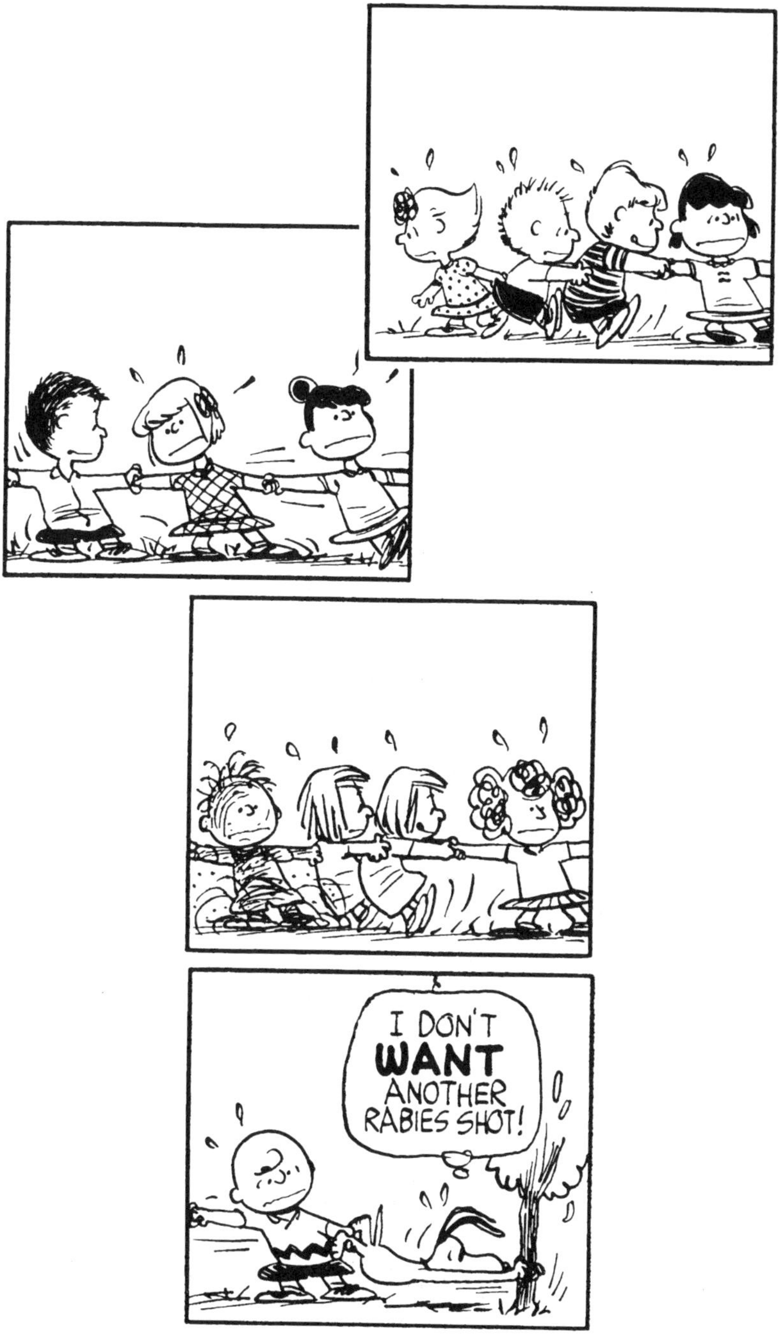
I DON'T WANT ANOTHER RABIES SHOT!

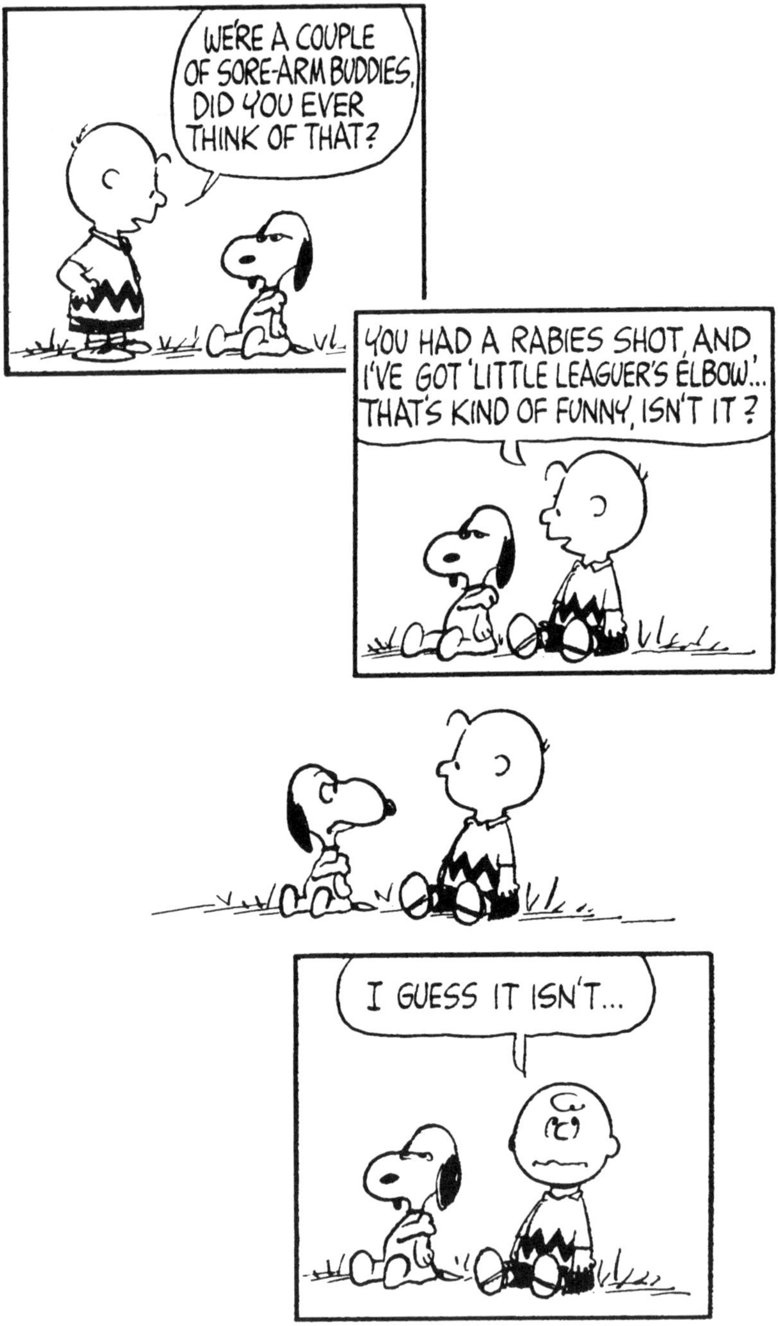
WE'RE A COUPLE OF SORE-ARM BUDDIES, DID YOU EVER THINK OF THAT?
YOU HAD A RABIES SHOT, AND I'VE GOT 'LITTLE LEAGUER'S ELBOW'... THAT'S KIND OF FUNNY, ISN'T IT?
I GUESS IT ISN'T...

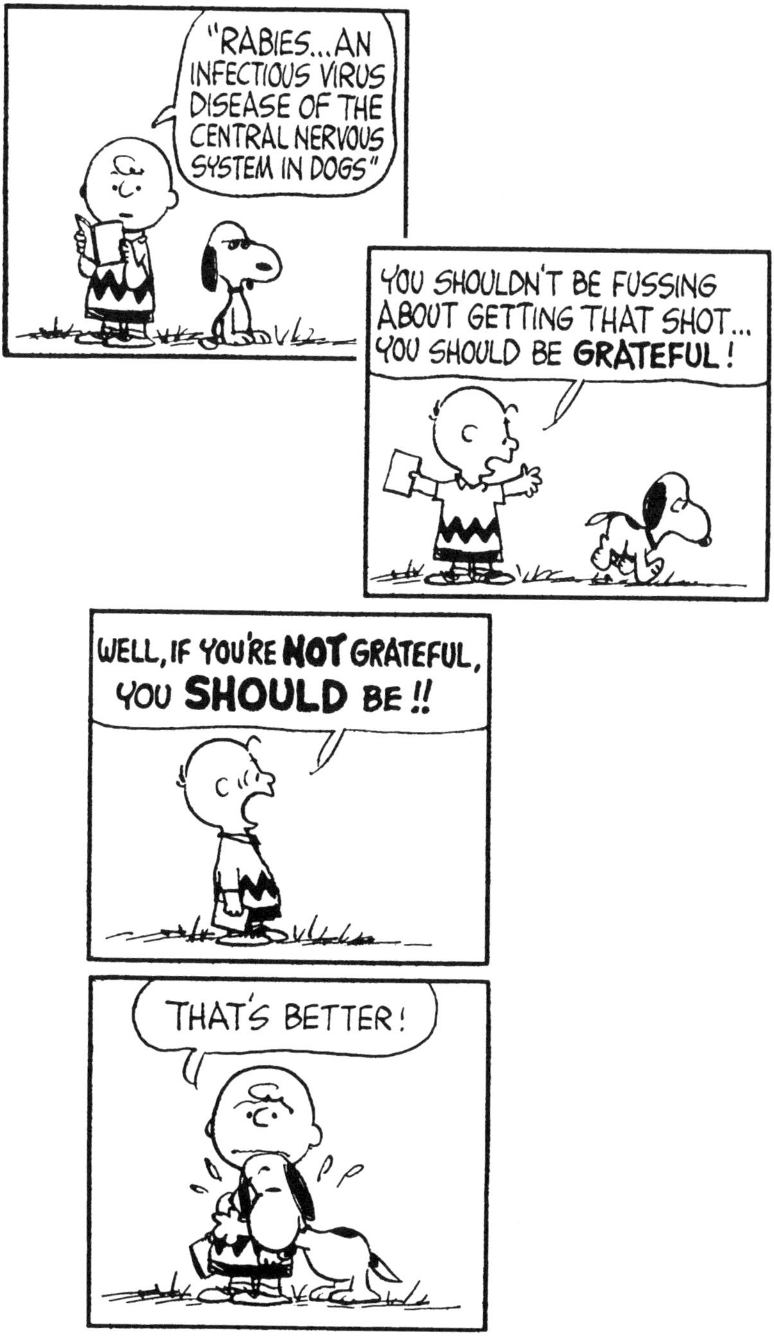
"RABIES...AN INFECTIOUS VIRUS DISEASE OF THE CENTRAL NERVOUS SYSTEM IN DOGS"
YOU SHOULDN'T BE FUSSING ABOUT GETTING THAT SHOT... YOU SHOULD BE GRATEFUL!
WELL, IF YOU'RE NOT GRATEFUL, YOU SHOULD BE!!
THAT'S BETTER!

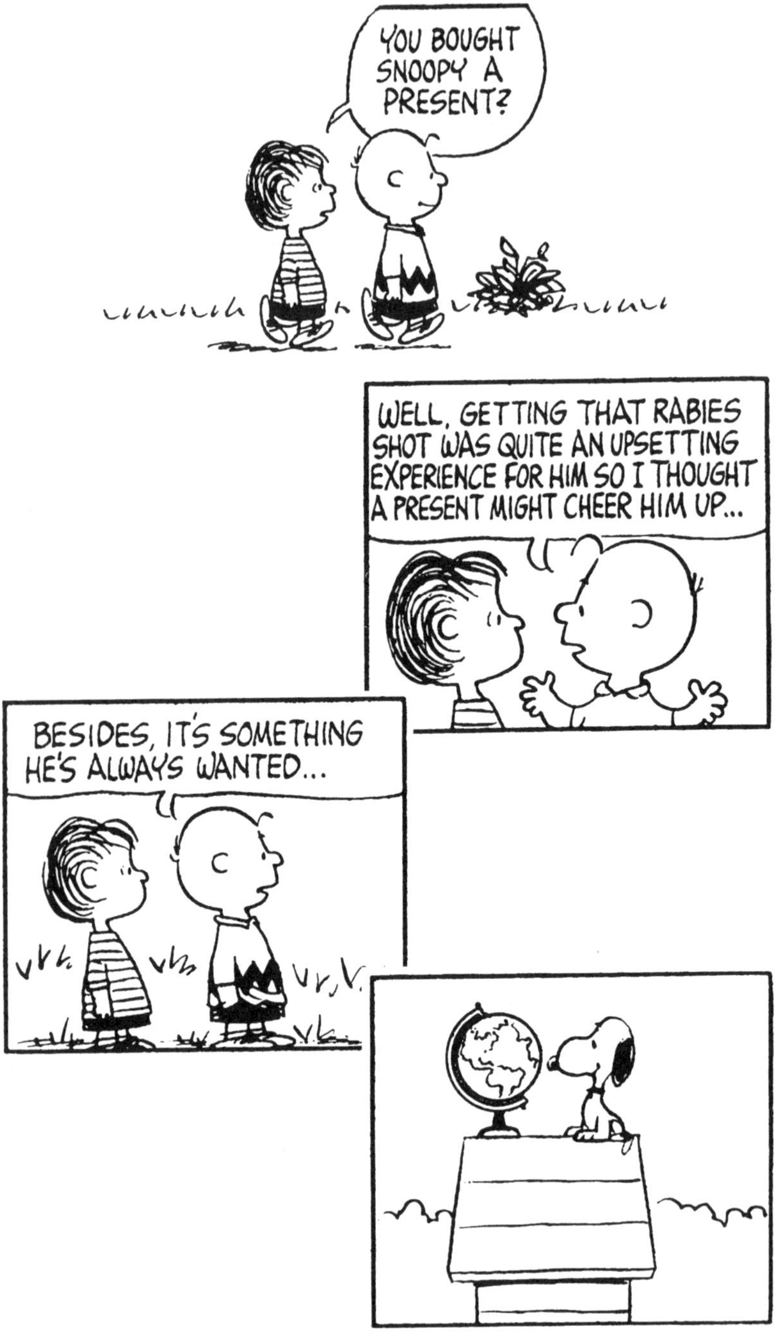
YOU BOUGHT SNOOPY A PRESENT?
WELL, GETTING THAT RABIES SHOT WAS QUITE AN UPSETTING EXPERIENCE FOR HIM SO I THOUGHT A PRESENT MIGHT CHEER HIM UP...
BESIDES, IT'S SOMETHING HE'S ALWAYS WANTED...

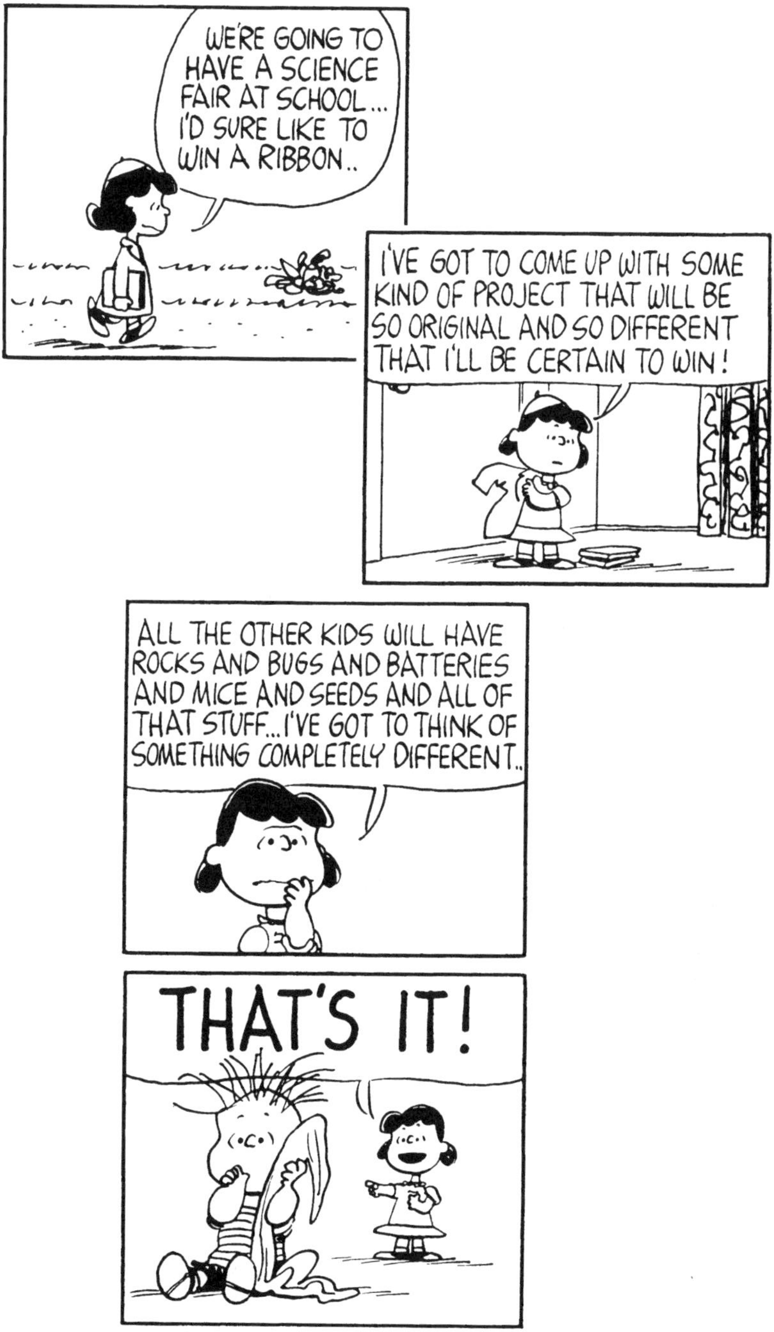
WE'RE GOING TO HAVE A SCIENCE FAIR AT SCHOOL... I'D SURE LIKE TO WIN A RIBBON..
I'VE GOT TO COME UP WITH SOME KIND OF PROJECT THAT WILL BE SO ORIGINAL AND SO DIFFERENT THAT I'LL BE CERTAIN TO WIN!
ALL THE OTHER KIDS WILL HAVE ROCKS AND BUGS AND BATTERIES AND MICE AND SEEDS AND ALL OF THAT STUFF...I'VE GOT TO THINK OF SOMETHING COMPLETELY DIFFERENT..
THAT'S IT!

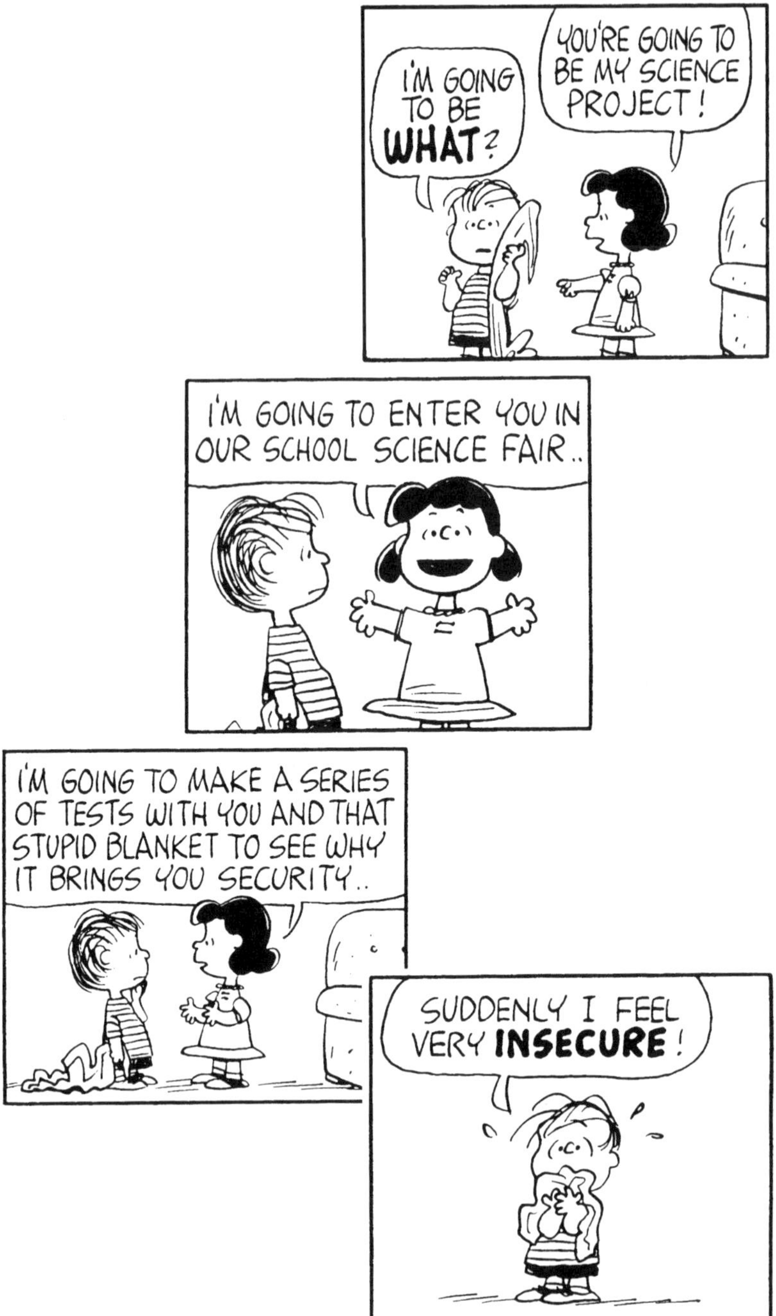
YOU'RE GOING TO BE MY SCIENCE PROJECT!
I'M GOING TO BE WHAT?
I'M GOING TO ENTER YOU IN OUR SCHOOL SCIENCE FAIR..
I'M GOING TO MAKE A SERIES OF TESTS WITH YOU AND THAT STUPID BLANKET TO SEE WHY IT BRINGS YOU SECURITY..
SUDDENLY I FEEL VERY INSECURE!

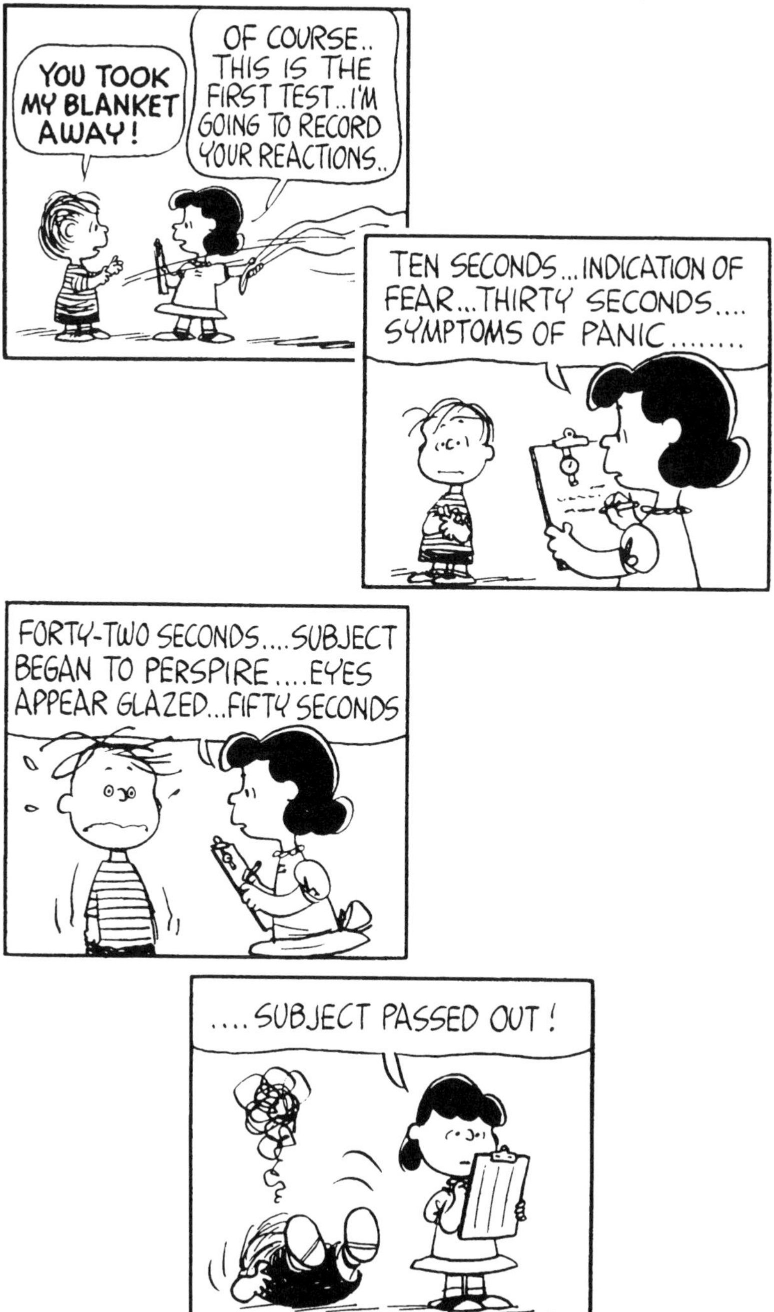
YOU TOOK MY BLANKET AWAY!
OF COURSE.. THIS IS THE FIRST TEST..I'M GOING TO RECORD YOUR REACTIONS..
TEN SECONDS...INDICATION OF FEAR...THIRTY SECONDS.... SYMPTOMS OF PANIC........
FORTY-TWO SECONDS....SUBJECT BEGAN TO PERSPIRE....EYES APPEAR GLAZED...FIFTY SECONDS
....SUBJECT PASSED OUT!

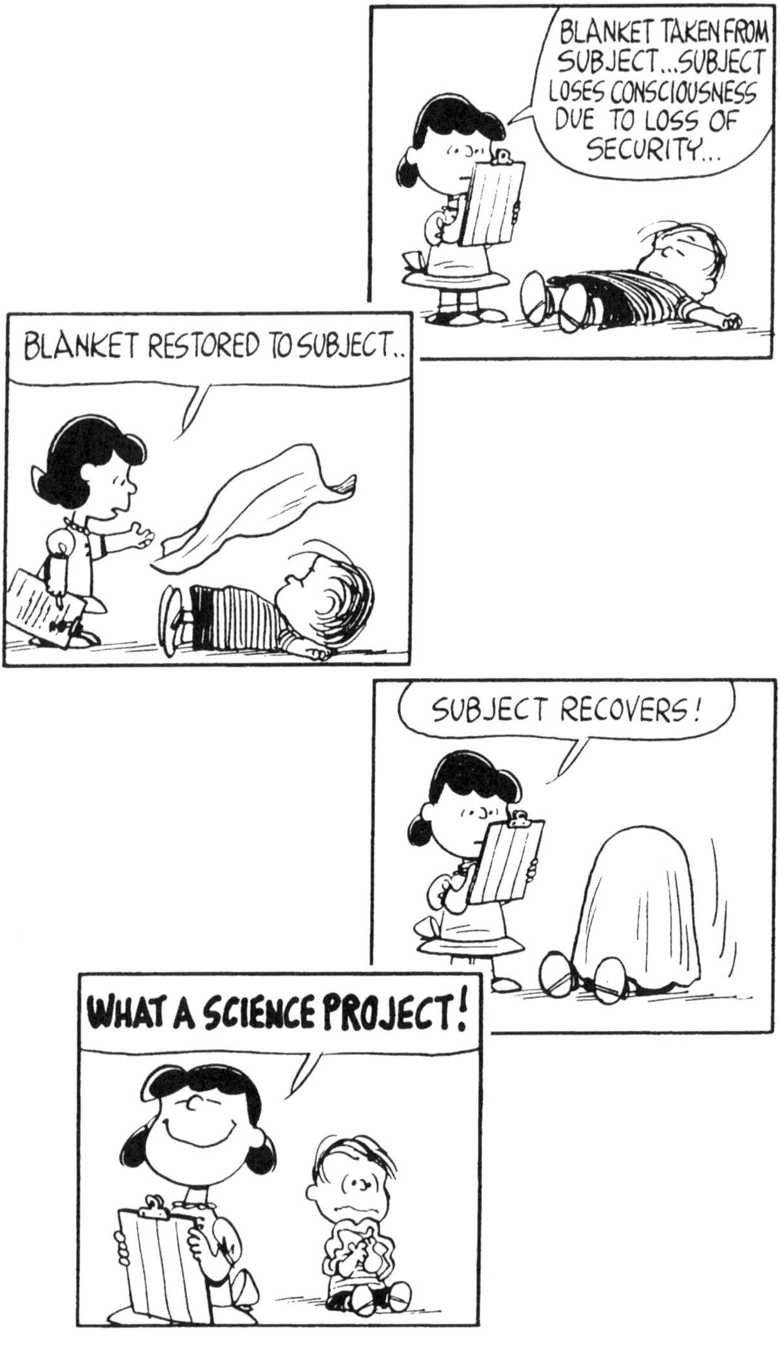
BLANKET TAKEN FROM SUBJECT...SUBJECT LOSES CONSCIOUSNESS DUE TO LOSS OF SECURITY...
BLANKET RESTORED TO SUBJECT..
SUBJECT RECOVERS!
WHAT A SCIENCE PROJECT!

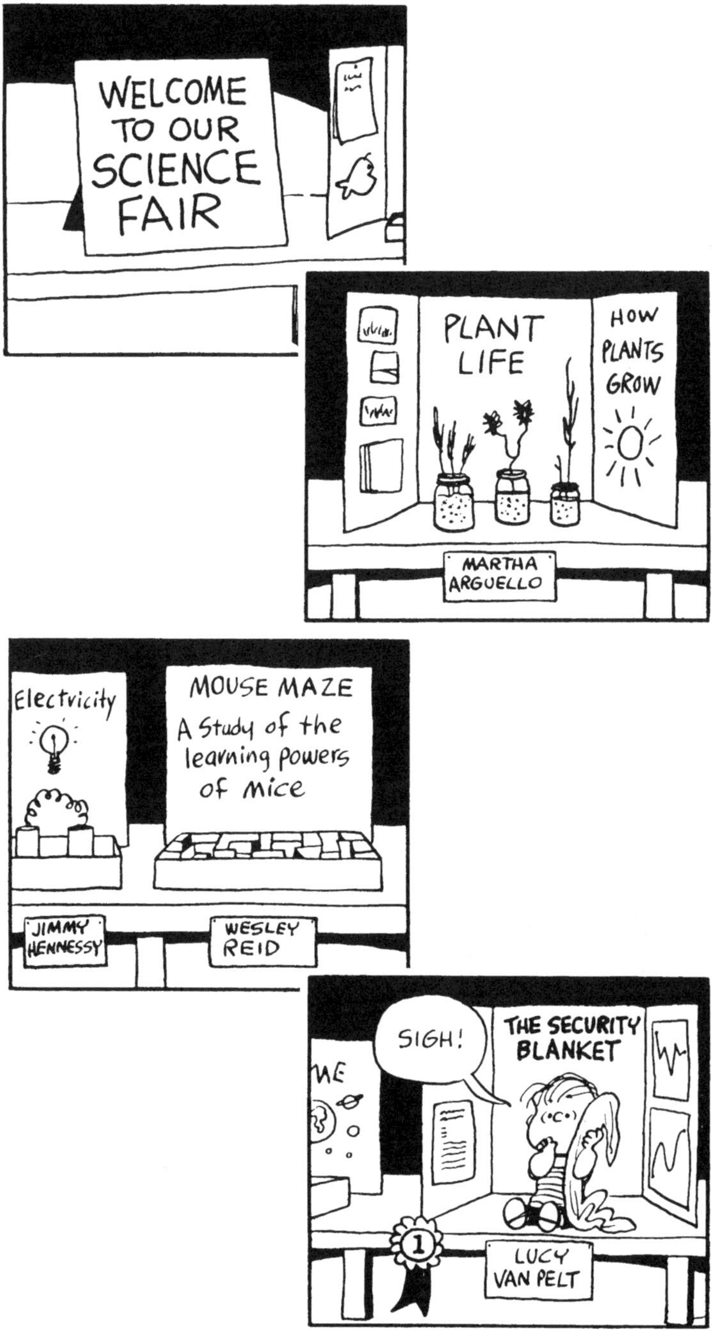

WELCOME TO OUR SCIENCE FAIR
PLANT LIFE
HOW PLANTS GROW
MARTHA ARGUELLO
Electricity
MOUSE MAZE
A Study of the learning powers of mice
JIMMY HENNESSY
WESLEY REID
SIGH!
THE SECURITY BLANKET
1
LUCY VAN PELT

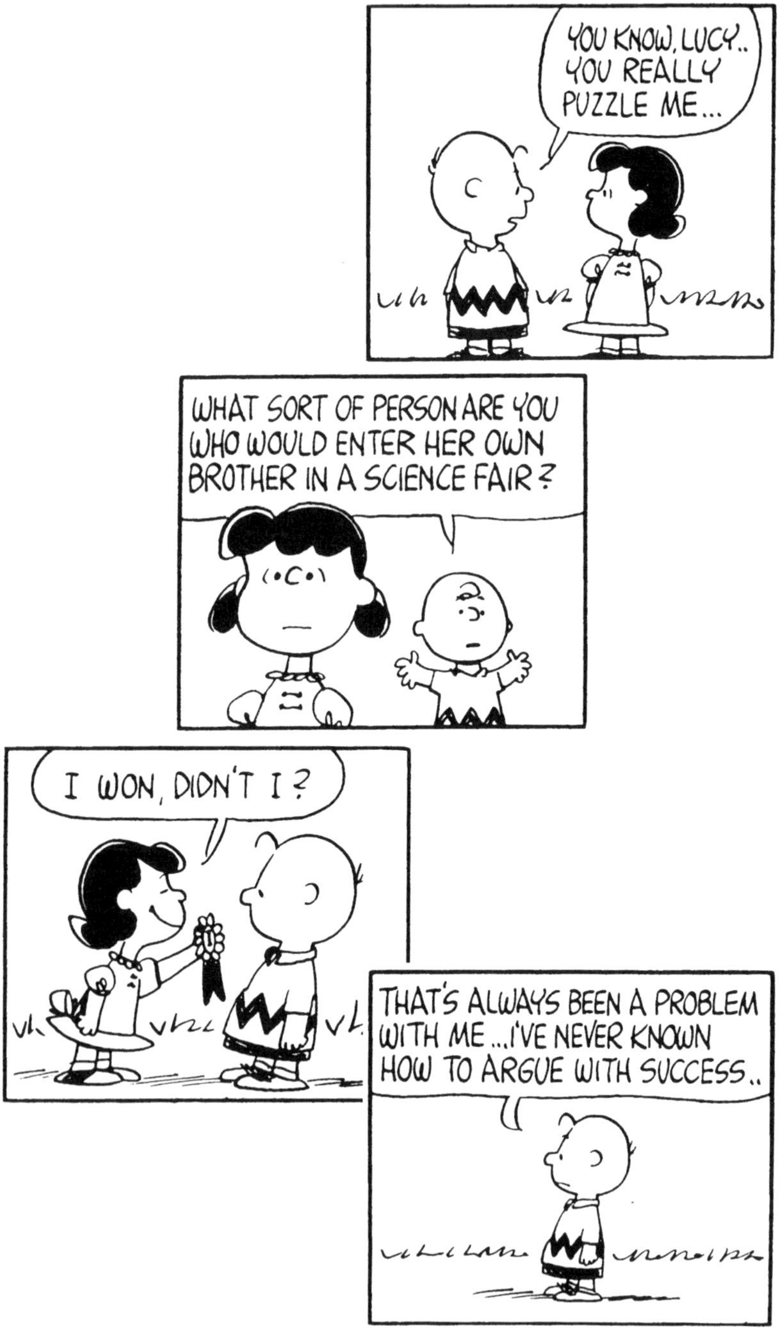
YOU KNOW, LUCY.. YOU REALLY PUZZLE ME...
WHAT SORT OF PERSON ARE YOU WHO WOULD ENTER HER OWN BROTHER IN A SCIENCE FAIR?
I WON, DIDN'T I?
THAT'S ALWAYS BEEN A PROBLEM WITH ME...I'VE NEVER KNOWN HOW TO ARGUE WITH SUCCESS..

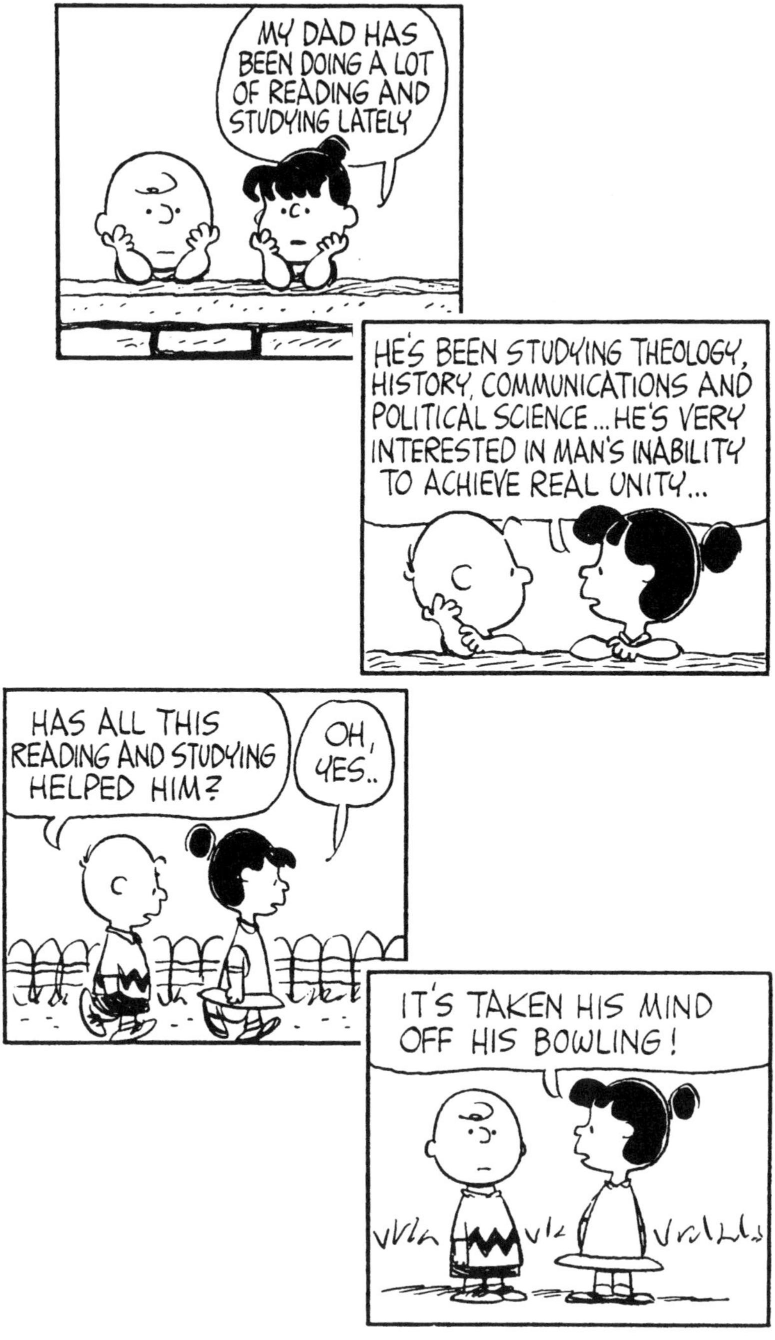

MY DAD HAS BEEN DOING A LOT OF READING AND STUDYING LATELY
HE'S BEEN STUDYING THEOLOGY, HISTORY, COMMUNICATIONS AND POLITICAL SCIENCE... HE'S VERY INTERESTED IN MAN'S INABILITY TO ACHIEVE REAL UNITY...
HAS ALL THIS READING AND STUDYING HELPED HIM?
OH, YES..
IT'S TAKEN HIS MIND OFF HIS BOWLING!

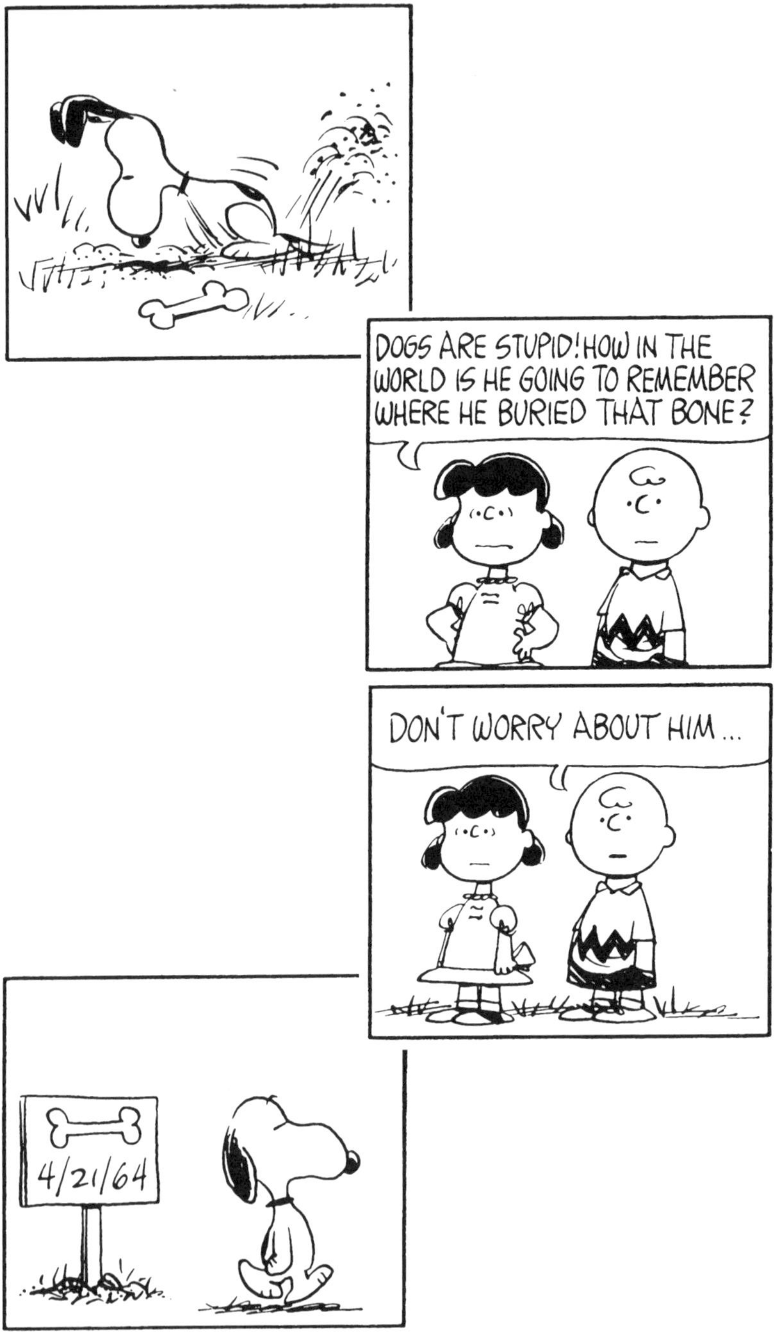
DOGS ARE STUPID! HOW IN THE WORLD IS HE GOING TO REMEMBER WHERE HE BURIED THAT BONE?
DON'T WORRY ABOUT HIM...
4/21/64

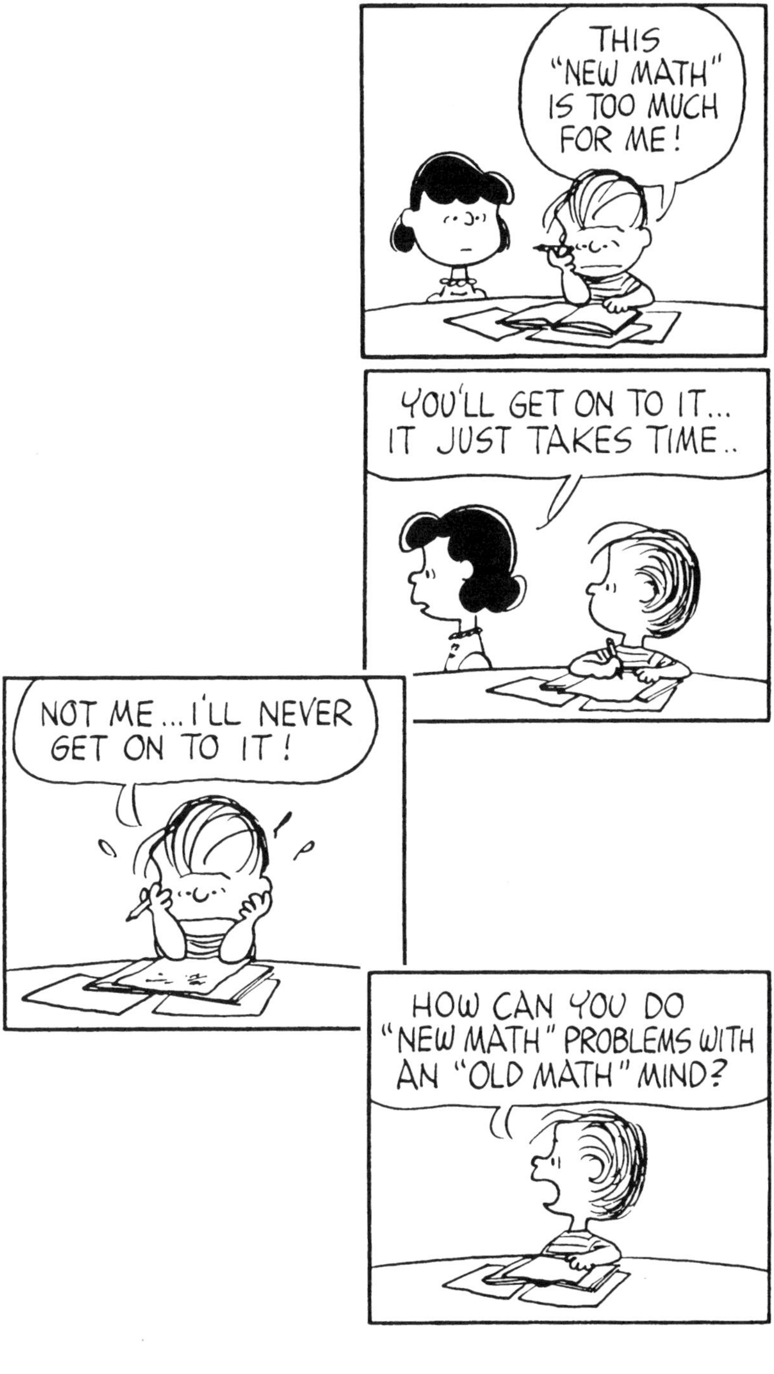
THIS "NEW MATH" IS TOO MUCH FOR ME!
YOU'LL GET ON TO IT... IT JUST TAKES TIME..
NOT ME...I'LL NEVER GET ON TO IT!
HOW CAN YOU DO "NEW MATH" PROBLEMS WITH AN "OLD MATH" MIND?

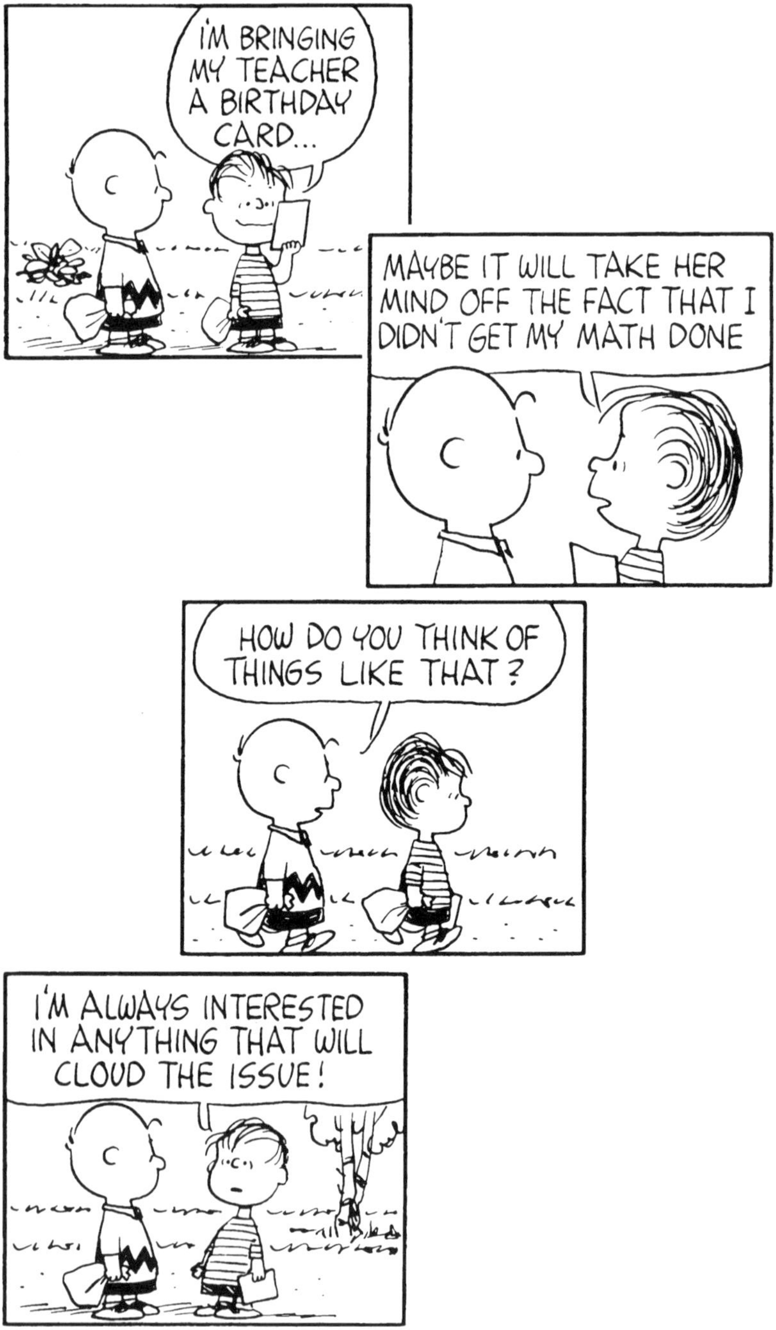
I'M BRINGING MY TEACHER A BIRTHDAY CARD...
MAYBE IT WILL TAKE HER MIND OFF THE FACT THAT I DIDN'T GET MY MATH DONE
HOW DO YOU THINK OF THINGS LIKE THAT?
I'M ALWAYS INTERESTED IN ANYTHING THAT WILL CLOUD THE ISSUE!

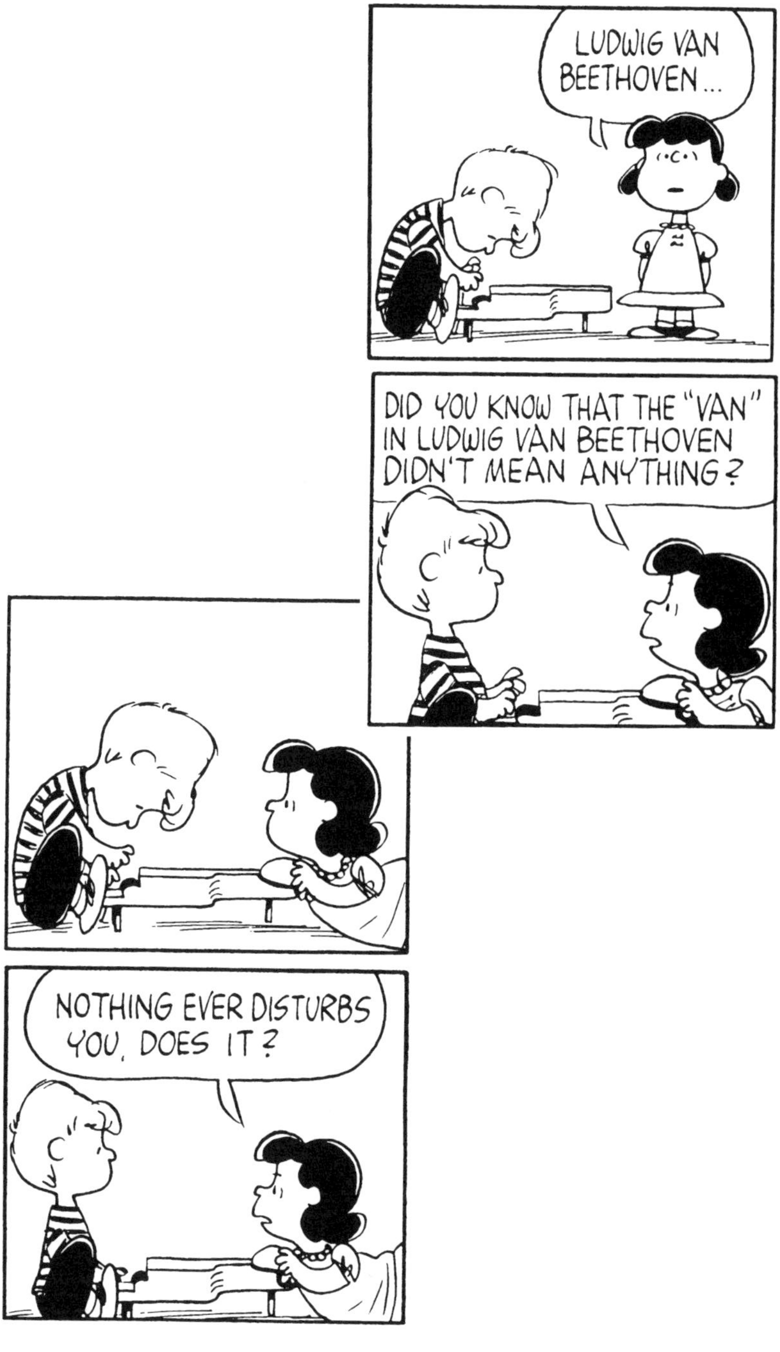

LUDWIG VAN BEETHOVEN...
DID YOU KNOW THAT THE "VAN" IN LUDWIG VAN BEETHOVEN DIDN'T MEAN ANYTHING?
NOTHING EVER DISTURBS YOU, DOES IT?

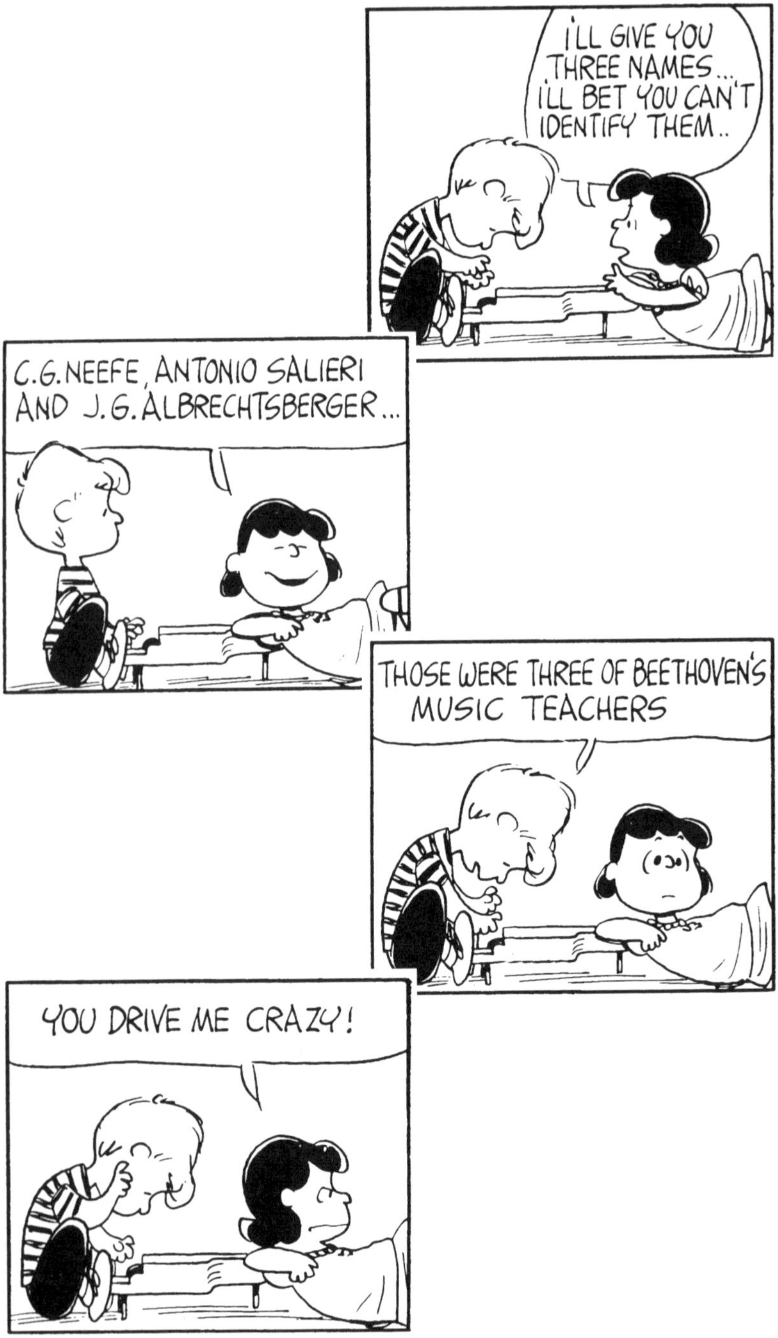
I'LL GIVE YOU THREE NAMES... I'LL BET YOU CAN'T IDENTIFY THEM..
C.G. NEEFE, ANTONIO SALIERI AND J.G. ALBRECHTSBERGER...
THOSE WERE THREE OF BEETHOVEN'S MUSIC TEACHERS
YOU DRIVE ME CRAZY!

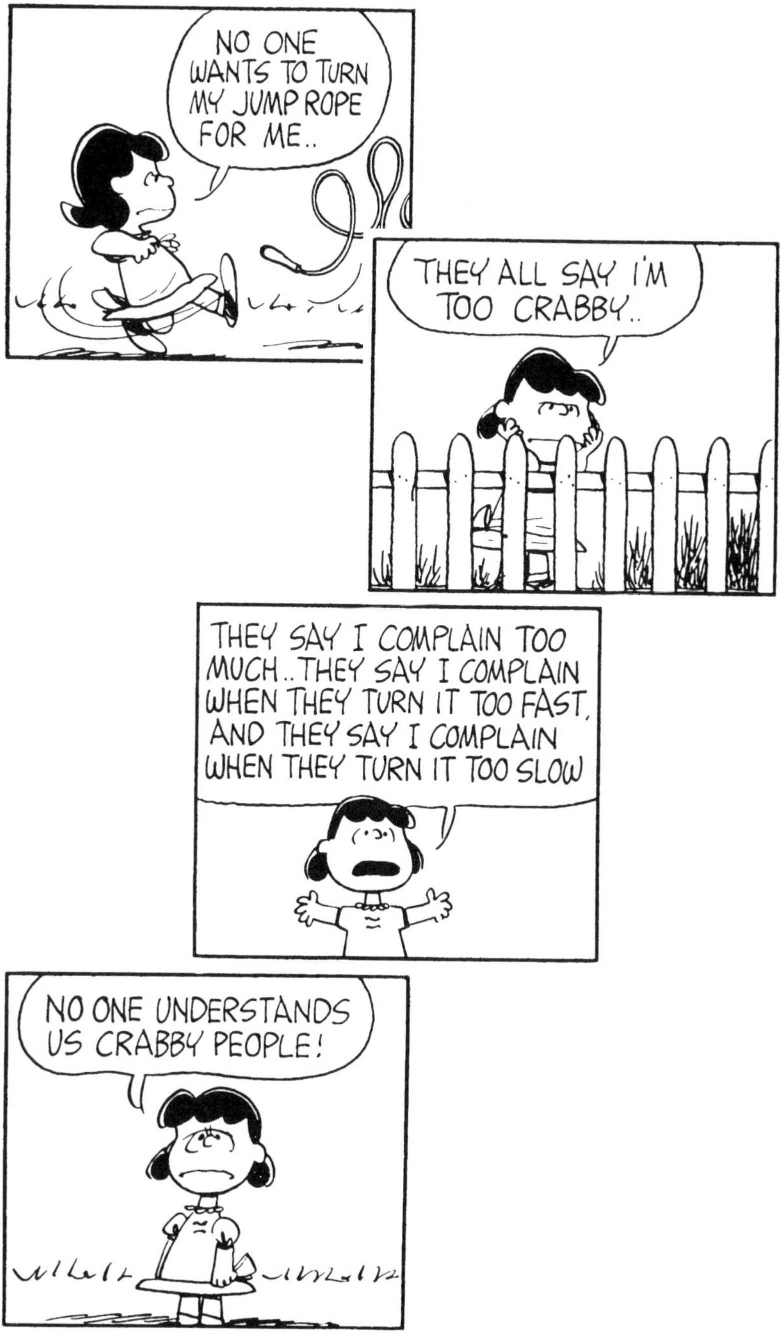
NO ONE WANTS TO TURN MY JUMP ROPE FOR ME..
THEY ALL SAY I'M TOO CRABBY..
THEY SAY I COMPLAIN TOO MUCH..THEY SAY I COMPLAIN WHEN THEY TURN IT TOO FAST, AND THEY SAY I COMPLAIN WHEN THEY TURN IT TOO SLOW
NO ONE UNDERSTANDS US CRABBY PEOPLE!

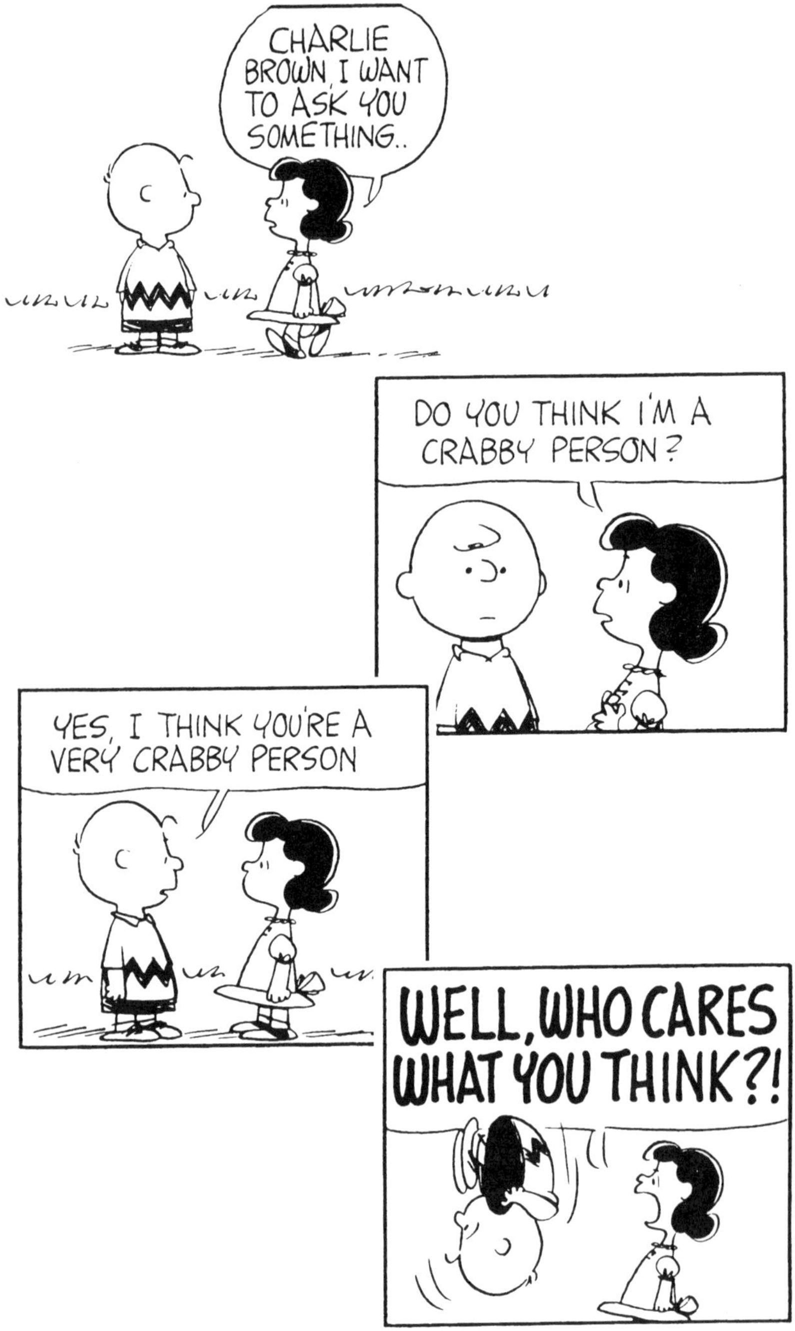

CHARLIE BROWN, I WANT TO ASK YOU SOMETHING..
DO YOU THINK I'M A CRABBY PERSON?
YES, I THINK YOU'RE A VERY CRABBY PERSON
WELL, WHO CARES WHAT YOU THINK?!

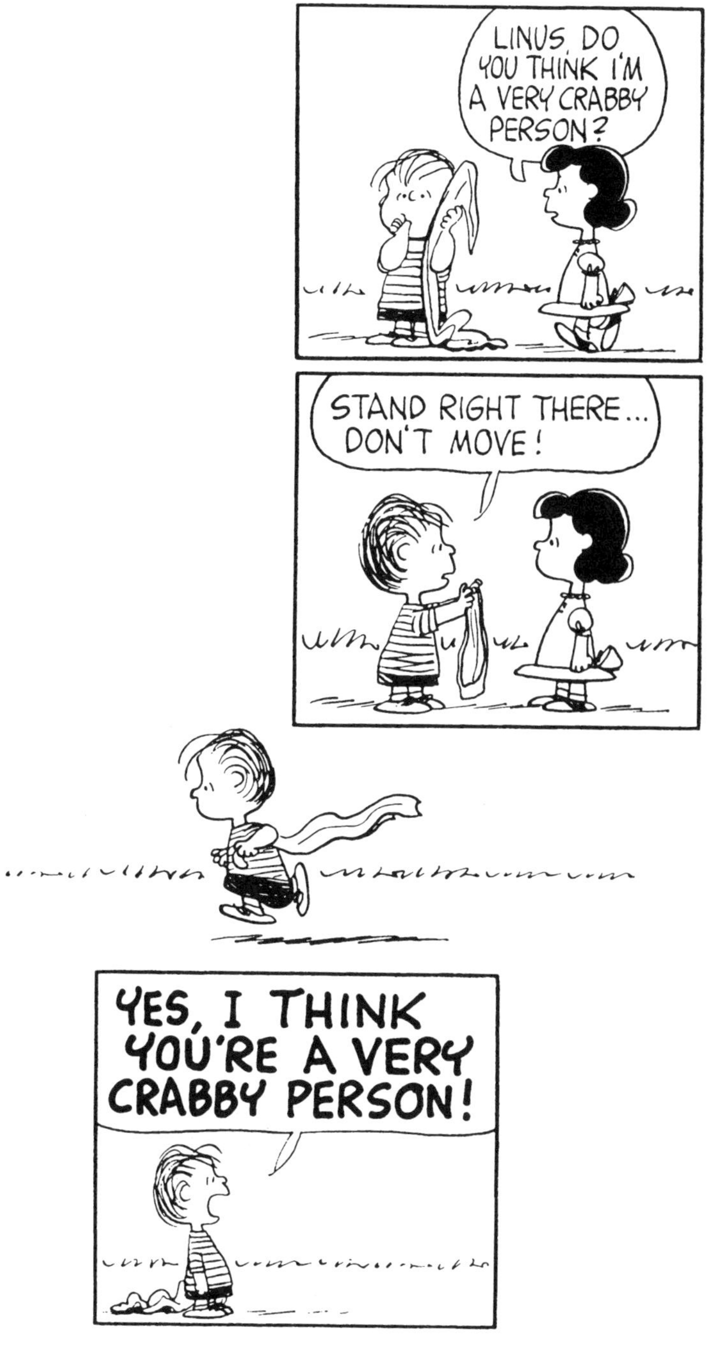

LINUS, DO YOU THINK I'M A VERY CRABBY PERSON?
STAND RIGHT THERE... DON'T MOVE!
YES, I THINK YOU'RE A VERY CRABBY PERSON!

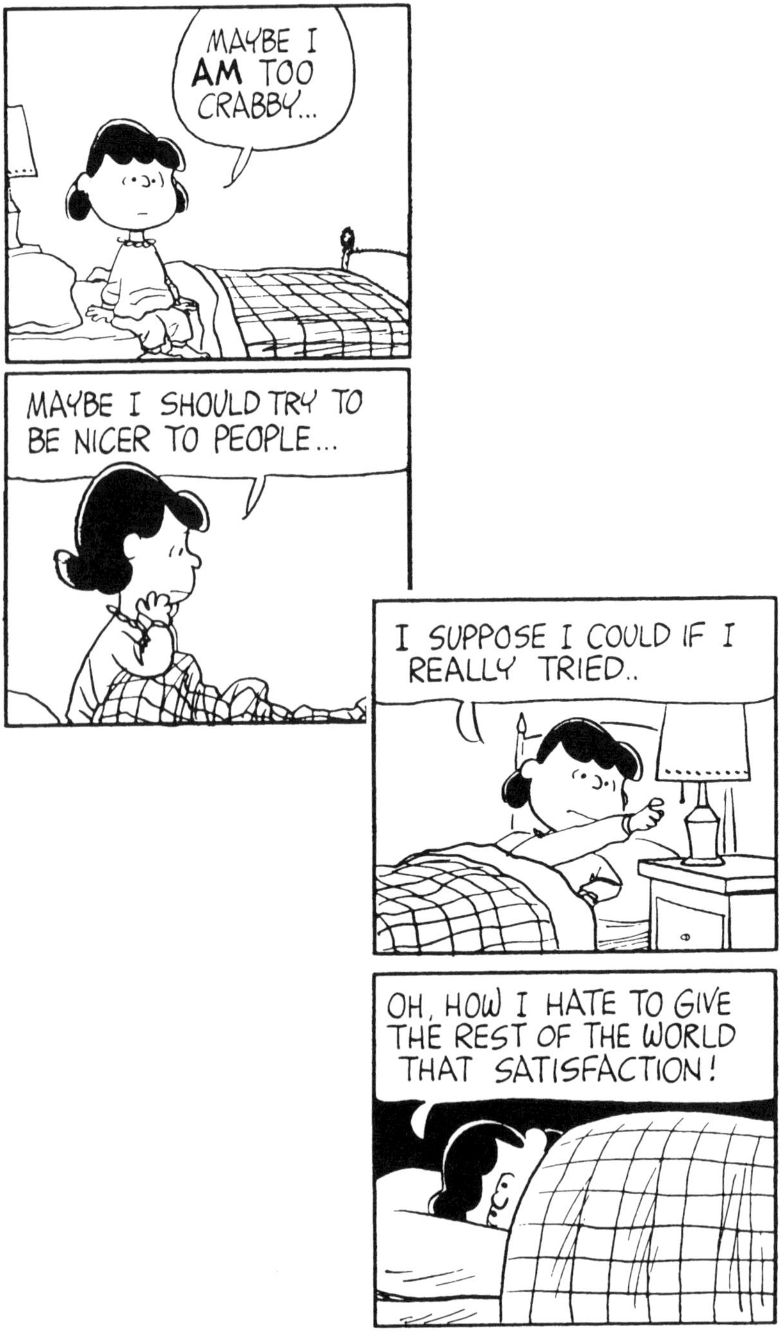

MAYBE I **AM** TOO CRABBY...
MAYBE I SHOULD TRY TO BE NICER TO PEOPLE...
I SUPPOSE I COULD IF I REALLY TRIED..
OH, HOW I HATE TO GIVE THE REST OF THE WORLD THAT SATISFACTION!

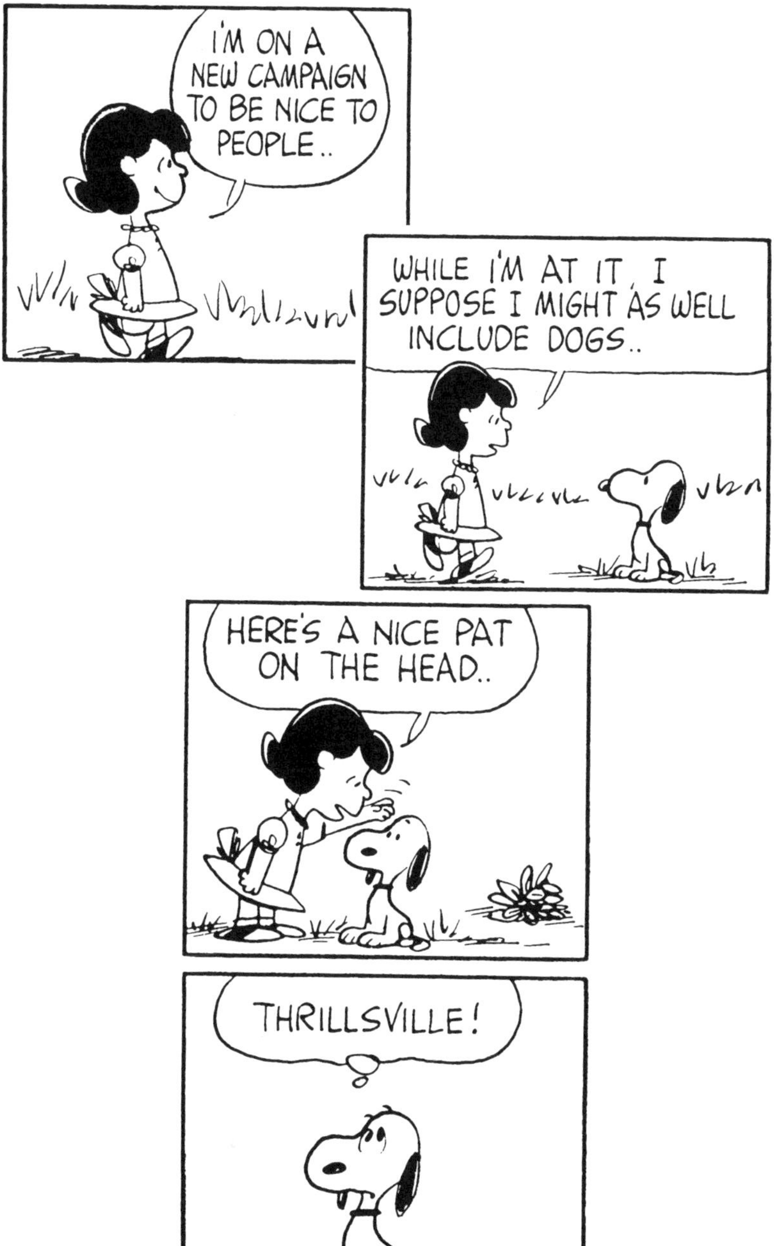
I'M ON A NEW CAMPAIGN TO BE NICE TO PEOPLE..
WHILE I'M AT IT, I SUPPOSE I MIGHT AS WELL INCLUDE DOGS..
HERE'S A NICE PAT ON THE HEAD..
THRILLSVILLE!

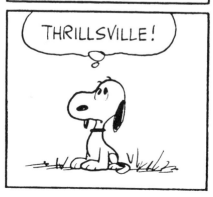

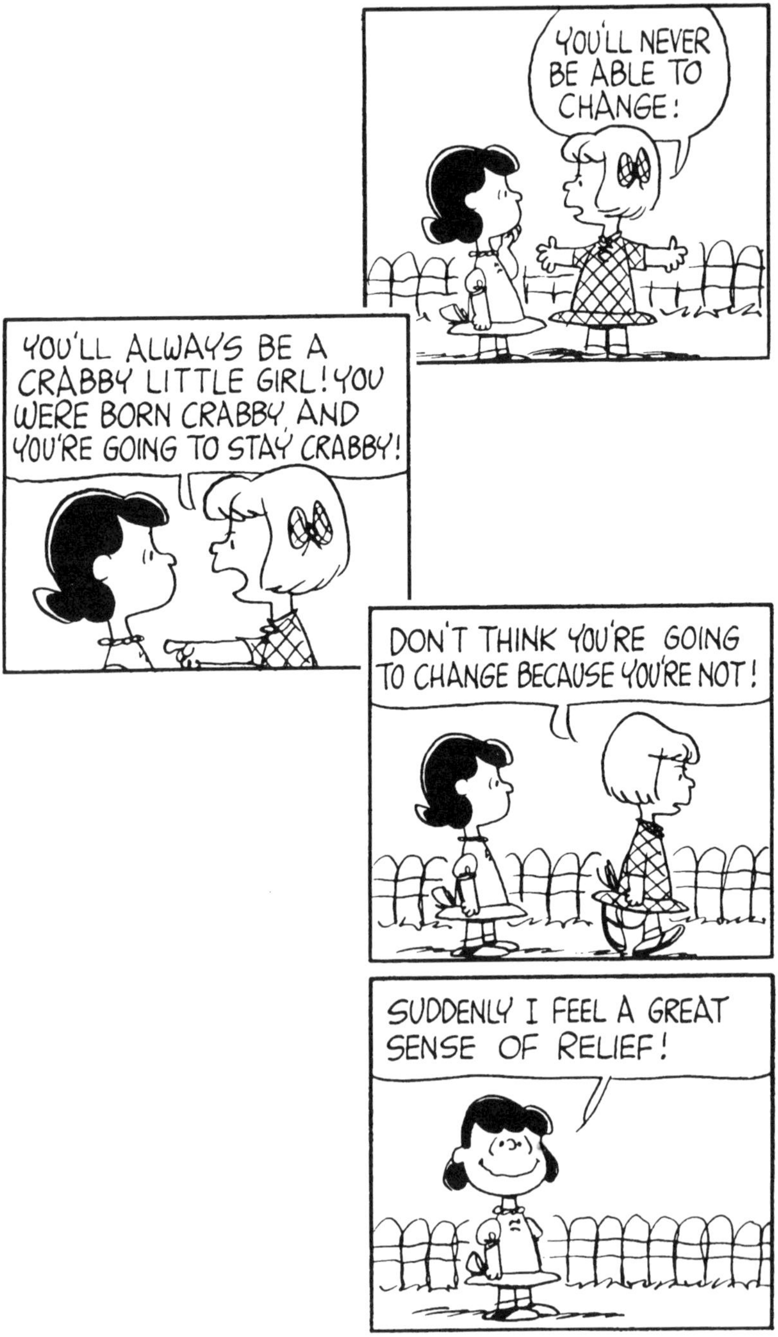
YOU'LL NEVER BE ABLE TO CHANGE!
YOU'LL ALWAYS BE A CRABBY LITTLE GIRL! YOU WERE BORN CRABBY, AND YOU'RE GOING TO STAY CRABBY!
DON'T THINK YOU'RE GOING TO CHANGE BECAUSE YOU'RE NOT!
SUDDENLY I FEEL A GREAT SENSE OF RELIEF!

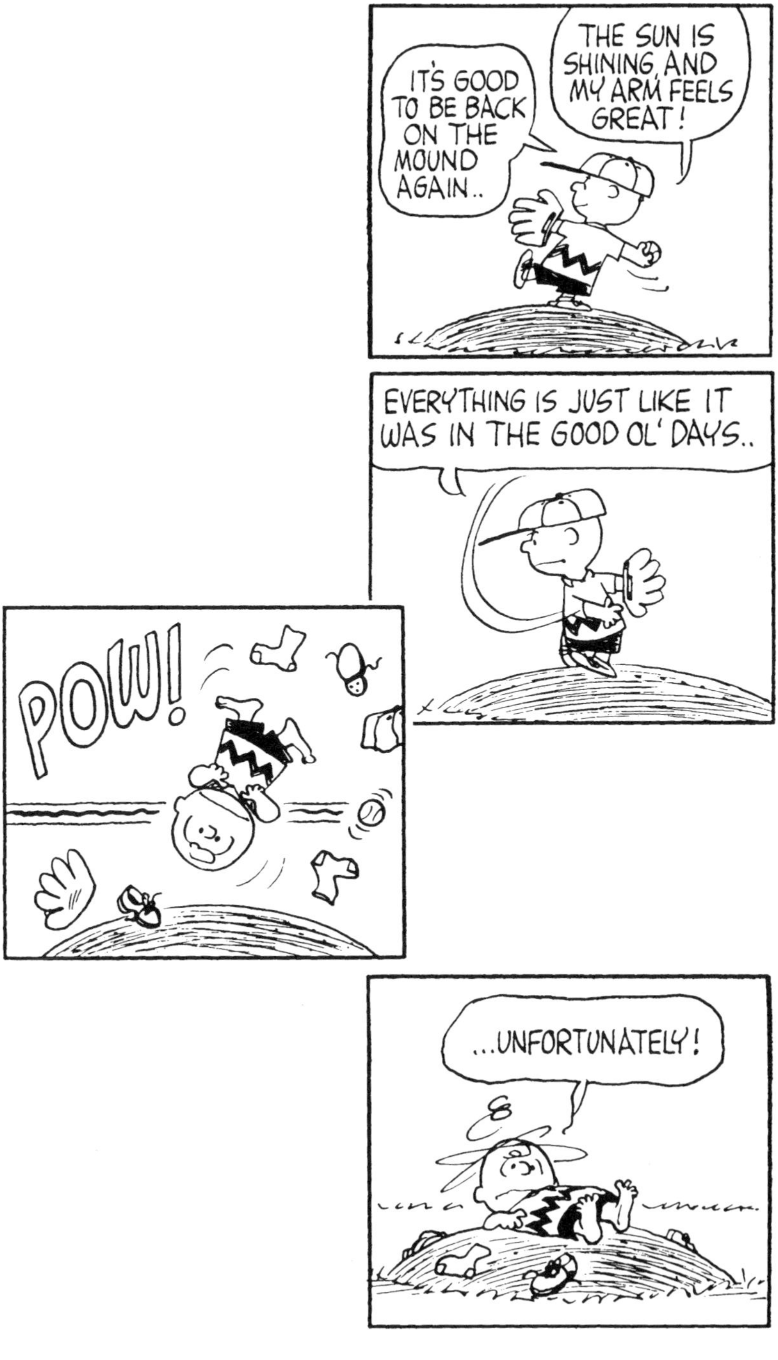
IT'S GOOD TO BE BACK ON THE MOUND AGAIN..
THE SUN IS SHINING, AND MY ARM FEELS GREAT!
EVERYTHING IS JUST LIKE IT WAS IN THE GOOD OL' DAYS..
POW!
...UNFORTUNATELY!

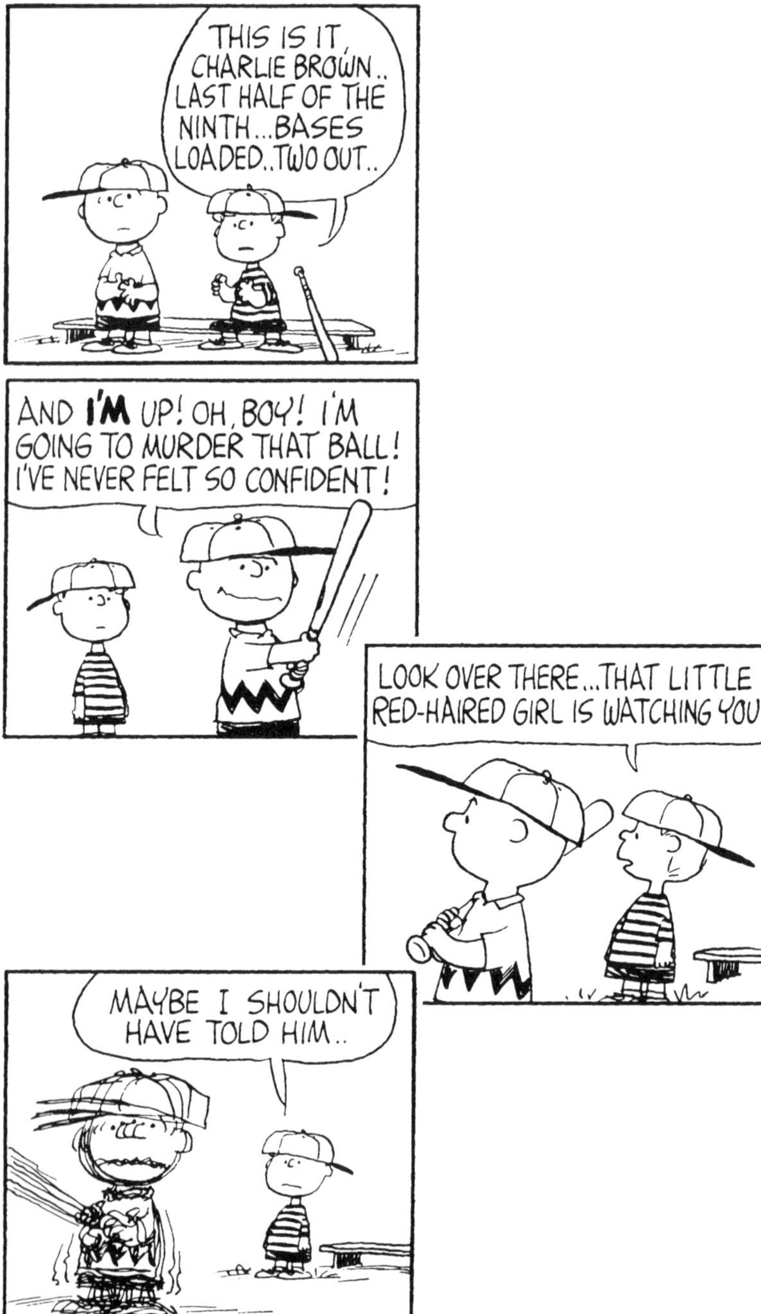
THIS IS IT, CHARLIE BROWN.. LAST HALF OF THE NINTH...BASES LOADED..TWO OUT..
AND I'M UP! OH, BOY! I'M GOING TO MURDER THAT BALL! I'VE NEVER FELT SO CONFIDENT!
LOOK OVER THERE...THAT LITTLE RED-HAIRED GIRL IS WATCHING YOU
MAYBE I SHOULDN'T HAVE TOLD HIM..

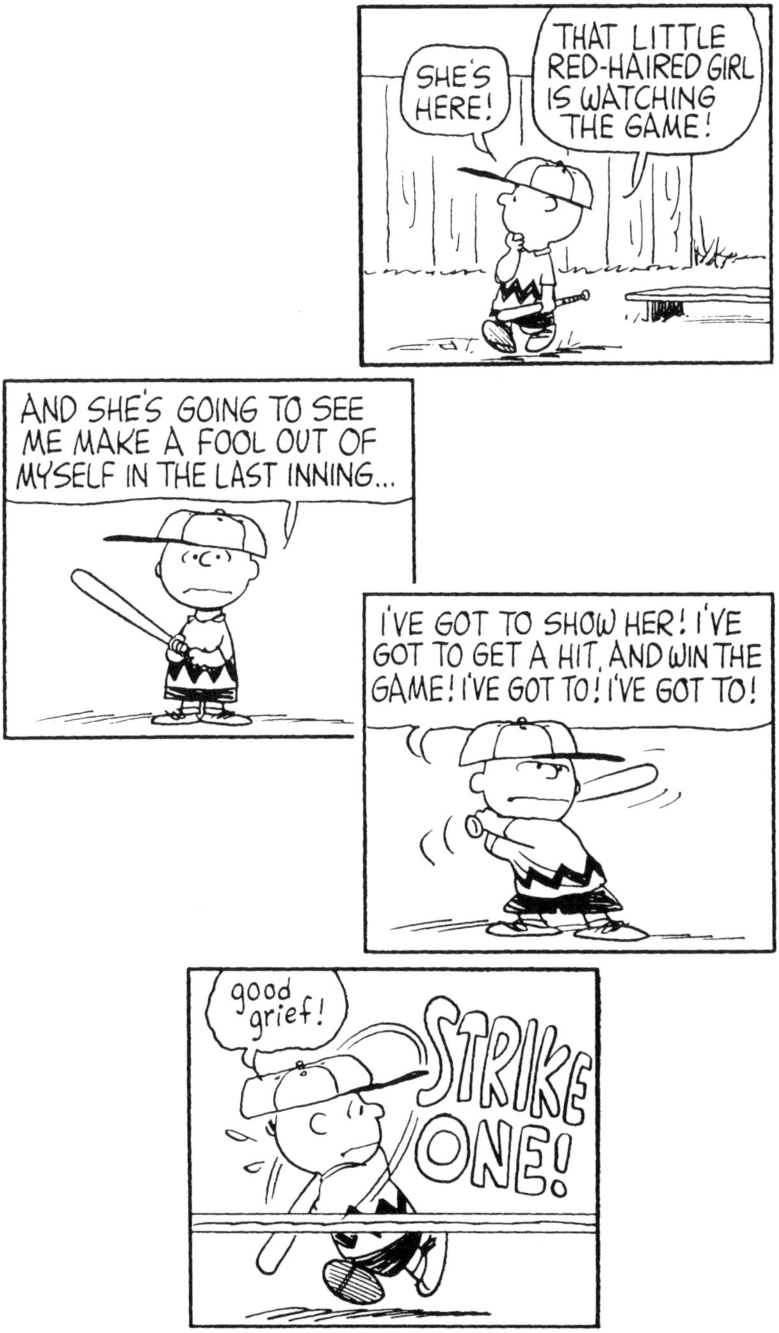

SHE'S HERE!
THAT LITTLE RED-HAIRED GIRL IS WATCHING THE GAME!
AND SHE'S GOING TO SEE ME MAKE A FOOL OUT OF MYSELF IN THE LAST INNING...
I'VE GOT TO SHOW HER! I'VE GOT TO GET A HIT, AND WIN THE GAME! I'VE GOT TO! I'VE GOT TO!
good grief!
STRIKE ONE!

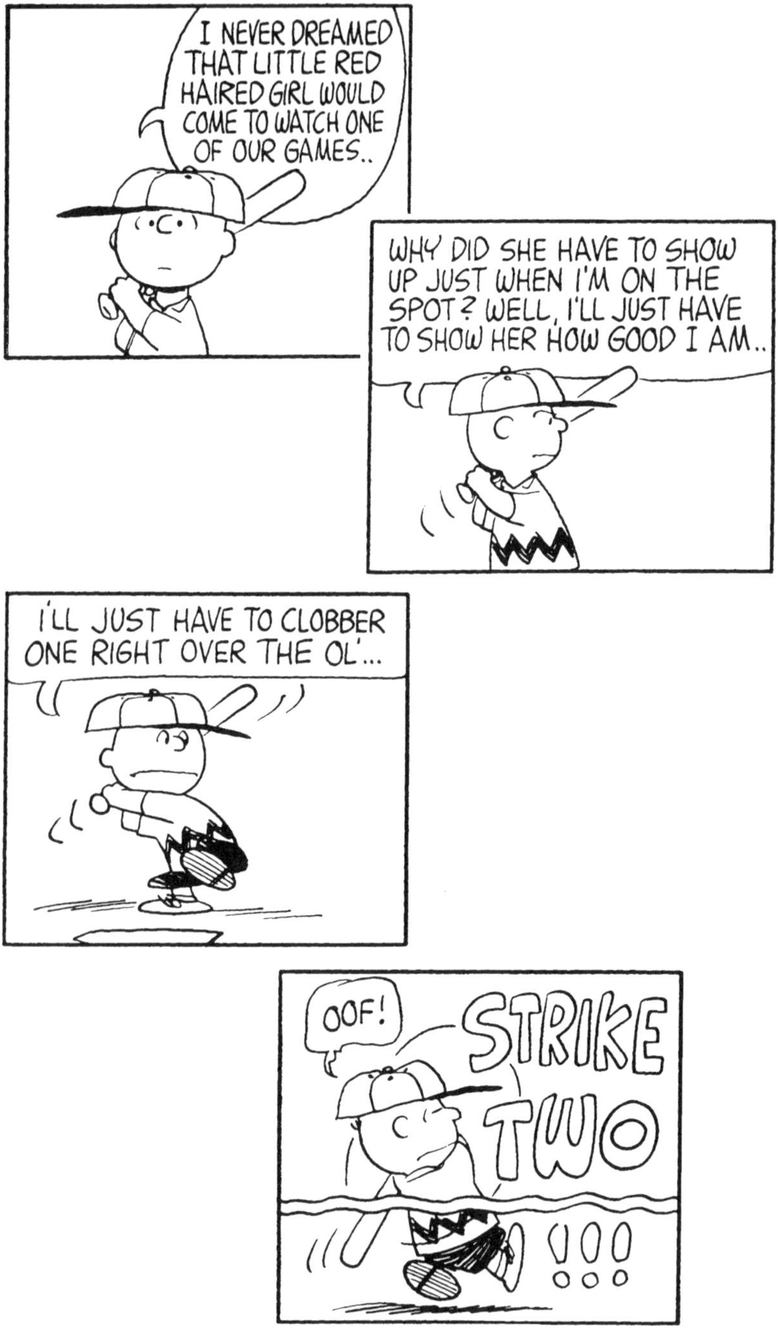
I NEVER DREAMED THAT LITTLE RED HAIRED GIRL WOULD COME TO WATCH ONE OF OUR GAMES..
WHY DID SHE HAVE TO SHOW UP JUST WHEN I'M ON THE SPOT? WELL, I'LL JUST HAVE TO SHOW HER HOW GOOD I AM..
I'LL JUST HAVE TO CLOBBER ONE RIGHT OVER THE OL'...
OOF!
STRIKE TWO
!!!

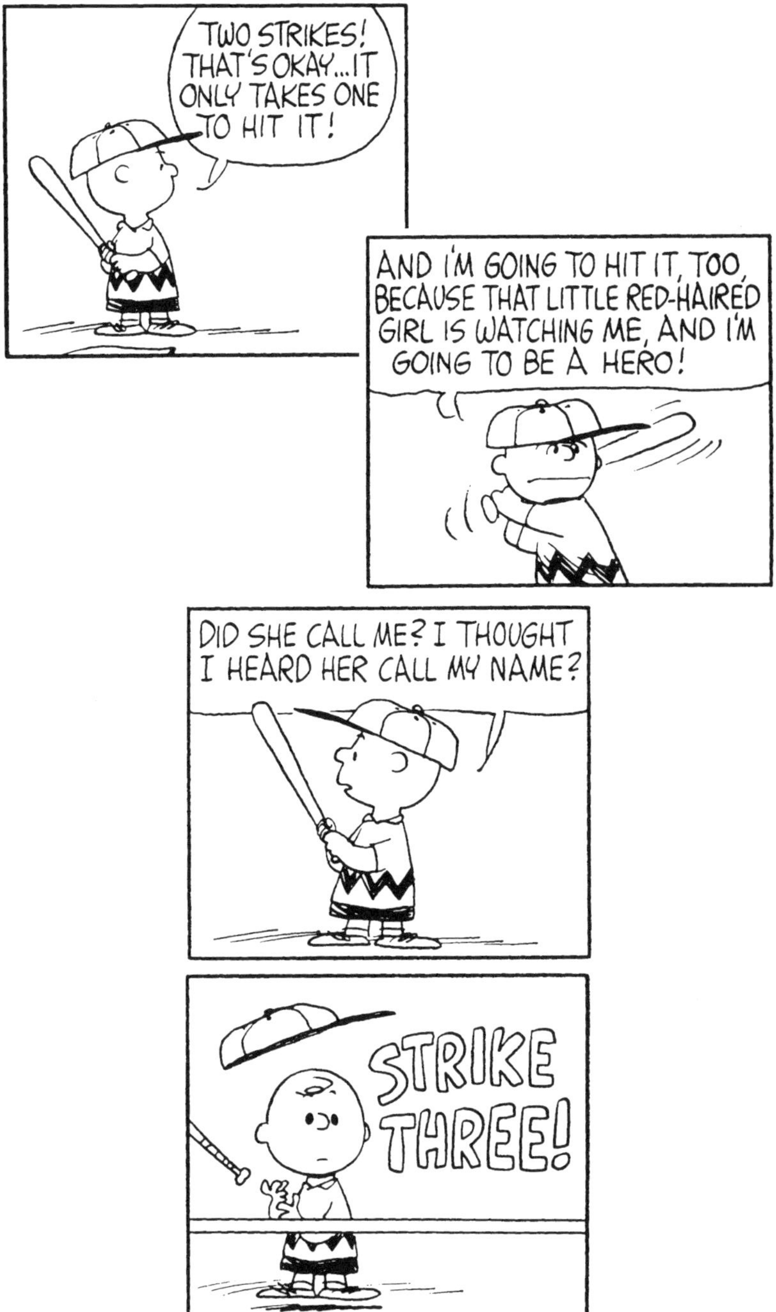
TWO STRIKES! THAT'S OKAY...IT ONLY TAKES ONE TO HIT IT!
AND I'M GOING TO HIT IT, TOO, BECAUSE THAT LITTLE RED-HAIRED GIRL IS WATCHING ME, AND I'M GOING TO BE A HERO!
DID SHE CALL ME? I THOUGHT I HEARD HER CALL MY NAME?
STRIKE THREE!

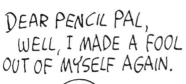

DEAR PENCIL PAL,
WELL, I MADE A FOOL
OUT OF MYSELF AGAIN.

SIGH

I STRUCK OUT WITH
THE BASES LOADED,
AND LOST THE BALL GAME.

A LITTLE RED-HAIRED
GIRL WHOM I ADMIRE VERY
MUCH WAS WATCHING ME.

COULD YOU TELL ME HOW TO
GET TO WHERE YOU LIVE?
I'M THINKING OF LEAVING
THE COUNTRY!

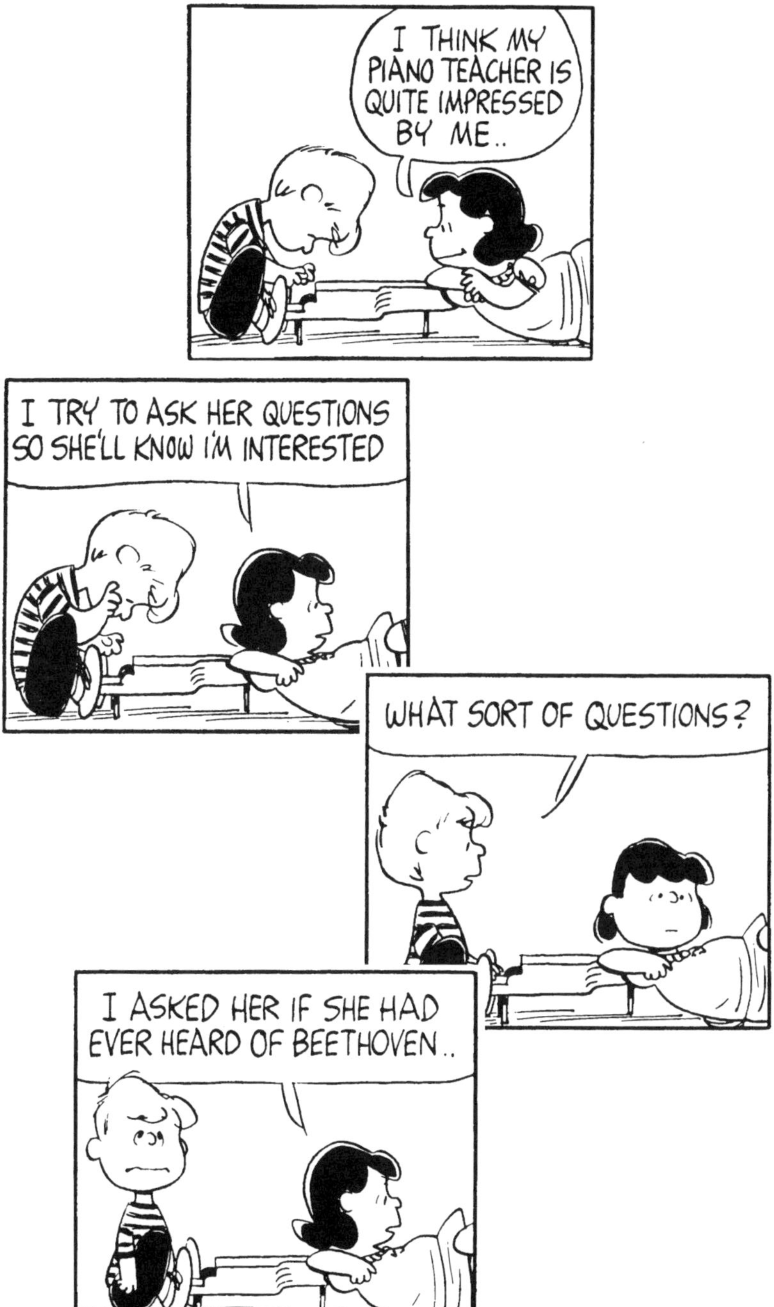
I THINK MY PIANO TEACHER IS QUITE IMPRESSED BY ME..
I TRY TO ASK HER QUESTIONS SO SHE'LL KNOW I'M INTERESTED
WHAT SORT OF QUESTIONS?
I ASKED HER IF SHE HAD EVER HEARD OF BEETHOVEN..

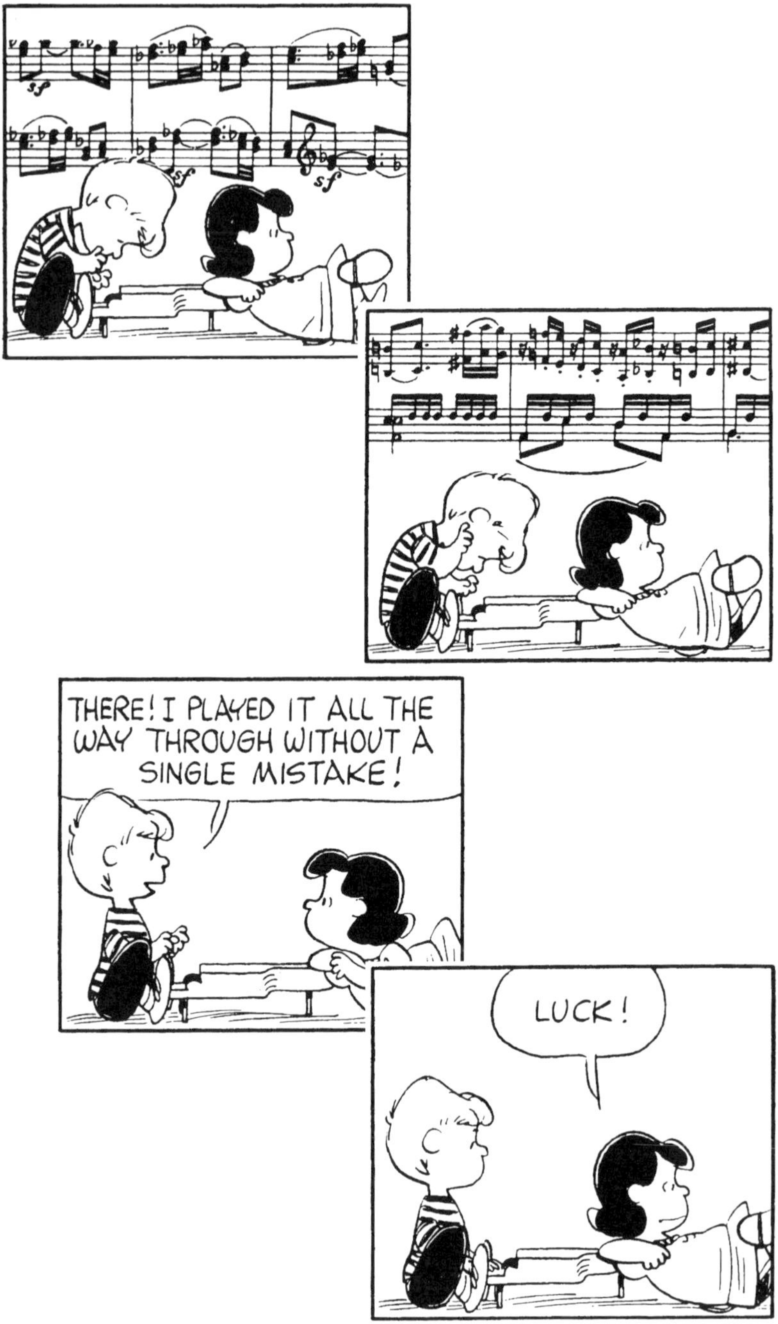
THERE! I PLAYED IT ALL THE WAY THROUGH WITHOUT A SINGLE MISTAKE!
LUCK!